For my husband and best friend, David.
—*Cheridan Kerr*

To my loving wife Bianca, our family, and bub to be. Praise to Cheridan for the patience. Special thanks to Chub Chub for the support and companionship on those late lonely nights.
—*Jon Keats*

CONTENTS AT A GLANCE

CONTENTS

ABOUT THE AUTHORS

Cheridan Kerr

Cheridan Kerr has been involved in web development and design since 1997, when she began working on a research team for the Y2K Millennium Bug. It was there she learned about the Internet and promptly fell in love with the medium. In her career she has been responsible for websites in the early '00's, such as www.weightwatchers.com.au and http://quicken.com.au, and worked as creative services manager of Yahoo!7 in Australia with clients such as Toyota, 20th Century Fox, and Ford. Currently she is working as an executive producer for an Australian advertising agency.

Jon Keats

Jon Keats has been using Flash since its early predecessor, Fantavision, and has continued using every incarnation since. He is a regular contributor to online Flash communities like flashkit and gotoAndPlay(). Over the years he has used his background in visual art, music, and programming to create interactive solutions for a host of major national and international clients. Jon holds a bachelor of design, specializing in stereoscopic 3D visualization and interactive systems, from the University of Newcastle, Australia. He has also studied computer and software engineering. He lives, armed with banjo in hand, atop a mountain nestled in the Australian outback with his loving family and an adopted crazy puglike alien life form.

ABOUT THE TECHNICAL REVIEWER

Leyton Smith is a multidisciplinary, diversely experienced industrial designer practicing architectural planning and design in Sydney, Australia. He has been working with and has supported the Flash community since the mid '90's and has designed and developed Flash-based visual-communication and motion-graphic projects for film, stage, and Web.

ACKNOWLEDGMENTS

It's always a shock when you're working on one of these books, the sheer number of talented people who are involved from inception to completion. We would like to list them in no particular order here, but offer our love and gratitude to each one.

Ben Renow-Clarke, for being a patient and wise editor with always-constructive and just feedback. Thanks for being an inspiration.

Richard Dal Porto and Candace English, the wonderful project managers who ensured this book was steered always toward the finish line.

Leyton Smith, a technical editor among technical editors, who picked up this book after a number of false starts and drove it home.

Once again Candace English and also Damon Larson for taking these pages and ensuring they became the beautiful structured pages you see before you.

Ellie Fountain for the wonderful production-editor work.

And last, but not least, to Spotty McGotty and Chub Chub, the pets who maintained the vigil with us during the late nights and early mornings as deadlines loomed and passed.

Cheridan Kerr and Jon Keats

INTRODUCTION

Over the last decade, we have seen a phenomenal change in the way we interact with sites online. Where the experience for the end user was once two-dimensional, there are now endless possibilities a Flash designer can create to introduce users to a whole new world of interaction with their animations, and ergo, their brands. Yet with all of these great new abilities comes a responsibility to your company and your users to present the best experience you can.

This book will not only help to demystify Adobe Flash CS4 for newcomers to the CS4 suite of products; it will guide you on current industry standards and marketing principles, with useful insights into the way your online banner-advertisement campaigns and websites can help you cut through the clutter and noise of online marketing.

The Essential Guide to Flash CS4 is aimed at the intermediate Flash user as well as the more advanced user who wants to become quickly familiarized with Flash CS4's awesome new capabilities.

Who is this book for?

A variety of professionals will find *The Essential Guide to Flash CS4* a useful tool when creating their online presence.

Animators

With more features than ever before, the new intuitive Flash CS4 interface will streamline animators' development time. *The Essential Guide to Flash CS4* will show you how.

Graphic designers

As well as enabling graphic designers to breathe life into their static designs, Flash CS4's new tools, such as the Deco and Bones tools, allow graphic designers to import their creations from any of the CS4-suite products, ready for animation.

Web designers

This book demonstrates how web designers can quickly integrate database back-end systems with functional and compelling Flash CS4 interfaces, creating for users a beautiful and informative experience.

Web developers

The Essential Guide to Flash CS4 serves as a quick course in integrating back-end databases and front-end dynamic content.

How is this book structured?

The Essential Guide to Flash CS4 covers all aspects of designing and developing within Flash CS4. It begins with a fundamental overview in Chapter 1 and works steadily through each important aspect of the program.

Chapter 1, "Welcome to Flash CS4," takes you through the differences between Flash CS4 and Flash CS3, and introduces you to Flash CS4's great new tools. Discover how the Motion Editor panel will save you precious development time, and enjoy a quick overview and intuitive exercises involving new features such as inverse kinematics and the Deco tool.

Chapter 2, "Getting Creative: How to Make Your Ideas Come to Life Through Project Planning," offers you a crash course in the project-development cycle and teaches you how to make the most of your projects with an introduction to wireframes and marketing-competitor analysis. New designers will find the comprehensive guide to design principles useful in assisting them with quickly creating comprehensive and attractive designs.

Chapter 3, "Getting Your Hands Dirty: Layers, Masks and Photoshop," teaches you about the importance of layers in the Flash CS4 universe, and defines the different kinds of layers you will encounter. Following a comprehensive overview of masks, we get down to brass tacks and demonstrate two ways mask layers can be used in an actual banner.

Chapter 4, "Draw Me a Picture: Using the Drawing Tools," takes you on a journey through different techniques that you can employ in Flash CS4 using the drawing tools. Following a series of step-by-step exercises, you will learn how to transform a hand-drawn logo into a usable and attractive digital asset, and you'll learn the differences between types of graphics and find out how to use them, discover the drawing modes, and learn to use the 3D rotation and translation tools.

Chapter 5, "Filters and Blends," teaches you how filters and blends in Flash CS4 can greatly streamline precious development time. You will learn, through a series of exercises, the impact that choosing the right filter and blend can have on your Flash CS4 design.

Chapter 6, "Let's Get Animated!," is designed to get you up and running in the world of animation. Here you will learn how to use Flash CS4's capabilities to build a banner ad that is customizable and ready for you to dispatch to clients.

Chapter 7, "Achieving Lifelike Motion with Inverse Kinematics," teaches you how to use inverse kinematics to give your animations a real-life perspective. In Chapter 1 you learned how to make an arm wave convincingly—now it's time to expand on that!

Chapter 8, "Lights, Camera, ActionScript!," is focused purely on ActionScript 3.0. In this chapter you marry back-end databases with front-end beautiful Flash designs. You will learn about variables and data types, and how decisions are made through programming in ActionScript 3.0. You'll also learn the date and function basics and how to use XML and ActionScript 3.0 to make a dynamic application.

Chapter 9, "Using 3D Space in Flash CS4," teaches you all about the z-axis, which enables you to manipulate objects on your Flash CS4 stage in the third dimension, providing them with depth. Also included is an overview of how to create a 3D carousel using Flash CS4 XML, as well as an overview of 3D engines.

Chapter 10, "Seeing and Hearing Are Believing!," is all about bringing sound and video into your Flash CS4 movies. Remember that banner you created in Chapter 6? Now you're going to apply a convincing sound to it. You'll also learn how to import a video and apply sound to that.

Chapter 11, "Utilizing Best Practices to Get the Most out of Your Flash CS4 Movies," is a lesson in making your Flash CS4 applications available to everyone. Learn about utilizing screen readers, tab controls, and universal industry standards. It's a boring but necessary part of every online campaign.

Chapter 12, "The End of the Beginning," shows you how to bring the previous parts of the book together in a convincing display.

Appendix A, "Installing Away3D and Other Class Libraries Using Subversion," is a demonstration on how to install Flash CS4 plug-ins, specifically a 3D engine, to help you further bring your Flash animations to life.

Appendix B, "Keyboard Shortcuts," is a handy summary of both Windows and Mac OS shortcuts to help you streamline your development times.

Layout conventions

To keep this book as clear and easy to follow as possible, the following text conventions are used throughout.

Code is presented in `fixed-width` font.

Menu commands are written in the form Menu ➤ Submenu ➤ Submenu.

Where I want to draw your attention to something, I've highlighted it like this:

> *Ahem, don't say we didn't warn you.*

Sometimes code won't fit on a single line in a book. Where this happens, I use an arrow like this: ➥.

```
This is a very, very long section of code that should be written all on ➥
the same line without a break.
```

 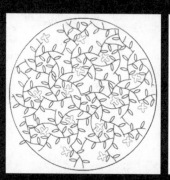 

The Internet is a massive, noisy, crowded place, and it can be difficult for both businesses and individuals to cut through the hordes of marketing collateral out there. Flash CS4 has revolutionized the layman's ability to produce professional Flash assets. Regardless of whether you are building a complex Flash website, producing a video for the Web, or building a simple banner campaign, Flash CS4 empowers you to produce dazzling executions.

This book has been written with the explicit intention of getting you up and running and creating animations with Flash CS4 in a matter of mere minutes, but also to ensure that you take the opportunity to harness your vision and creativity and build comprehensive and compelling Flash executions. Whether you are a seasoned Flash user or a novice, within the pages of this book you will find anecdotes, hints, and exercises to help you build Flash applications immediately.

You can either work through exercise by exercise or download the source files for each of the chapters. This book relies heavily on the source files, so please ensure that you have downloaded them from the friends of ED website (www.friendsofed.com) to get the maximum benefit.

Welcome to the Future!

Think about almost every website that you have visited in the last decade. Chances are most of these sites will have some elements of Flash within them, from complicated (and often not recommended!) full-screen Flash animation introductions, to banner advertisements. Flash is here to stay—and it just got better.

Flash CS4 was developed to take the smoke and mirrors away from advanced web design. Now with the adaptability of a graphics program and simplifying what used to be, Flash CS4 brings an advanced digital studio to your lounge room.

It appears that every day there is a new technology to enhance our online experiences—the way we do business, browse the Web—and seemingly every part of our lives. Once the domain of the Internet, Flash now infiltrates more and more: in movies, in websites, and in user interfaces such as e-commerce or subscription systems that we use every day.

Beautiful executions combined with supreme usability and functionality are very much the order of the day. Flash CS4 has taken the guesswork out of building complex Flash executions with a host of new functions and an intuitive new layout, including vertical property panels that take advantage of today's wider screens. There is a lot more flexibility in customizing the way that you want your defaults to appear than there was in previous versions, as shown in Figure 1-1.

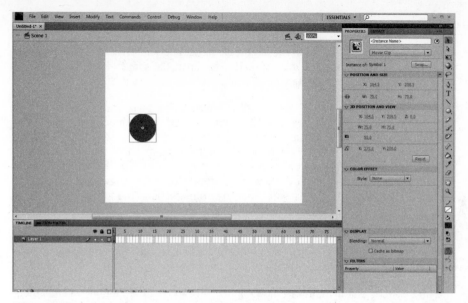

Figure 1-1. The new Flash CS4 interface provides users with maximum screen real estate for the stage, but also great flexibility in customizing to individual tastes.

Take a moment to play with the Essentials drop-down as shown in Figure 1-2 to explore how the Flash CS4 interface changes. A number of presets enable you to organize your workspace in many different and intuitive ways. You also have the ability to drag all components of Flash CS4 around the stage to suit your monitor size.

You are now going to discover how Flash CS4 is a viable and vastly improved alternative to Flash CS3.

Figure 1-2. Changing the look and feel of the workspace to suit you

How Flash CS4 is different from Flash CS3

Flash CS3 revolutionized the way we used Flash. It introduced ActionScript 3.0 to the mix and better allowed code and animations to be converted to ActionScript. It offered better integration with other programs in Adobe Creative Suite, such as Photoshop, and integrated graphical and drawing abilities such as Adobe Fireworks and Adobe Illustrator.

Flash CS4 takes all of the good bits of Flash CS3 and pushes them to the limits, as well as introducing a number of new tools that allow Flash users to create professional, innovative, and cutting-edge Flash applications. This section provides an overview of some of these features, and exercises to introduce some of the new features before we get into the nuts and bolts of Flash CS4.

Object-based animation

Object-based animation is one of the largest differences between Flash CS4 and its predecessors. Simply put, it enables you to create great animations much faster and with less difficulty than ever before, giving you a better control of your animation.

In Flash CS4 a *tween* is a kind of animation that is placed within a layer of a Flash execution and enables you to animate objects from shape to shape, or via motion. To convert an object you have placed on a layer in the timeline to a tween, select the object, right-click, and choose one of the Create Tween options from the menu that appears. Another way to create a tween is to select the object on the stage that you wish to convert, and choose the option from the Insert menu. In the predecessors to Flash CS4, tweens were applied to keyframes. We will further investigate tweening in the section "The Motion Editor panel gives you greater control" later in this chapter, and in Chapter 3.

By allowing tweening to be applied directly to objects instead of keyframes, Flash CS4 takes a lot of the finessing and guesswork out of creating tweens. This empowers users by giving them exact control over each animation attribute.

The first exercise will demonstrate how simply you can create a motion tween without ever touching the timeline, and we will then investigate how it affects the Motion Editor panel, and what wonderful things you can do with the Motion Editor panel.

1. Open a new blank document in Flash CS4 by selecting File ➤ New from the menu, as shown in Figure 1-3.

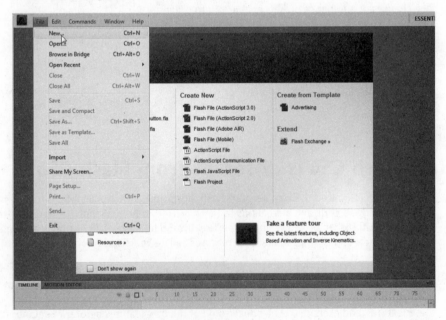

Figure 1-3. Creating a new document in Flash CS4

2. Select Flash File (ActionScript 3.0) from the Create New menu.

The animation that we are going to create is a circle moving across the screen, so now we need to specify that we are creating a circle.

3. Left-click and hold on the Rectangle tool. A set of options will appear as shown in Figure 1-4.

4. Choose the Oval tool as shown in Figure 1-4.

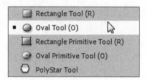

Figure 1-4. Left-clicking and holding on an item that has a small triangle next to it on the Tools panel displays the available options.

> *A few tools on the* Tools *panel let you choose which iteration of the tool you want to use. These include the* Transform, Pen, Rectangle, Brush, *and* Paint Bucket *tools.*

5. With the Oval tool still selected, draw a circle on the left side of the canvas, as shown in Figure 1-5.

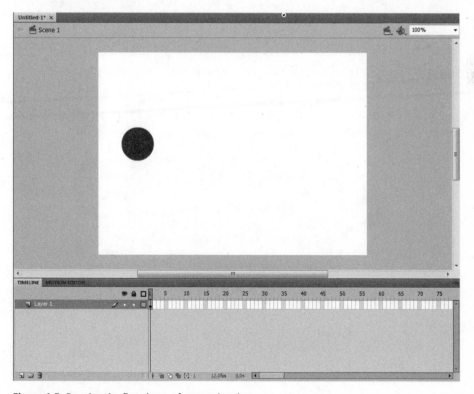

Figure 1-5. Drawing the first shape of your animation

To create a motion tween, we need to convert the image on the screen into a symbol.

6. Clear the Oval tool by clicking on the Selection tool as shown in Figure 1-6.

7. Right-click the oval on the stage and select Convert to Symbol as shown in Figure 1-7.

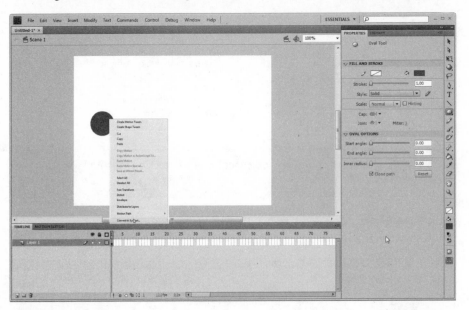

Figure 1-6. Click on the Selection tool to clear the Oval tool.

Figure 1-7. Selecting Convert to Symbol transforms the oval into a symbol that is ready to have animation effects applied to it.

8. The Convert to Symbol dialog box will appear, asking you to rename your symbol.

9. In the Name field, rename the symbol to Ball as shown in Figure 1-8, and click OK.

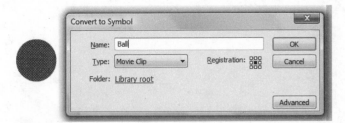

Figure 1-8. Ensuring an intuitive name for your symbol makes it easier to identify when you are dealing with large-scale Flash animations.

You will see the new Ball symbol appear in the Library area. Now that the shape has become a symbol, it's time to create our motion tween—and this is where the ease of Flash CS4 is really on display!

10. Right-click once more on the Ball symbol and select Create Motion Tween from the menu. We are now going make the ball move!

11. Drag the shape to the right side of the screen as shown in Figure 1-9. You will notice that a path appears behind the oval. This is the path the animation will travel along.

Figure 1-9. Dragging your ball to the right defines the path of animation.

12. Select from the menu Control ➤ Test Movie to test your movie.

13. Save the file as chapter1_motiontween.fla.

You will see the path that the ball will take as it moves.

You can also download the flash file to instantly see the movement by opening chapter1_motiontween.fla in the files that are available for download from www.friendsofed.com.

Now you understand how easy it is to create a simple motion tween. The same principals apply to more advanced graphics, as you will see as we get further into the book.

In the next section we will examine how the Motion Editor panel allows you even greater control over your animations.

The Motion Editor panel gives you greater control

The Motion Editor panel, shown in Figure 1-10, enables you to control every keyframe parameter using the keyframe editor, such as size, scale, rotation, positioning, and filters, and it also allows you to visually control easing using curves. It gives you the ability to quickly and easily add effects and details to your tweens.

Represented as a series of graphs, the Motion Editor panel symbolizes tween property values by displaying a graph for each property. When a tween property is affected on the stage, you will see its corresponding graph change on the Motion Editor. This is incredibly useful for Flash designers because it gives us the ability to create complex animations without having to create complicated motion paths and tweening.

Each graph on the Motion Editor panel represents time horizontally on an x-axis as well as the value of the change of the keyframe property on the y-axis. The previous image, Figure 1-10, shows the value of the x and y properties of the animation from the first exercise.

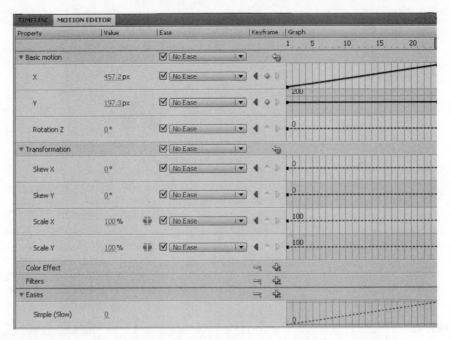

Figure 1-10. The Motion Editor panel gives you greater control over keyframe properties.

We will briefly divert into an exercise now, which will take the FLA file created earlier and enable the ball to move along a preset curve. Then we'll examine the effect that this has on the Motion Editor, and specifically the Basic Motion y-axis.

1. Open chapter1_motiontween.fla. If you skipped the previous exercise, you can open a file of the same name from the downloadable material available on the friends of ED website.

2. With the Selection tool selected and the drawing path unselected, drag the middle of the object path toward the top of the stage, as shown in Figure 1-11.

Figure 1-11. Changing the trajectory of your animation

3. Select Control ➤ Test Movie to see the effect of adding the curve to the trajectory will have on your animation.

You will see that your ball now travels along the curve that you have set, and adds more interest to your animation. But more interesting than this is what has happened to your Motion Editor panel.

4. Select the drawing curve with the Selection tool, then use your cursor to drag the Motion Editor panel to full view, as shown in Figure 1-12. What do you see? The second panel on the Basic Motion section has changed on the y-axis to reflect the vertical height of the curve upon the stage.

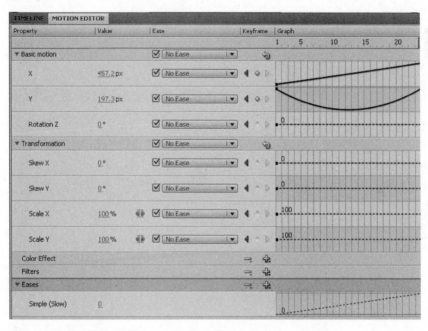

Figure 1-12. The Motion Editor panel reflects changes to your animation.

> *If you click on the Timeline tab now, you will see that it has automatically been set by the Motion Editor, depending on the frame rate that you have established. The Motion Editor panel is a no-muss, no-fuss way of easily animating your movie clips.*

This has been a very quick introduction to the Motion Editor panel. We will be using this tool more thoroughly in Chapter 6, when you learn the difference between Motion, Shape, and Classic tweens and begin to learn about inverse kinematics.

Motion tween presets gets you started quickly!

Motion tween presets are motion tweens that were installed with Adobe Flash CS4. They are a great way of learning basic animation in Flash CS4, so if you are a newcomer, we recommend that you experiment with them as you create your animations and movie clips.

The following exercise will teach you about the Motion Presets panel and how to apply motion presets to objects.

1. Create a new blank ActionScript 3.0 document in Flash CS4 by selecting File ➤ New.

2. Left-click and hold the Rectangle tool and select the PolyStar tool from the menu that appears.

3. In the same way that we placed the circle on the stage in the first exercise, place a polygon on the stage, as shown in Figure 1-13.

Figure 1-13. Placing a shape on the stage

We now need to convert the shape into a symbol as we did in the first exercise.

4. With the Selection tool selected, right-click the polygon and select Convert to Symbol.

5. At the Convert to Symbol screen, rename the symbol polygon 1 and click OK.

Your polygon is now ready to apply a motion preset to!

6. Select Windows ➤ Motion Presets as shown in Figure 1-14.

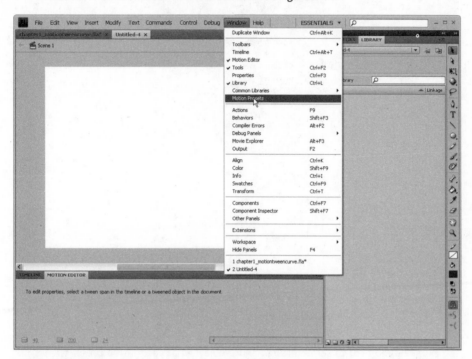

Figure 1-14. Opening the Motion Presets panel in Flash CS4

The Motion Presets panel will open as shown in Figure 1-15. This is where we begin to see how valuable these presets are in creating animations quickly.

Figure 1-15. The Motion Presets panel comes preconfigured with dozens of ready-to-go animations.

7. Take a moment to scroll through and preview what each of the preset tweens do, then choose one you like. We have chosen fly-out-bottom.

8. Select your shape.

9. Highlight fly-out-bottom in the Motion Presets panel and click Apply. The path of the animation will appear on the screen as shown in Figure 1-16.

10. Select Control ➤ Test Movie to test your movie.

You will see the shape follow the animation that you have chosen.

The large exercise in the section "Advertising templates in Flash CS4" will show you how to create a basic but effective advertising banner using motion presets. We will investigate motion presets in more detail in Chapter 3.

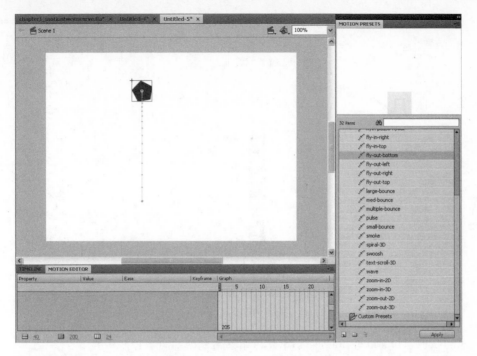

Figure 1-16. The green line indicates the preset path for the object's journey on the stage.

Achieve pure motion with inverse kinematics

Using inverse kinematics (IK) with the Bone tool allows you to create truly smooth and lifelike animations. Inverse kinematics is the manner in which you can determine the boundaries of an object that possesses joints. It is widely used in programming for games such as World of Warcraft and Far Cry to ensure that characters relate realistically to their environments, and for 3D animation.

With Flash CS4 you can create two kinds of IK animations: using shapes and using symbols. The symbol IK animation has bones that are linked together in a chainlike effect as detailed in the following exercise, and the shape IK animation converts the shapes that you have selected into an IK shape object.

Creating an IK animation with symbols

1. Create a new blank document in Flash CS4.

2. Create two rectangles, one above the other as shown in Figure 1-17.

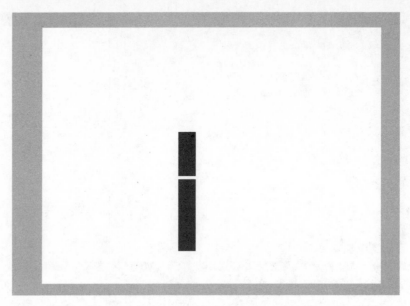

Figure 1-17. Careful consideration of your bonework makes for better animation.

Complete your arm by drawing an oval on the stage for a hand.

   3. Choose the Oval tool and draw a circle on the top of the rectangles as shown in Figure 1-18.

Figure 1-18. Three shapes compose your arm.

We have just drawn the basics of an arm. The first rectangle represents the arm from shoulder to elbow, the second from elbow to wrist, and the circle the hand. The next step is to turn the individual shapes into movie clips in preparation for animating them.

   4. Right-click on the first rectangle you created. From the menu, select Convert to Symbol.

5. At the Convert to Symbol pop-up, rename it Arm1.

6. Repeat this step for the forearm and the hand, naming them Arm2 and Hand, respectively.

The preparation for animation is done; we are now going to apply the Bone tool to link the symbols together for lifelike animation.

7. Select the Bone tool from the tool menu, as shown in Figure 1-19.

Consider where the movable joints need to be. In the case of an arm, you need to ensure that it leads from the upper edge of the bottom rectangle to the bottom edge of the upper rectangle.

Figure 1-19. The Bone tool enables you to create movable skeletons of your animations.

8. With the mouse, select the upper edge of the lower rectangle and drag a small line to the bottom of the upper rectangle, as shown in Figure 1-20.

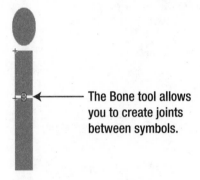

The Bone tool allows you to create joints between symbols.

Figure 1-20. The Bone tool creates movable joints.

9. Repeat the preceding step from the top of the second rectangle to the bottom of the hand oval, as shown in Figure 1-21.

Figure 1-21. The completed bone structure

You now have your bone structure in place. Compare it to your own arm—so far we have placed an elbow joint and a wrist joint. Now we will make it wave like an arm!

10. On the Armature layer of the timeline, shown in Figure 1-22, right-click frame 5 and choose Insert Pose.

Figure 1-22. The Armature layer of the timeline

11. With the Selection tool drag the "hand" of your arm to the left so it appears that it is waving, as shown in Figure 1-23.

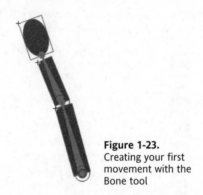

Figure 1-23.
Creating your first
movement with the
Bone tool

12. On the Armature layer of the timeline, right-click frame 15 and choose Insert Pose.

13. Drag the hand of your "arm" to the right so that it waves to the other direction, as shown in Figure 1-24.

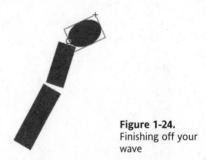

Figure 1-24.
Finishing off your
wave

14. Test your movie by selecting Control ➤ Test Movie.

The result is a more natural-looking animation created in minutes rather than hours. This is just a very small part of what IK and the Bone tool can do. We will revisit inverse kinematics and the Bone tool in Chapter 5, when we further investigate kinds of tweens, and in Chapter 6, where we will create some truly awesome IK animations.

Instant 3D transformations using Flash CS4

Flash CS4 empowers users to position and animate objects in 3D space. You can create sophisticated 3D animations from 2D objects. It also introduces the ability to rotate and animate across three axes: the traditional horizontal x-axis, the vertical y-axis, and the 3D z-axis.

Two kinds of 3D executions can be performed in Flash CS4: a *translation*, which is when an object is moved in 3D space, and a *transformation*, which is when an object is rotated in 3D space. Using both of these tools, Flash CS4 users can create sophisticated 3D animations.

In Chapter 7 you will learn how to travel through time and space with the Flash CS4 3D tool.

An artist is born with the Deco drawing tool

The Deco (Decorative) drawing tool enables you to turn shapes into intricate and complex geometric patterns via algorithmic calculations. Any graphical shape can be transformed into a tool for designing patterns that can be utilized via tools such as Brush or Fill, or you can create effects with the Deco Symmetry tool.

Although Chapters 4 and 5 will take a closer look at creating imaginative graphics, let's find out how the powerful Deco drawing tool can take your drawing to the next level.

The Vine fill

In the following exercise, you will see how the Deco tool allows you to create a background very easily, first using the default Vine fill. We will then create our own custom fill.

1. Create a new Flash ActionScript 3.0 file.
2. Using the Oval tool, shown in Figure 1-25, draw a circle in the center of the screen.

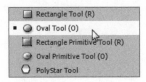

Figure 1-25. Selecting the Oval tool

Holding down the Shift key as you drag a circle outward locks both axes together, making a perfect circle like the one shown in Figure 1-26.

Figure 1-26. Drawing a circle

3. Select the center fill of the circle.

4. Press Delete to remove the filler, leaving the circumference, shown in Figure 1-27.

Figure 1-27. Deleting the circle's fill

5. Select the Deco tool or press U.

6. Open the Deco tool's Properties Inspector and select Vine Fill as shown in Figure 1-28.

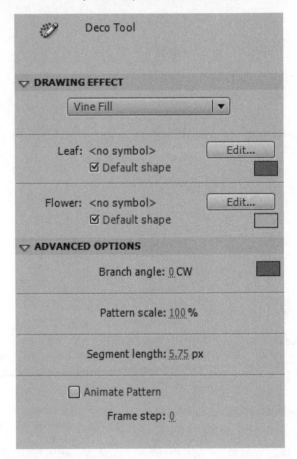

Figure 1-28. Selecting the Vine Fill drawing effect in the Deco tool

7. Click the middle of the outlined circle.

8. Watch the vine grow to fill the bounds of the circle, as shown in Figure 1-29.

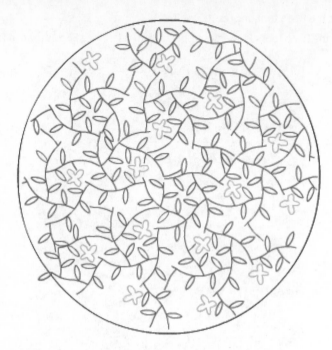

Figure 1-29. Your vine

If you want to create customized leaf and flower shapes, you will need to draw both leaf and flower shapes, then convert them to movie clips. Use the Deco tool panel to edit the symbol type. Then fill your desired area. The following exercise covers creating a custom Vine fill.

1. Select the fill created with the Deco tool.
2. Select the Brush tool, and give it a red color.
3. Draw a small flower shape with the Brush tool, as shown in Figure 1-30. Use different colors to fill it in if you like.

Figure 1-30. Drawing a flower

4. Select the whole flower using the Selection tool.

5. Convert the flower to a Movie Clip by right-clicking on the graphic and selecting Movie Clip from the Convert to Symbol dialog box. Call it Flower, as shown in Figure 1-31.

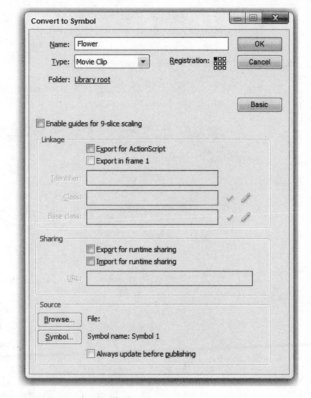

Figure 1-31. Select the flower then convert it to a movie clip.

6. Select a leaf color from the palette.

7. Using the Brush tool draw a very small leaf. This leaf will populate the branches of the Vine fill as shown in Figure 1-32.

Figure 1-32. Select the leaf then convert it to a movie clip.

21

8. Select the whole leaf and convert it to a movie clip called Leaf, as we did previously with the Flower movie clip.

9. Select the Deco tool and locate the Properties Inspector.

10. With the Deco tool still selected, click the Edit button next to the Leaf field in the Properties Inspector, as shown in Figure 1-33.

We will now repeat this for the Flower symbol.

11. With the Deco tool still selected, click the Edit button that is to the right of the Flower field in the Properties Inspector, also show in Figure 1-33.

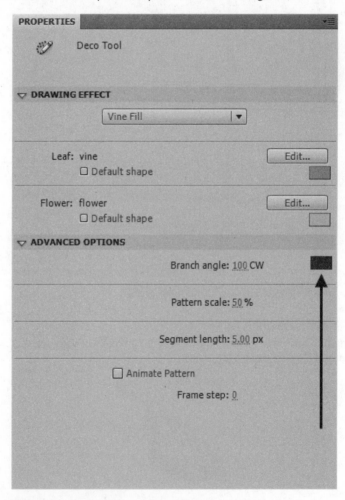

Figure 1-33. The Properties Inspector allows you to choose custom graphics for your fill.

12. In the Deco tool's Properties Inspector, set the Branch Angle to 100 CW, Pattern Scale to 50%, and Segment Length to 5.00px, as shown in Figure 1-33.

The color of the branch is controlled by the colored square adjacent to Branch Angle.

13. Fill the middle circle with the new Deco fill tool as shown in Figure 1-34.

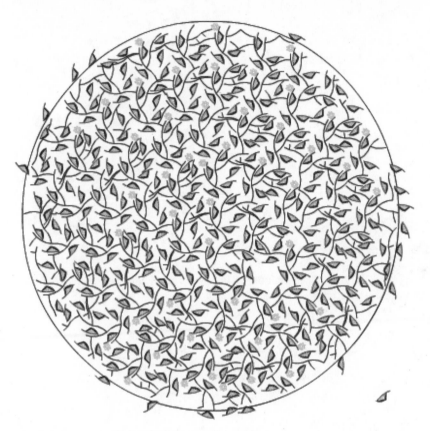

Figure 1-34. The customized Vine fill

The Grid fill

We are now going to use the customized flower and leaf symbols we created in the previous exercise to generate the customized fill.

1. Starting from where you left off with the Vine fill, delete the Vine fill within the oval.

2. Select the Deco tool and change the drawing effect to Grid Fill. Make sure the Fill movie clip is set to Flower. Change Horizontal Spacing and Vertical Spacing to 3.00px. Also change the scale to 300% to match Figure 1-35.

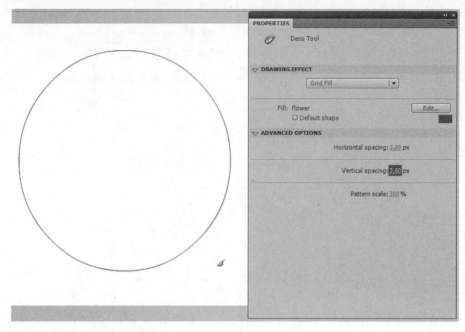

Figure 1-35. The Grid fill settings

3. Using the Deco tool, fill the middle of the oval. You should see the oval populate with evenly spaced flowers, as shown in Figure 1-36.

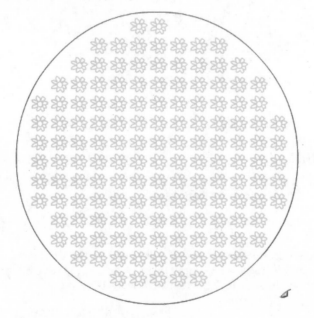

Figure 1-36. The Grid fill drawing effect

The Symmetry brush

The Symmetry brush allows you to create kaleidoscope effects using the Deco tool and one or more symbols.

1. Starting from where you left off with the Grid fill, delete the Grid fill within the oval.

2. Select the Deco tool and change the drawing effect to Symmetry Brush. Make sure the module is set to Flower as shown in Figure 1-37.

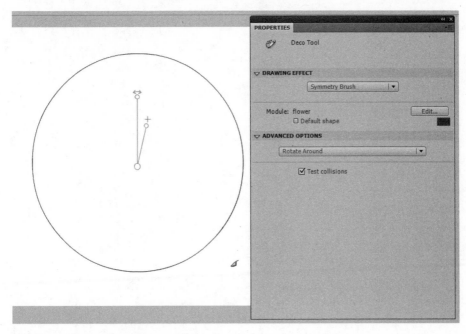

Figure 1-37. The Symmetry brush settings

3. Adjust the Symmetry brush's arms on the center of the stage to bring the arms close together.

   The number of movie-clip duplications you need depends on the angle between the Symmetry brush's arms. The smaller the angle and the closer the arms are to each other, the more movie clips will be duplicated to the stage.

4. Use your mouse to drag a pattern onto the stage.

   The further you drag your mouse, the larger the radius of the Symmetry brush, as shown in Figure 1-38.

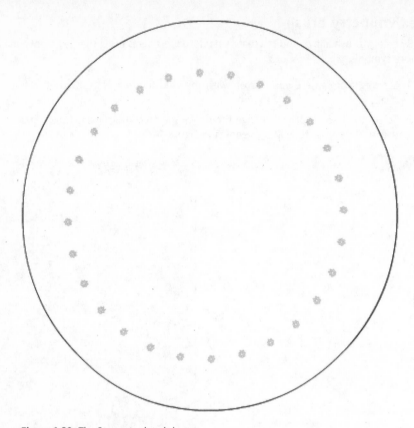

Figure 1-38. The Symmetry brush in use

Just how do all these great things benefit us?

Not only is Flash CS4 designed to get you up and running as quickly and painlessly as possible, it also contains templates designed to get you up and running in the *marketing world*. These enable you to create advertising banners that act as conduits between your potential clients and your website.

Online advertising uses the Internet to promote your brand to consumers. Online advertising can take many forms, but one of the most popular is banner advertising. Banner advertising allows you to bring your unique designs, animations, and audio to the mass market. You can see banner ads on almost any major site; simply visit www.yahoo.com or www.msn.com to see a selection.

In the distant past, banner ads were capped at a 20KB file weight. Today this specification has doubled for most online publishers to 40KB for a standard banner ad, which enables you to include more graphics and animations than before. There are also nonstandard ads called *rich media* and *polite download* banners that enable you to create ads with a total of 100MB to run video, sound, and larger animations. We will investigate how to set up rich media templates in Chapter 8, as they rely heavily on ActionScript to run. For now we'll focus on the banner templates that come standard with Flash CS4.

> *You can find out more about advertising standards and tracking the success of your online banner campaign in Chapter 11.*

Advertising templates in Flash CS4

Flash CS4 is equipped with standard banner templates that you can implement immediately. In the next section, you'll find out how to use the templates and you'll implement some of the techniques you learned previously in this chapter to see how quickly you can create a marketing campaign in Flash CS4. Let's waste no more time—check out the Flash CS4 advertising template.

1. Open Flash CS4.

The Welcome screen will appear as shown in Figure 1-39.

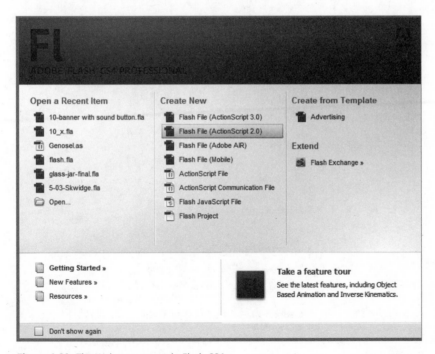

Figure 1-39. The Welcome screen in Flash CS4

2. Click on the Advertising link under the Create from Template section.

A screen will appear with a choice of 16 advertising templates that are commonly employed on large-scale websites. To learn more about Internet industry standards, see Chapter 11 of this book.

3. Select the 160✕600—Wide Skyscraper banner ad and click OK.

On the stage you will see the Flash CS4 document appear in the size 160✕600, the size of the industry-standard wide skyscraper banner advertisement. We are going to place a small amount of animated text on it to create the advertisement.

4. Click on the Text tool to select it. On the stage, type the word Gene as shown in Figure 1-40.

Because we are going to animate the text by having it fly in from off the banner, we need to convert it to a Movie Clip symbol type.

5. Right-click the Gene text and select Convert to Symbol from the menu that opens, as shown in Figure 1-41.

Figure 1-40.
Adding text to a wide skyscraper banner advertisement

Figure 1-41. Converting static text to a symbol

6. The Convert to Symbol dialog box will appear. Name the movie Gene.

7. Rename Layer 1 of the timeline where the Gene symbol is placed; name it Gene.

8. Click on the Selection tool and then the Gene movie clip on the stage to select it.

Remember earlier in the chapter when we investigated motion presets? You're now going to see how easily we can use them to create an informative advertising asset.

9. From the menu, select Window ➤ Motion Presets.

You will see the Motion Presets panel open, as shown in Figure 1-42.

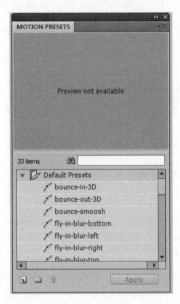

Figure 1-42. The Motion Presets panel

We're going to have the first line of the text, Gene, fly in from the left hand side.

10. Scroll down the Motion Presets panel and select the fly-in-left option as shown in Figure 1-43.

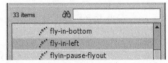

Figure 1-43. Selecting the fly-in-left option in the Motion Presets panel

11. Click Apply.

You will see the timeline on the Gene layer is populated, and a path has appeared on the page, as shown in Figure 1-44.

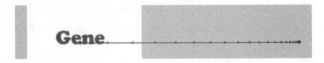

Figure 1-44. The motion preset path on the stage

12. Test your movie by selecting Control ➤ Test Movie.

You will see that your movie begins with Gene in the middle of the 160x600 stage, then moving off it to the right. We don't want this. We would like to have it move from the left of the banner into the middle of the banner. We'll make this happen now.

13. Click on the Selection tool, then click on the motion path on the stage.

14. Using your arrow keys or your mouse, drag the path and the movie clip to the left side of the stage so that the path ends in the middle of the stage, as shown in Figure 1-45.

Figure 1-45. Moving the path to end the animation on the banner

15. Test your movie again by selecting Control ➤ Test Movie.

16. Save your movie as 160x600.fla.

You will see that the movie now animates with the Gene movie clip sliding from the left of the banner to the middle of the banner. It will loop rapidly, but we will fix that soon. The next exercise will allow us to add animation to finish off the advertisement.

1. Open the 160x600.fla document as completed in the previous exercise.

2. Create a new layer on the timeline by clicking the New Layer button .

3. Call the new layer With, as shown in Figure 1-46.

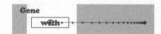

Figure 1-46. Creating a new layer in the banner advertisement

4. Right-click frame 10 on the With layer of the timeline and select Insert Keyframe from the menu.

5. Select the Text tool, and in the same font as Gene, type with on the stage as shown in Figure 1-47.

Figure 1-47. Adding more copy to the stage

6. Right-click the *with* text on the stage and choose Convert to Symbol.

7. Choose Movie Clip from the Convert to Symbol dialog box and call it With.

8. Select Window ➤ Motion Presets to open the Motion Preset panel and once again scroll down to select fly-in-left and click Apply.

Your stage will appear similar to Figure 1-48.

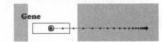

Figure 1-48. Creating a preset motion path on the With layer

9. Click the Selection tool and then click on the With motion path on the stage.

10. Using your arrow keys or your mouse, drag the path and the movie clip to the left side of the stage so that the path ends in the middle of the stage.

11. Test your movie.

What happens? You begin to see the animation build. Motion presets are very basic Flash CS4, but suddenly you can see how easy it is to create compelling animations using them. Over the course of this book, you will learn how to make truly interactive and compelling banners and websites, but this exercise shows you how quickly you can have a marketing campaign up and running.

12. Create a new layer on the timeline.

13. Call it Envy.

14. Right-click on frame 20 of the timeline and select Insert Keyframe.

15. Select the Text tool and type Envy onto the stage.

16. Convert the *Envy* text on the stage to a movie clip called Envy.

17. Open the Motion Presets panel and apply the fly-in-left preset to the Envy movie clip.

18. As before, move the preset path to conclude in the middle of the banner as shown in Figure 1-49.

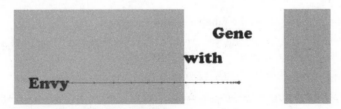

Figure 1-49. The stage with all three animations on it

19. Test and save your movie.

We have one last step to complete the animation. We are going to give the viewer of the banner advertisement a reason to want to click on it—by promoting a sale. The next exercise is basically a repetition of the animation that we have applied to the words *Gene with Envy* previously.

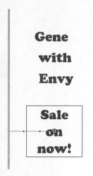

Figure 1-50.
Adding the final copy to the animation

1. Open 160x600.fla in Flash CS4, taking up where we left off with the previous exercise.

2. Add a new layer called Sale on the timeline.

3. On the Sale layer, insert a keyframe at frame 40.

4. Using the Text tool add the words *Sale on now!* as shown in Figure 1-50.

5. Convert the *Sale on now!* text into a movie clip called Sale.

6. Open the Motion Presets panel and apply the fly-in-left motion path to the Sale movie clip.

7. Relocate the motion path to end in the middle of the banner as we did with the previous animation.

8. Test and save your movie.

You will notice the message Gene with Envy Sale on now! appear in the animation and quickly disappear. The following exercise will enable the text to stay on the screen for a short while before the animation loops again.

1. On the Sale layer of the timeline, scrub along to frame 100 and insert a frame.

2. Repeat this with the remaining layers.

3. Test and save the movie.

When you test your movie you will see the message appear nicely and stay on the screen for a few seconds before looping.

We have one final step before we could theoretically send the advertisement, with accompanying backup GIF, to a publisher to run on their network. We need to give the ad a button to enable the user to click through to the site. Bear in mind that the following exercise is a very quick overview of buttons. In Chapter 6 we will revisit the Banner button, and in Chapter 10 you will discover how to create a Mute button.

Figure 1-51.
Creating a large button on the stage

1. Open 160x600.fla in Flash CS4, taking up where we left off with the previous exercise.

2. Create a new layer on the timeline. Call it Button.

3. On frame 1 of the Button layer create a shape on the stage that covers the entire 160×600 banner as shown in Figure 1-51.

4. Right-click the button and choose Convert to Symbol from the menu.

5. Choose Button from the Type drop-down in the Convert to Symbol dialog box.

6. Name your button Button.

7. Click on the Properties Inspector and give your button the instance name of Button.

8. With Button layer selected, go to Window ➤ Actions.

The Actions - Frame window will appear, as shown in Figure 1-52. Don't worry much about ActionScript now, because Chapter 8 will show you how to become a script wizard. We are simply going to place the click-through code onto the button.

9. Type the following code into line 1 of the ActionScript panel, as shown in Figure 1-52.

```
Button.addEventListener(MouseEvent.MOUSE_DOWN, mouseDownHandler);

function mouseDownHandler(event:MouseEvent):void {

    navigateToURL(new URLRequest("http://www.gene-envy.com/"));

}
```

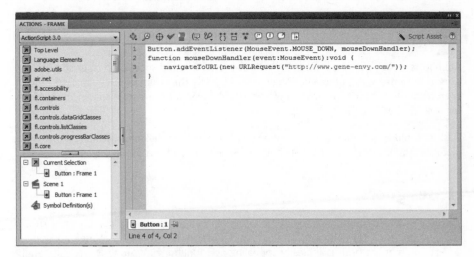

Figure 1-52. Your code in the Actionscript panel

All that is left to do is to remove the opacity from the button.

10. Double-click the button on the stage to select it.

11. Click on the Properties Inspector, and then click on the Fill button 🖼.

12. Click on the 100% value in the Alpha channel, and amend it to be 0%.

13. Save and test your movie.

You banner advertisement is complete. If you had purchased a media schedule on a network such as Yahoo! or MSN, you would have been able to create a backup GIF and send the banner to the client to display.

> *On clicking you will be taken to the Gene-with-Envy website. This website contains many Flash CS4 applications that you will be building throughout the course of this book.*

Who uses Flash CS4?

No longer the realm of dedicated web designers alone, a number of professionals will find Flash CS4 helpful in their day-to-day work.

Graphic designers

A graphic designer creates designs using images, photographs, fonts, and motion graphics. Traditionally graphic designers designed for print executions only, but crossover between the mediums is increasingly common.

Flash CS4 allows graphic designers to take their static designs to new levels. Using components such as the Deco and 3D tools, graphic designers can make their visions come alive.

Animators

Animators create multiple images that are displayed in rapid succession to create the illusion of movement. Animators no longer exist in solely the realm of television and movies. With technology becoming increasingly accessible, animators are able to join the ranks of mainstream designers and developers.

Flash CS4 reduces the amount of time animators spend on making their animations work, thanks to sophisticated functions such as the Bone tool, 3D transformation, and translation.

Web designers

The goal of web designers is to combine design and interaction. They combine the knowledge of design, information technology, and systems to produce websites and online advertising that are both graphically appealing and functional. Web designers will benefit from Flash CS4 because more than ever it is a design tool and an animation tool rolled into one.

Web developers

Web developers are software developers or engineers who work specifically on projects that exist online. Front-end web developers specialize in user-side technology and the way that users interact with websites and online applications.

Flash CS4 will hold special interest for web developers because it offers easier integration between back-end databases and displaying dynamic content on demand.

Summary

Adobe Flash CS4 provides users with the ability to quickly design and produce comprehensive, professional animations. With a number of new abilities that were discussed in this chapter, such as 3D modeling, which enables you to apply a sense of weight and perspective to your animations; inverse kinematics, which allows you to create lifelike movements in your movie clips; and object-based animation, which gets you animating quicker than ever before, Flash CS4 brings professional design and animation to everyone.

In Chapter 2 we will begin to work on developing the platform for a larger project. A thorough project plan will help readers breach the abyss between the "big idea" and final published execution. You will learn how to set out ideas in such a way that you will be able to clearly determine how to implement them in Flash and beyond, and you'll learn the preliminaries of online marketing. The chapter will detail the design flow, as well as teach you how to break your project into workable chunks so that that big idea doesn't get out of control.

CHAPTER 2

GETTING CREATIVE: HOW TO MAKE YOUR IDEAS COME TO LIFE THROUGH PROJECT PLANNING

Over the course of this book, you will be creating a website and associated banner campaign for marketing the site in Flash CS4.

To get the most out of the time you spend creating your site and assets, you should first invest time planning exactly what it is you are going to build. This is important because not only will it allow you to plan your timeline for the build, but also identify any "seeds of destruction" early—that is, elements of your project that could prove to be harder than they first seem and allow you to prepare for the difficulties ahead.

This chapter delves into the realm of best practices, and how to plan your build so that your users have the best possible experience. Chapter 3 will see you beginning to build Flash CS4 animations, starting with a 300×250 medium rectangle advertising banner. A **medium rectangle** banner is a standard-sized banner as defined by the Internet Advertising Bureau.

The development cycle: Implementing the design flow in your Flash CS4 project

Design flow is a design methodology that was originally created for working with electronics. It enables you to plan the order of project progress through conception, design and build, quality assurance testing, and project deployment. It's the comprehensive plan of your project because it is a step-by-step guide to concepts that you must consider.

When you are contemplating a project that users will interact with, such as a website or Flash application, you need to consider the way that the user will navigate through to achieving what you want them to achieve. Using a design flow ensures that you consider everything that you need to include in your website or application before you have invested the time designing and building it.

There are four stages to a design flow: concept and planning, design and build, quality assurance testing, and deployment and implementation, as shown in Figure 2-1. Let's now examine each of these steps.

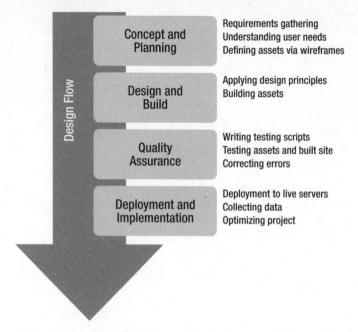

Figure 2-1. The design flow

Phase 1: Concept and planning

It all starts with an idea. If you can dream it, you can do it. So how do you go about dreaming it? There are many techniques used to enhance creativity and problem solving. One crucial step is to remove criticism from your train of thought. Children are creative for this very reason. Doodle everything that comes to mind. Some people see ideas in words, so grab a blank piece of paper and just jot it down. Above all, try not to filter your thoughts, even if the ideas are silly or don't fit the situation. Often a great solution comes from left field. While you are considering raw ideas, browse as much media as you can. Flip through magazines, surf the Web, and watch random Internet video clips. The aim of this stage is to get a feel for a concept. Too many people fall into the trap of thinking that the first step is the final finished idea. Ideas are fluid, as are Flash designs. The final design will grow under personal experience and external feedback. Also, people are afraid to borrow ideas from other concepts. Imagine where art and music would be today if ideas weren't cross-pollinated in mimetic fashion. Borrow and modify—just remember to make it your own.

So you've got a page full of gibberish, some stick drawings, and a coffee stain that looks like a blob. Unless you have a definite feel for your end design, the next step is crucial. This involves using your cognition and perception to draw workable concepts from the cacophony of ideas on the page.

When trying to decide on ideas for the main project in this book, a heap of ideas were thrown onto the table. Some were funny, some were stupid, some were even good enough to use. For instance, I considered making the end project in this book a radio station, a video game, a toaster simulator, and even a virtual zoo. After research, deliberation, and brainstorming, I decided on the website for a pet store in the end. However, note that the first concepts were nothing like the final idea.

So, after you have settled on a few big ideas, the next phase of the design process is to translate one of the concepts into something concrete, something "Flashable." Research will help you decide which concept best suits the situation. Research the time it may take to do a particular task. Look at a competitor's offerings. What can you offer that they do not?

The source files and exercises in this book will enable you to build a site for a fictional fantasy pet store. The exercises in this chapter will detail the steps in implementing the concept and planning stage of your project's design flow.

Researching what your users want to do

One of the most important things to consider in this phase is the way that users will interact with the site. You need to ensure that it is immediately recognizable to your user what it is they can accomplish on your Flash site.

In the case of this book, we are going to create a site and a banner campaign for a fictional company called Gene with Envy that specializes in breeding and selling little critters with a difference.

Your research phase in the concept and planning section of your website design should involve researching your target demographic and researching competitor sites.

Generally, people take the path of least resistance when they visit a website. This behavior is observed in the dogma of "form follows function." That is, make it easy for users to navigate a website and a style will evolve from the navigation. This is the difference between the psychologies of art and design. Art is a vehicle of expression used to satisfy the creator. Art can often neglect the needs of the user. Design is more cerebral, and considers the needs of the user. Both mentalities can create beauty, but go about it in a different way. As you become a Flash designer, it is your duty to guide the user journey, even if you don't feel the design matches your own internal taste. Succumbing to the art side could leave your website users lost and confused. So just remember, "communication before decoration."

Ask yourself, what are the key objectives for users to achieve before they leave your site? What can you do to ensure that they achieve these quickly and easily? What assumptions can you make about the familiarity they have in navigating the technology that you have chosen to build your site on? What are the three most important tasks you want your users to complete, and how can you ensure that these are the easiest and most easily achievable? How do users navigate through your application?

When you are researching your competition, take note of what they do well and what could be improved. An easy way to summarize what level your competitors are at is to perform what is commonly known as a SWOT analysis on their websites. SWOT stands for "strengths, weaknesses, opportunities, and threats."

Strengths. When you are analyzing a competitor's site, you need to look at the attributes of that site and note what is helpful in getting users to achieve their goals.

Weaknesses. Note what is not done well on your competitor's site, and compare it to your own goals. What weaknesses on the sites of others can you change to become strengths on yours?

Opportunities. Where do opportunities lie externally for a site such as yours? Is there a niche market that you can take advantage of in getting your site out into public consumption? We will be investigating opportunities later in this book when we look at the marketing campaign that will accompany your site.

Threats. What is happening externally? Is your business one of many attempting to achieve cut-through in the market? Does a large company already offer what your business offers at greater value for money, or quicker turnaround?

Figure 2-2 shows an example SWOT analysis of our fictional company Gene with Envy.

Strengths	Weaknesses
- New, never-before-seen product receiving lots of media attention - Youth market demographic	- Nature of product means that you need to direct people into the store rather than purchase over the Internet
Opportunities - January pet convention - Incentivize prospective buyers with loyalty program	**Threats** - Pets-R-Us local market competing chain

Figure 2-2. A SWOT analysis of the Gene with Envy business

From the SWOT analysis shown in Figure 2-2, we can begin to draw conclusions about what kinds of assets we need to build to capture our demographics needs. From the Strengths section, we can see that the new product is receiving lots of media attention. It would be beneficial to have a news section that displays the latest news about the gene-with-envy product. We can see from the weaknesses that we need to make it easy for people to contact the company, so we need to ensure we create a prominent contact section on the site. We also need to ensure that we have a comprehensive gallery to display our wares.

In the next section, we will generate wireframes that will form the skeleton of your site.

A **wireframe** is a basic visual guideline of what a page in your site will look like. It enables you to structure your content in a preferred hierarchy prior to investing the time and effort building the site. It enables you to decide where the fundamental elements of your site will sit.

In a real-world scenario, wireframes are a vital communication tool when you are communicating with clients and project stakeholders. It enables people to visualize the site and make amendments without the actual work being invested.

You will face many decisions to ensure that users get the most out of your site, and you will be forced to make priorities about the most important goals of your site.

Defining your concept with wireframes

As you know, the most important part of any website is deciding what content you will have on it and how the user will interact with it. As noted before, we are going to create a site for Gene with Envy. From our SWOT analysis, we know that we want the user to be able to watch videos of the critters, send videos to friends, browse a complete gallery of all available products, read news via an RSS feed, and contact the store via an inquiry form. We will set the site up in such a way that you will be able to customize it relatively easily for your own needs.

Wireframes dictate the user journey and interactivity

To plan your website, you need to create a wireframe about what content you will have on it and how the user will interact with it. A wireframe allows you to define the information architecture of the site, which will in turn influence your design. A wireframe is the representation of the Flash CS4 execution. It instantly accomplishes a number of important things such as identifying all of the features on the page, prioritizing them in order of prominence, and most importantly, communicating what needs to be on the page to your design team.

Figure 2-3 is the basic wireframe of the gene-with-envy one-page website. Over the course of this book, you will be animating a logo, creating a video and associated audio, developing a contact form and a viral component, designing your "plants" to be animated and displayed in a carousel gallery, and creating two standard-sized banners for an accompanying marketing campaign.

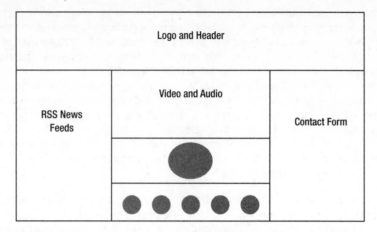

Figure 2-3. Wireframes define the functionality and information architecture of your application.

Phase 2: Design and build

The second phase is the one that most of this book encompasses: the design and build of your project. From Chapter 3, you will be learning how to incorporate beautiful and functional designs into your Flash CS4 website and banner campaign, and how best to use the advanced Flash CS4 tools to create optimum functionality on your site—but let's first investigate what constitutes a good design.

Design is a philosophy that encourages you to think about the problem at hand and solve it using a strategy employed by simple elements and principles. All complex solutions are built from simple, fundamental strategies. Some of the design problems you will encounter in Flash CS4 are likely to be visual design problems. Use the elements and principles of design to ensure a good solution.

Design elements

Design elements and principles envelop basic visual problem solving tactics. The elements are the basic words of design and the principles are the broader grammatical rules of design. These concepts and elements drive all intentional design strategies.

Many design elements are described in the following sections.

Color. Color describes our sensitivity to the flow of energy in the form of light. Energy vibrates at an infinite number of frequencies. Some forms of energy vibrate back and forth very fast, while other forms of energy limp like snails. Humans can only see a small number of the infinite range of frequencies, or colors. The mnemonic "Roy G. Biv" spells out the sequence of seven colors that make up white light, also known as the visible color spectrum. Starting with the most intense energy is red. Then comes orange, yellow, green, and blue. Finally are the low-intensity indigo and violet. Infrared refers to colors that vibrate faster than red, while ultraviolet refers to colors that vibrate more slowly than violet. Knowing about energy levels can help create the illusion of depth. Utilizing intense colors such as red against a laid-back green can make the red appear to come forward while the green recedes into the distance. Color is also particularly useful to draw the eye to an important part of the design. This can be achieved using the color wheel. If the visible colors of the spectrum appear in a radial circle, certain relationships become apparent. Red sits opposite to green, orange opposite to blue, and yellow opposite to violet. To generate user interest, make the background one color and the foreground focus spot the opposite color. Disney cartoons have been using this trick for years. Aside from color being a visual aid, it also plays an important part in psychology. How do you feel when you picture blue for foods? How about green for medicine? Red for the environment? Pay attention to the gut feeling colors give you.

Form. Visual perception is great at creating a sense of volume. The brain uses light and line to calculate our perceived sense of form. We need a sense of form as it helps us to navigate the world we live in. In understanding this need, form can be used to re-create the world we live using line, color, and shape to mimic the real world. Think how a gradient fill on a button uses the highlight at the top and a shadow on the bottom to paint the illusion of a rounded surface. The rounded form creates a greater sense of tangibility, and thus a more intuitive user experience.

Motion. The idea of motion as a design element is created using multiple images, repeating figures, or blurring. Think back to the speed lines placed on cartoon characters to illustrate frantic motion. Geometric shapes placed at increasingly regular intervals can also create a sense of motion in a static picture. Just think of Marcel Duchamp's *Nude Descending Staircase* to see motion in a static image. Motion can also be created using juxtaposing vivid colors.

Space. You can consider space to be one of the most important design elements. This intriguing element is created using discrete areas to let your focal point "breathe." Space can also be perceived in three dimensions through the use of visual cues such as the horizontal positioning of a graphic relative to the vertical location, the size of elements, transparencies, vanishing points, and the amount of detail. Space is used to focus a viewer to a particular region. Clutter is used to diffuse focus, scattering the viewer's attention. The use of space is often referred to as **design space** or **whitespace**.

Line. This element is the mark that is made by the collision of two or more shapes or forms. This can be reproduced using a moving point, such as a pencil, or in the case of Flash CS4, the various design tools, such as the Pencil Line and Pen tools, as shown in Figure 2-4.

Shape. Shape in design can be defined as an area that is enclosed by a line, but, at the same time, it is also definable as an area not enclosed by a line. The shape exists in the negative space. Flash CS4 enables you to easily create shapes through the Shape tool, as shown in Figure 2-5. Any shape in your design will automatically create a negative space around it. Shape becomes important in design when dealing with familiarity and attraction.

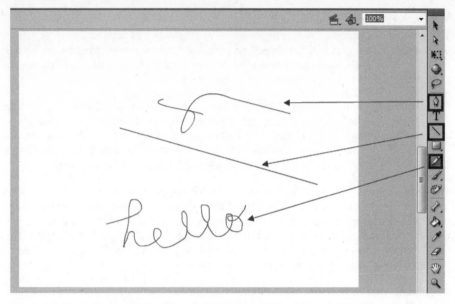

Figure 2-4. Flash CS4 provides useful tools for creating the line element of design.

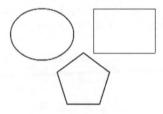

Figure 2-5. Flash CS4 provides a useful Shape tool for creating the shape elements of a design.

Size. This design element is the relative proportion of objects on the canvas to each other. Practically, you can use differences in size to encourage viewer focus to a particular area.

Tone. Also known as value, the design element tone is the lightness or darkness of a surface. It's one of the most potent ways to direct the perception of form.

Now that we have identified all of the elements about design, it's time to talk about exactly what constitutes a design; from there on we will investigate design principles.

Design principles

Visual design is defined as the arrangement of elements and principles. Design principles are the enforcers of the entire design composition. Design principles structure design elements in a way that enables your design to instruct users on how to navigate your layout so that they achieve exactly what you need them to do.

Never are design principles more important than in Flash executions. Consider a painting. The artist is trying to convey a message to the viewer. Flash executions can convey a message and much more. For example, they could be used to get users to fill out a form to receive more information about a product, to browse a gallery, to sign up for a newsletter, or to read the latest news. Flash combines elegance of design with functionality.

There are many schools of thought regarding what exactly design principles are, but all agree that the designer needs to be aware of the elements of design to understand design principles. Broadly put, design principles encompass alignment, balance, contrast, repetition, and whitespace. When using Flash, these form the overriding concept of design principles, which is the art of interactively communicating an idea that includes the use of images, sounds, mouse gestures, animation, and words.

Alignment. Alignment is the horizontal or vertical positioning or arrangement of design elements. It's the way that text and graphics are lined up on the stage. Alignment allows you to create a hierarchy of importance of information upon the stage, organize the order of information, group elements and chunks of information, and create visual connections that will ultimately funnel your users to the place where they can best transact with your brand. Figure 2-6 shows the three kinds of horizontal alignment: left, center, and right.

Figure 2-6. Left, center, and right alignment

Balance. The design principle balance is interesting because it can be executed in many different ways to achieve the desired effect from the user. When considering balance, the most important thing to assess is the content hierarchy. This is often overlooked, and every element in the design ends up fighting for your attention. Developing a content hierarchy involves you going through every element in the layout and ordering information importance. For instance, the homepage of www.google.com has been correctly balanced. The branding/logo dominates the page, followed by the search field and buttons, ending with the minor links. Imagine what the page would look like with those elements in reverse order. In some cases, it's appropriate to misbalance the content hierarchy to highlight what the reader really needs to digest. Remember, the scales of balance can be offset using all the elements of design, not just size and position. You can use tone to give a bigger object depth and push it back into the layout. You could use an opposite color to balance contrast between fighting elements. There are three basic kinds of balance: asymmetrical, radial, and symmetrical.

Typically, an asymmetrical design is off-center, as shown in Figure 2-7. Asymmetrical balance is distributing the objects in your design unevenly to highlight certain visual information. Asymmetrical design also allows you to highlight aspects of your design that are important for the user to acknowledge.

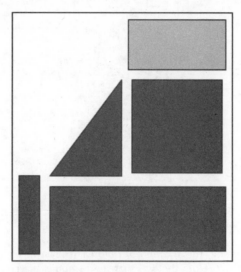

Figure 2-7. With asymmetrical balance, you distribute objects in your design unevenly to highlight certain visual information.

An example of this is *Christ at the Sea of Galilee*, the classical painting by Tintoretto, as shown in Figure 2-8. Examine the structure of the painting. Jesus is the central figure, yet he is not at the center of the painting. The eye is drawn through tone, light, and lines to him standing at the left side of the painting.

Figure 2-8. An example of an asymmetrical piece of art

Radial balance is simply a design in which the visual importance flows outward from the center point, like light rays from the sun, as shown in Figure 2-9. Common places to see radial balance are in circle-based navigation systems.

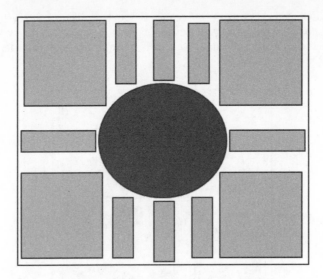

Figure 2-9. The radial balance design principle dictates that information hierarchy flows from a central point in the design.

Raphael's famous painting, the *Triumph of Galatea* (shown in Figure 2-10), is a classic example of radial balance. Note the way that the nymph is the central balance with the lines of the painting—for example, the arrows of the cherubs in the sky draw the eye to the central figure.

Figure 2-10. The *Triumph of Galatea* is an example of radial balance.

Symmetrical balance is the most easily recognized and understood. It's achieved by evenly placing design elements upon the stage, as shown in Figure 2-11; it can also be referred to as mirror imaging. Be aware that your axis of symmetry does not need to fall down the center of the image. It can actually occur in more complicated ways, like an M. C. Escher tessellation.

Figure 2-11. Symmetrical balance is basically a mirror image.

One of the most famous paintings in the world is an example of symmetrical balance. Da Vinci's *The Last Supper* creates a mirror image with Christ as the central point, as shown in Figure 2-12.

Figure 2-12. *The Last Supper* is an example of symmetrical balance.

Contrast. *Contrast* is the word we give to differentiate between objects in a design. Traditionally, contrast is defined by color and tonality, but it can also be applied to all the other design elements. It's an effective way to add visual interest to your Flash CS4 design, and again it works the same way as balance in creating a visual hierarchy. Contrast can be used to focus the viewer's eyes in your design.

Color contrast is most easily recognized, and it is a very important aspect of your Flash CS4 design. Figure 2-13 displays a bad color contrast as it is difficult to read, and Figure 2-14 displays a good color contrast, as it is immediately easy to read. Contrasting colors appear at opposite ends of the color wheel. That is, red vs. green, orange vs. blue, and yellow vs. violet. Be careful not to confuse color contrast with tonal contrast. Tonal contrast refers to how light or dark an object is, while color contrast refers to a position on the color wheel.

This color contrast is hard to read

This color contrast is easy to read

Figure 2-13. Similar tones have low contrast and are hard to differentiate.

Figure 2-14. Tones that are strikingly different from one another have good contrast and are easier to differentiate.

Repetition. This design principle is also often referred to as rhythm or pattern, and defines elements that recur within a design. It can consist of any of the design elements, such as lines, shapes, or even color. It creates visual consistency within a design, subconsciously directing the reader to a focal point, as shown in Figure 2-15. Repetition can also provide a sense of visual timing. Closely placed patterns give a faster, frantic feel, whereas more distantly spaced patterns provide a slower, sleepy feel.

Figure 2-15. Repetition creates visual cues that tie your information together.

Design space. Design space is perhaps the most intriguing of the design principles, and using it is a lot like cooking a soup. Basically, design space is like the liquid—the fluid holding the design together. The contents you place into the soup are like the fresh vegetables, herbs, and wontons. Some soups are thick and chunky, while others beg for emptiness. Design space can be called negative space or whitespace, but these definitions are too literal to be considered good definitions (especially the term *negative space*, which can be confused with *wasted space*). Emptiness can be cleverly used to draw attention to where you want your user to click or visit. Figure 2-16 shows intentional design space.

Figure 2-16. Design space can emphasize knowledge.

Navigation in Flash CS4

Flash CS4 gives you the opportunity to bring a static design to life. It offers the user an engagement and interactivity that can be both functional and beautiful. While the ability to wow your audience with multimedia is easy to do with Flash CS4, it is also easy to alienate your audience with multimedia. This is especially true if you are a newcomer to dynamic design.

Having the means to create amazing animations doesn't warrant a license to do so. Just as animated GIF sites in the late '90s rapidly became pedestrian, so does too much Flash. Recognize the best technology, whether it be Flash CS4, HTML, Ajax, or JavaScript, and utilize it to communicate in the best possible way.

Typography: A powerful communication tool

Reading these pages, you probably haven't given much thought to the typography used.

If this book were set in Comic Sans, the publishers would probably receive complaints.

You may know typefaces as fonts. A **font** represents one particular typeface in a size and style from a family of many. The anatomy of type is shown in Figure 2-17.

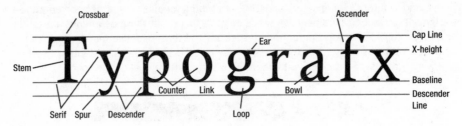

Figure 2-17. The anatomy of type

Important elements to remember are serifs, x-height, and descenders. **Serifs** are little marks at the ends of type characters that help differentiate them. **X-height** is the distance from the baseline to the top of a lowercase x. Typefaces with small x-heights are more efficient, and can fit more words in a sentence. **Descenders** are the dangly bits that hang from the character's baseline. It's important to give your type enough line spacing so the descenders can "breathe."

Typography is as much about psychology as it is about aesthetics. Typography is all about communication. Choose a wrong typeface and you risk sending the wrong message. This especially applies to the Internet and Flash. The typeface you choose should have a reason, just like your composition. To understand which font fits best, you first need to look at a brief history of type. Type has always been about communication. Typefaces evolved from glyphs and scripts—hand-drawn lines that either represented whole words or phonemics. **Phonemics** are word sounds compiled and arranged to an alphabet. For thousands of years, the thoughts of people were drawn, carved, or sculpted by hand. While carving and sculpting was quite permanent, it also occupied time to do effectively. Drawing letters—writing—was much more efficient, but the downfall to drawing was that the media was fallible. Papyrus in particular was prone to erosion and decay. So after putting up with this for a few thousand years, a clever fellow named Johannes Gutenberg decided to automate the process of writing. Around the year 1440, Gutenberg established the first little collection of stamps that could be used to string together words and print pages of sentences. In doing so, he solidified a common letterform, thus giving birth to some of the world's first typefaces.

Early typefaces adopted serifs from their handwritten counterparts. Before Gutenberg, books were all handwritten with a calligraphic style. The first moveable type, the blackletter script shown in Figure 2-18 (also known as Humanist), adapted this look. Blackletter typefaces carry an archaic and dark feel while preaching authority. Some of the first blackletter typefaces include Rotunda and Fraktur.

𝔗𝔥𝔦𝔰 𝔦𝔰 𝔞 𝔟𝔩𝔞𝔠𝔨𝔩𝔢𝔱𝔱𝔢𝔯 𝔱𝔶𝔭𝔢𝔣𝔞𝔠𝔢. 𝔗𝔥𝔦𝔰 𝔦𝔰 𝔞 𝔟𝔩𝔞𝔠𝔨𝔩𝔢𝔱𝔱𝔢𝔯 𝔱𝔶𝔭𝔢𝔣𝔞𝔠𝔢. 𝔗𝔥𝔦𝔰 𝔦𝔰 𝔞 𝔟𝔩𝔞𝔠𝔨𝔩𝔢𝔱𝔱𝔢𝔯 𝔱𝔶𝔭𝔢𝔣𝔞𝔠𝔢.

Figure 2-18. The blackletter typeface

Serifs make text easier to read. Serif fonts, shown in Figure 2-19, carry a very real prestige; strict and serious with a get-the-job-done attitude. Considering serifs are quite small, and video displays are in the range of 72 to 96 dpi, it is not the best idea to use serifs online—that is, unless they can be rendered at a large enough size. Avoid using serif type online that is 10 point or smaller. Some good serif families to use are New Baskerville, Garamond, Palatino, and Century Schoolbook.

This is a serif typeface. This is a serif typeface. This is a serif typeface.

Figure 2-19. Examples of serif typefaces

The **slab-serif** typeface (shown in Figure 2-20), also known as Egyptian, is characterized by its rectilinear, straight-edged serifs. Slab-serifs evolved from the serif family. The super-massive weighting of some slab-serifs give them a strong appearance. They are often adopted by sports teams and university fraternities due to this strength. Some common slab-serif families include Rockwell, Archer, Antique, and the slightly anorexic Courier.

This is a slab-serif typeface. This is a slab-serif typeface. This is a slab-serif typeface.

Figure 2-20. The slab-serif typeface

Another variation is **sans-serif** (*sans* is French for *not*). Sans-serif typefaces (shown in Figure 2-21) lack the little serif bits. This makes them ideal to use online. Some sans-serifs are also rounded, for which they're often given the name Gothic. Sans-serif fonts also have a chic about them. This probably stems from the Bauhaus school of thought, which asked, if something doesn't need to be there, should it be there at all? This attitude gives sans-serif type a punk edge. The best thing about sans is its neutrality. It can be used for many applications without miscommunication. However, due to this neutrality, it can come across as unemotional and boring. So choose wisely. Some great sans-serif families to use are Futura, Century Gothic, Gill Sans, News Gothic, and the ubiquitous Helvetica.

This is a sans-serif typeface. **This is a sans-serif typeface.** This is a sans-serif typeface.

Figure 2-21. The sans-serif font

Handwritten typefaces are known as **script** or **cursive**. Some scripts sing of soft sensitivity. Some scripts mimic a child's first attempts at letterform. Others can be scratchy, decadence-inspired grunge. This gives the family a charm and sensibility not seen in other typefaces. However, some scripts can be very hard to read. Hard-to-read fonts kill communication and must be avoided at all costs. Some common scripts include Caflisch, Edwardian, Mistral, Lucinda, Corsiva, Brush, and the dreaded, never-to-be-used-at-any-cost Comic Sans. Examples of script typefaces are shown in Figure 2-22.

This is a script typeface. This is a script typeface. This is a script typeface.

Figure 2-22. Examples of script typefaces

Computerized typography made it possible to re-create virtually any graphical idea and package it into a typeface. This has lead to an explosion of typefaces known as **ornamental** type (see Figure 2-23). Sometimes ornamental type is called **display type**. This is a category for the freaks of type that escape classification. Ornamental typefaces have often been designed for a particular use, to evoke a distinct feel—for example, Halloween or the military. Ornamental type can be cutting-edge and funky, but hard to read, especially in large chunks. So beware of overuse and be sure to use ornamental typefaces for headlines only. Remember, the purpose of typography is first to speak to an audience, and second to aesthetically balance the layout design.

THIS IS AN ORNAMENTAL TYPEFACE. THIS IS AN ORNAMENTAL TYPEFACE.

This is an ornamental typeface.

Figure 2-23. Examples of ornamental typefaces

The digital age has produced its own breed of type, known as **pixel fonts** (see Figure 2-24). These are also known as **screen fonts** or **bitmap fonts**. These fonts stem back to the early days of home 8- or 16-bit computing; the Commodore 64 and Amiga, Sinclair/ Spectrum, and Atari ST. A pixel font is built from a grid or array of pixels. The great thing about pixel fonts, apart from looking geeky, is their legibility at minuscule point sizes. Most other typefaces are vector-based. This means that they are mathematically shrunk or enlarged at runtime. Most times, the mathematics isn't accurate, which results in small points sizes becoming ugly and hard to read. Pixel fonts were designed to work at a precise point size, commonly 7 or 8 point. Due to this, no strange, mathematically induced artifacts are created, and the font renders correctly. However, the fact that these fonts are legible at such small sizes is not a license to use them without reason. Always consider the end user. A common pixel font is MINI 7.

This is a pixel font. THIS IS A PIXEL FONT. THIS IS A PIXEL FONT.

Figure 2-24. Examples of pixel font

As an exercise, pick the typeface family from Figure 2-25 that you think works best for each of the following situations:

- Nail polish banner ad
- NCAA basketball website
- Government of Estonia's YouTube viral campaign
- Wedding invitation website
- Thrash metal band Dark Maggot's MySpace page
- Garden nursery Happy Trees' e-commerce site
- New Armani menswear microsite
- Daily News portal

𝕭𝖑𝖆𝖈𝖐𝖑𝖊𝖙𝖙𝖊𝖗, Serif, **Slab-serif**, Sans-serif, *Script*, ORNAMENTAL, P I X E L .

Figure 2-25. Different fonts are appropriate for different situations.

You will find there is no one correct answer, only that some typefaces work better than others.

Phase 3: Quality assurance testing

Ensuring your Flash application has been correctly tested is as important as the build phase. This stage is called quality assurance testing (also known as QA testing). Quality assurance testing ensures that every part of your Flash CS4 website has been tested prior to deploying it to public consumption (using a testing script and via methodical and logical examination of each function of your Flash application).

When you are designing Flash applications, you need to be aware of a number of Flash-specific conditions, which are detailed in the following sections.

Testing over multiple connection speeds

Testing over multiple connection speeds ensures everyone can see your Flash animation. This part of quality assurance testing is the most important part of quality assurance, and one that many traditional web developers often overlook. This is because this kind of testing in languages such as HTML fulfills one sole function: ensuring that the download speed is acceptable for a wide range of users. Flash testing over different connection speeds will help you pinpoint much more than just download issues.

Testing your Flash application on your computer's local hard drive or a server on your local network may hide a plethora of issues that would otherwise be evident if testing on a remote server. For example, when you test off your local hard drive, image display, SWF streaming, and server communication are instant, and it is easy to write ActionScript and other code that is dependent on the instant response time of your computer.

Flash CS4 and its predecessors have a tool that allows you to simulate Internet connection speed to ensure that your movies work properly in a real-life environment. The following exercise demonstrates how to use it:

1. Open `Chapter1_motiontween.fla` from the source files for this book in Flash CS4.

2. From the menu, choose Control ➤ Test Movie, as shown in Figure 2-26, to open the movie in Flash Player.

3. Select View ➤ Simulate Download in the window that plays your Flash movie, as shown in Figure 2-27.

4. To simulate different connection screens, select View ➤ Download Settings to change the value of the download settings (also shown in Figure 2-27).

Figure 2-26. Testing your movie in Flash CS4

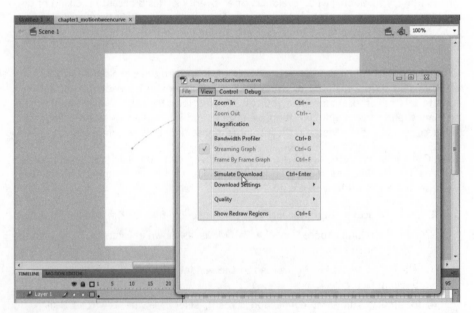

Figure 2-27. Flash CS4 allows you to simulate connection speeds.

This tool is especially valuable when building preloaders for large Flash movies. As valuable as this tool is when developing your Flash movie, you should always ensure that you test thoroughly on the web server that faces the public as well.

Testing across browsers

It is just as important to test your Flash sites as it is your traditional HTML sites, but for very different reasons. When you test your HTML code across browsers, you are generally looking to identify page display and client-side scripting issues. The Flash SWF file handles this for you in Flash interfaces, so you don't need to test Flash for it. However, you do need to test across browsers the way that the Flash movie is embedded into the page.

Different browsers require different HTML code to embed your Flash CS4 movie into your web page in order to display the movie on the page. You also need to test the way that browsers resolve URLs when they attempt to load external assets such as images or XML content. We will look at this more when we create news feeds and the dynamic gallery.

Flash Player 10 includes a number of security upgrades, including the ability to locally save and load, which means that you will be able to allow your users to save and load data from a SWF file to their hard drive. It also allows users limited keyboard use, including the Tab key, the space bar, and the arrow keys when viewing a SWF file in full-screen mode. It also allows peer-to-peer communication via the RTMFP protocol, and the ability to read data from the clipboard via a paste event handler.

> *There are multiple services across the Internet that offer a multibrowser download for testing purposes, which allows you to install different versions of the same browser on the same computer. A good example is Microsoft SuperPreview, which you can download from www.microsoft.com/expression/try-it/superpreview.*

Testing across more than one version of Flash Player

Adobe Flash Player is a cross-platform player that allows browsers to display Flash movies. If you want to view Flash, you must have Flash Player installed. It's important to ensure that you test across multiple versions of Flash Player. Doing so ensures that you'll catch any publishing errors that may occur when an FLA file is published as a SWF file, as well as any Flash detection issues.

As a rule of thumb, you should always test your Flash movie in the player it has been designed for. For example, we will be testing all of the animations built in the course of this book in Flash Player 10, but also in another common player. If you are building banner ads to be distributed to publishers such as MSN or Yahoo, you should check with their advertising operations department what Flash Player version their specifications prescribe, and also test in that. Many of the larger publishers these days will accept Flash Player 8 and Flash Player 9, with the banners containing only ActionScript 2.0, not ActionScript 3.0. This will change as later versions of Flash players become more prevalent. Flash Player 9 is currently dominating market penetration at almost 99 percent, while Flash Player 10 is currently sitting at over 55 percent and is growing daily. Chapter 11 will cover guidelines and Internet industry advertising standards in greater depth.

> *Adobe Flash Player is a free program, and the latest version can be downloaded from the Downloads page at www.adobe.com. All versions of Flash Player are archived for testing purposes, and can be downloaded from www.adobe.com/go/tn_14266.*

Testing your Flash movie on different computers

Traditional websites built and designed in HTML use very few computer resources. Because of this, web developers have not had to consider the power of the user's computer. This is not the case with Flash CS4. The user's computer—specifically the CPU, video card, and RAM—significantly impacts their Flash experience.

Larger Flash projects should be built with a specific minimum hardware requirement in mind. It's worth noting that it's possible for a SWF file to detect certain things about a user's computer, such as the Flash Player version and the hardware acceleration, which harnesses the available hardware on the user's computer to provide an optimum experience.

Phase 4: Deployment and implementation

When you have built your Flash CS4 project and are satisfied that it has been sufficiently debugged and is working correctly, it is time to deploy it. This is when you upload your project and associated files to your web server.

It's important to note that a website project isn't finished when the site has been uploaded. To ensure that your Flash CS4 website is a success, you need to monitor how people are interacting with it. In Chapter 11, you will learn how to insert Google Analytics code into your site so you can begin to find out the most popular parts of your site, and accordingly plan upgrades to encourage people to visit the parts of your site you most want them to.

Proceed with caution: Using Flash wisely

Though Flash CS4 has some wonderful tools that enable you to create beautiful websites and animations, it's easy to fall into the trap of overwhelming the user with animation. If your website is distracting to look at, people will not use it the way you want them to and may be reluctant to return.

Jakob Nielsen is often referred to as the King of Usability. His famous 2000 article, "Flash: 99% Bad," has become a kind of unofficial guideline about the things to avoid when you are designing a Flash website. Nielsen subscribes to the belief that just because you *can* make something move doesn't necessarily mean that you *should*. Animation should have a purpose, and if the site's objective can be achieved without adding great amounts of animation, designers should consider removing it. Also, for a site to succeed, you need to allow your users to get to the information that they want easily. Though Flash introductions are becoming less popular, if you have one on your site, you should place a prominent Skip Intro button on the introduction page to allow users to quickly navigate past it.

Summary

Achieving the best possible result for your Flash CS4 project isn't simply a matter of knowing everything about Flash CS4, it's also about knowing certain design and marketing principles. A successful movie is one that allows users to easily achieve what it is you want them to be able to do on your site. Keeping track of competitors is also invaluable for ensuring that you are ahead of the market. The aim of this chapter has been to arm you with the design principles and quality assurance guidelines that are the basis to creating any great design, regardless of the medium.

We will now begin to build Flash applications. In Chapter 3, you'll learn about layers and layer exports, which form the basis of any Flash CS4 application. Then in Chapter 4 and beyond, you'll take the wireframe created at the beginning of this chapter and build the assets defined by it.

2

CHAPTER 3

GETTING YOUR HANDS DIRTY: LAYERS, MASKS, AND PHOTOSHOP

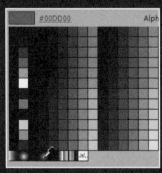 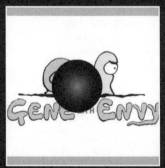 

In this chapter we will examine layers in Flash CS4, which are extremely important in organizing your Flash CS4 movies. We will then spend some time looking at mask layers and finally we will investigate the compatibility between Photoshop and Flash CS4.

Layer upon layer upon layer!

If you are familiar with previous versions of Flash or if you've used a graphics application like Photoshop, you will be familiar with layers. Layers are transparent sheets that are placed on top of each other, very much like making a bed that contains a bottom sheet, a top sheet, a blanket, and a bedspread. Figure 3-1 shows layers on the timeline in Flash CS4. Layers can be reordered, and you can add and delete layers.

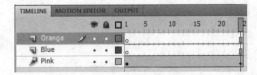

Figure 3-1. Layers are sheets that are placed on top of one another on the timeline.

Most importantly, layers organize your movie. You can place a single object on a layer that, when played with the rest of the Flash movie, appears to be very much an integrated part of it. But the beauty of layers is that you can edit them independently of the rest of the movie. Editing one layer doesn't necessarily change the entire movie or affect other layers.

Flash CS4 has four types of layers that you need to be familiar with. These are "normal" layers, mask layers, guide layers, and motion guide layers. In the next sections we are going to investigate each of these layers thoroughly.

Normal layers

Normal layers are exactly as they sound. They are layers in Flash CS4 that have not been transformed into any other kind of layer. A layer is a normal layer until you transform it into another kind of layer. Normal layers are made up of a frame or a sequence of frames in a timeline, and can contain graphical elements, actions, and instructions.

Mask layers

Remember when you were a child and had crayons? You could apply the crayon to the paper in different layers. I used to cover layers of colored crayon with a thick layer of black crayon and then use a knitting needle to create holes through the layers to reveal the different colors beneath. The harder you pressed down with the knitting needle, the more lower layers you would expose. Masked layers are exactly like that; they enable you to reveal selected parts of your Flash animation as you choose.

Mask layers are especially useful for spotlight effects and transitions. In the following exercise we will create a mask on a 300×250 banner document that will reveal our *Gene with Envy* (see Chapter 1) slowly when the SWF movie is played. We will then diverge into pairing a masking layer with a little ActionScript to create a realistic spotlight that will reveal the logo.

To get the most out of this exercise, ensure that you have downloaded the source file from www.friendsofed.com.

1. Open Flash CS4.

2. Click on the Advertising link under the Create from Template section on the welcome screen.

3. From the Templates list, select 300 × 250 – Medium Rectangle as shown in Figure 3-2.

Figure 3-2. Choosing the Medium Rectangle from the list of advertising templates

4. Click OK.

You will be presented with the screen shown in Figure 3-3.

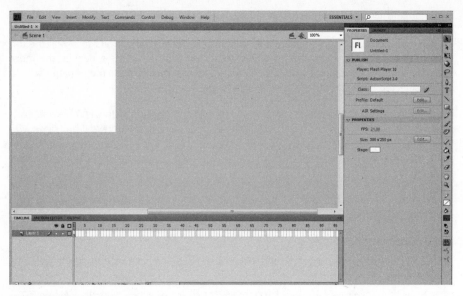

Figure 3-3. The blank Flash banner

The gene-with-envy logo will be the layer below the masked layer. We are now going to import the logo onto the stage.

5. From the File menu, select Import ➤ Import to Library as shown in Figure 3-4.

6. Browse to where you have saved the gene-with-envy logo and click OK.

7. Click the Library tab that is behind the Properties tab. You will see that genelogo. jpg has been imported, as shown in Figure 3-5.

> *Remember, if your tabs and windows get rearranged, you can reset your work space using the drop-down menu to the left of the search button at the top-right corner of the screen.*

We are now going to place the logo onto the stage.

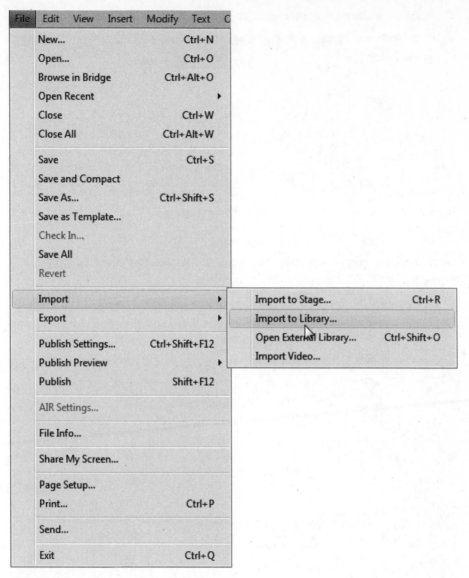

Figure 3-4. Importing a graphic to the Flash Library

8. From the Library, drag genelogo.jpg onto the stage as shown in Figure 3-5.

Figure 3-5. Dragging the logo from the Library onto the stage

9. Rename the Layer 1 on the timeline Image.

We now need to convert the image to a Movie Clip symbol, just as we did in Chapter 1 when we created a motion tween.

10. Right-click the image on the stage and choose Convert to Symbol.

11. Ensure that Type is set to Movie Clip and give the symbol the name of logo as shown in Figure 3-6.

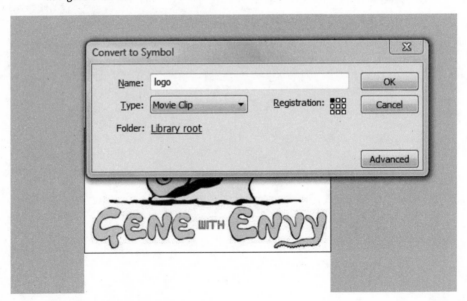

Figure 3-6. Renaming your movie clip

The movie clip is now set up. Next we are going to create a layer above it, where we'll place the shape of the mask.

12. Click OK to close the Convert to Symbol dialog box.

13. Create a new layer on the timeline by clicking the New Layer button . Name it Mask Shape as shown in Figure 3-7.

> Remember: to rename a layer, simply double-click on the layer name and type the new name over it.

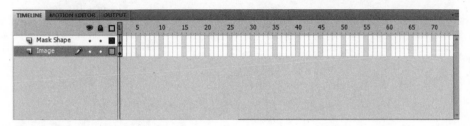

Figure 3-7. Adding a new layer to your timeline

With the new layer created, it's time to place the shape on it.

14. Draw a solid circle on the Mask Shape layer with the Oval tool as shown in Figure 3-8. Before you draw the circle on the stage, remove any stroke in the Properties Inspector. You can draw a perfect circle by pressing the Shift key as you draw the circle on the stage.

> The Oval tool is one of five tools available as part of the Shape toolset. By default, the Rectangle tool is displayed. To select the Oval tool, simply click and hold the Rectangle tool, and all of the options will become available for you to select.

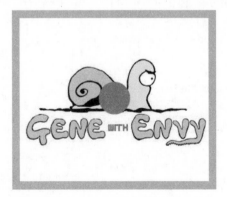

Figure 3-8. Click and hold the rectangle tool to reveal the Oval tool.

67

15. Right-click frame 15 on the timeline of the Mask Shape layer and select Insert Keyframe.

16. Right-click on frame 15 on the timeline of the Image layer and select Insert Frame. Your timeline should appear as shown in Figure 3-9.

Figure 3-9. Setting up the timeline for the masked-layer animation

17. Click on the Selection tool, and then right-click on the oval on the stage and select Convert to Symbol.

18. Convert the symbol to a movie clip and give it the name spotlight_mc in the Convert to Symbol dialog box.

19. Click OK to close the Convert to Symbol dialog box.

20. With keyframe 15 selected on the Mask Shape layer, click on the Free Transform tool and drag the oval by one of its control handles until it completely covers the logo, as shown in Figure 3-10.

21. Right-click between the first and last keyframes on the Mask Shape layer and select Create Classic Tween.

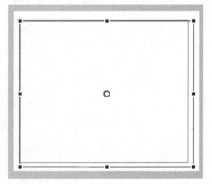

Figure 3-10. Creating the mask animation by dragging the oval outward

22. Select Control ➤ Test Movie from the menu to see what has happened to your movie.

The Mask Shape layer expands to cover the logo and loops. All that is left now is to make the white expanding circle into a mask layer.

23. Right-click on the Layer icon  next to the Mask Shape text on the timeline.

24. Select Mask from the menu, as shown in Figure 3-11.

25. Select Control ➤ Test Movie from the menu to see what has happened to your movie.

You will notice that the oval on the stage has been effectively reversed—it has become a porthole that expands to display the entire logo. This is just a simple demonstration of using a mask in a Flash CS4 movie. Through careful planning and design, masks can help to create truly compelling Flash movies.

Figure 3-11. Converting a normal layer to a mask layer

Combining mask layers and ActionScript

In this section we will create a Flash CS4 movie that combines mask layers with ActionScript. This exercise will demonstrate how combining the different features of Flash CS4 can take your movies to the next level of interactivity.

To complete the following exercise, you will need to download the ch4_masked_as.FLA file from the Downloads section at www.friendsofed.com.

1. Open the ch4_masked_as.FLA file in Flash CS4.

You will see that we have already imported the logo onto the stage for you. Now let's create a new layer as we did in the previous exercise.

2. Create a new layer on the timeline. Call it Mask Shape, as shown in Figure 3-12.

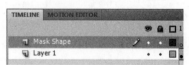

Figure 3-12. Creating a new shape for the mask on the timeline

3. With the Oval tool selected, go to the Properties Inspector and remove the stroke altogether, then select the green radial gradient from the color picker, as shown in Figure 3-13.

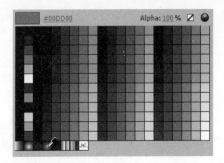

Figure 3-13. Selecting the radial gradient from the color picker

4. Draw a circle on the Mask Shape layer roughly in the middle of the logo on the stage, as shown in Figure 3-14.

> *To expand the circle in a way that keeps its dimensions, simply hold down the Shift key as you drag it.*

Figure 3-14. Using the Oval tool to draw a circle in the middle of the logo

Let's change the gradient slightly to create a realistic spotlight. In the next part of the exercise, we will apply a transparent gradient on the edge of the circle.

5. Click on the Gradient Transform tool and then click on the oval on the stage.

> *If you can't find the Gradient tool, type F (the shortcut for the Gradient tool) or click and hold the Free Transform tool.*

6. Open the Color panel (Figure 3-15) by choosing Window ➤ Color from the menu bar.

> *You can also open the* Color *panel via the Shift+F9 shortcut.*

7. In the Color panel select Radial from the Type drop-down list if it is not already selected.

8. Set the right handle on the gradient bar to the same value as the left handle. The value is R: 0 G: 255 B: 0.

The gradient will become solid. To complete it for use as our spotlight, we need to make the edges transparent.

9. With the right handle still selected, change the Alpha field to 10% as shown in Figure 3-16.

We're going to create the "spotlight" effect on the circle on the stage by manipulating the gradient just a little further.

10. Drag the left handle toward the middle to ensure that only the edges of the shape are transparent, as shown in Figure 3-17.

Figure 3-17. The gradient handles enable you to specify the degree of transparency.

You've finished the spotlight for this section. Your stage should look like Figure 3-18. You might be thinking that this doesn't look like a spotlight, and you're right, it doesn't—yet! Next we will apply masking to transform our banner ad.

Figure 3-15. The Color panel is opened by selecting Window ➤ Color.

Figure 3-16. When you manipulate the Alpha value of a color, you are manipulating its transparency/opacity settings.

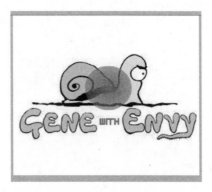

Figure 3-18. The "spotlight" on the stage

11. Transform the green oval on the stage into a movie clip by right-clicking with the Selection tool and selecting Convert to Symbol.

12. Name the movie clip Spotlight, as shown in Figure 3-19.

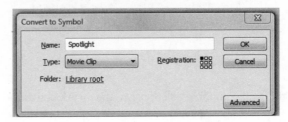

Figure 3-19. Renaming the movie clip Spotlight

We need to change the registration point to the middle of the stage because the final animation will be tied to the movement of the mouse pointer, which we want defaulted to the center of the stage, not the top of it.

Figure 3-20.
Changing the registration enables you to specify where the object is tied to the stage.

13. Click the middle square of the Registration area as shown in Figure 3-20 and click OK to close the Convert to Symbol screen.

We're now going to use ActionScript 3.0 to associate the Spotlight movie clip to the mouse pointer. This is an action we will be completing multiple times, as we want the spotlight to be constantly tied to the location of the mouse cursor. To achieve this we will create an ENTER_FRAME ActionScript 3.0 event. This event will continually check the location of the mouse pointer when it rolls over the movie and will ensure that the spotlight follows it accordingly.

> *Events are the processes that you employ in ActionScript to make your Flash CS4 movie react to mouse clicks, mouseovers, and the like. Chapter 8 will investigate event-handling procedures in ActionScript 3 in depth.*

Before we do this, however, we need to give the Spotlight an instance name on the stage.

14. Click on the oval on the stage to select it.

15. In the Properties tab, give the oval the instance name of spotlight_mc, as shown in Figure 3-21.

Figure 3-21. Naming the spotlight_mc instance

We need to create a new layer, called Action, on which to place the ActionScript.

16. Create a new layer by clicking the New Layer button.

17. Name the new layer Action by double-clicking the layer's name, as shown in Figure 3-22.

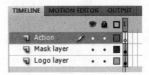

Figure 3-22. Naming the new layer Action

18. Select Frame 1 of the Action layer.

19. Select Windows ➤ Actions on the menu bar to open the Actions panel, which will allow you to write ActionScript, as shown in Figure 3-23.

> *You can also open the Actions panel via short-cuts. Press F9 to open the panel in Windows, and Option+F9 to open the panel in Mac OS.*

20. Type the following code into the Actions panel:

```
spotlight_mc.addEventListener(Event.ENTER_FRAME,
moveMask);
function moveMask(e:Event):void
{
spotlight_mc.x = mouseX;
spotlight_mc.y = mouseY;
}
```

21. Save your movie.

22. Test your movie by selecting Control ➤ Test Movie.

> *Remember that you can also test your movie by pressing Control/Command+Enter on your computer's keyboard.*

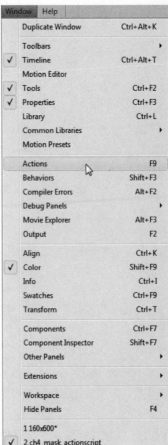

Figure 3-23. Opening the Actions panel

What happens when you mouse over the movie? That's right! The green oval follows your mouse pointer. In the next part of the exercise we will create the mask layer that will give the Flash CS4 movie a spotlight to highlight the logo.

Unlike its predecessors, Flash CS4 does not offer a movie class method called mask(). Masking is now a property. For the masking animation to work correctly, you need to apply it to the movie clip you wish to mask. This is simply a matter of adding a small piece of code to the first line of the ActionScript.

23. Add the following code to the first line of the script, as shown in Figure 3-24:

```
logo_mc.mask = spotlight_mc;
```

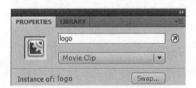

Figure 3-24. Adding the ActionScript to your animation

24. Click on the logo movie clip to select it, and give it an instance name of logo as shown in Figure 3-25.

Figure 3-25. Giving your movie clip object an instance name enables the ActionScript to reference it.

25. Test your movie by pressing Control/Command+Enter on your keyboard.

> Remember: you can also test your movie by selecting Control ➤ Test Movie in the Control menu.

Upon testing your movie you will see that it has been completely masked in black, with a little spotlight that enables you to mouse around the movie to reveal the logo. But we're not finished! We are now going to ensure that the gradient appears to give the spotlight a realistic look. Again, we need to employ ActionScript to do this.

26. Add the following code into lines 2 and 3 of your ActionScript, as shown in Figure 3-26:

```
spotlight_mc.cacheAsBitmap = true;
logo_mc.cacheAsBitmap = true;
```

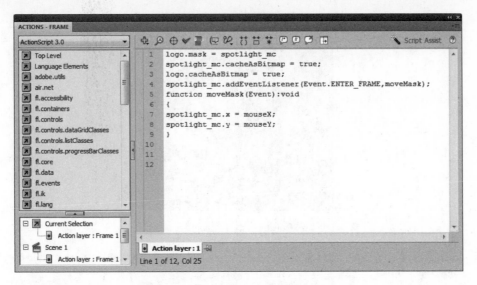

Figure 3-26. Adding code to your ActionScript to give a realistic gradient

The cacheAsBitmap command in ActionScript was designed to give an ease of movement to Flash movies that contain many moving vector graphics. Vector graphics are very light graphics that are composed of lines and curves to reproduce images. When you are building large-scale Flash movies, with many different kinds of movement and animations, you may notice your vector graphics moving across the stage in a jerky fashion when your movie is published at a high frame rate, particularly with slower machines and connection speeds. This jerkiness is caused by the computer redrawing the graphic on every single frame.

cacheAsBitmap dynamically converts a vector image into a bitmap image. Bitmap images do not need to be redrawn for each frame, which alleviates the jerkiness in the animation. The trade-off is that bitmap files can be much larger than vector images. We will cover more about different kinds of graphics in Chapter 4.

We're now at the final step, where we transform a normal layer to a masked layer.

27. Right-click on the Mask Shape layer and select Mask, as shown in Figure 3-27.

28. Test your completed movie by selecting Control ➤ Test Movie.

As you can see, the mask layer adopts the background color, and the code has provided interactivity. When you move the mouse pointer over the Flash CS4 movie, the spotlight moves with the mouse to reveal the image underneath, as shown in Figure 3-28.

Figure 3-27. Creating a mask layer

Figure 3-28. The completed animation

Special layers can be created that allow you to draw and edit with greater ease and achieve some really funky effects.

Guide layers

Figure 3-29. Creating a guide layer

Guide layers enable you to tweak your animations to ensure that everything in your movie is precisely where you want it. They assist you in aligning objects on one layer with objects on another layer.

While you can use animation paths like in Flash CS3, guide layers enable you to lock objects into place in relation to other objects. The beauty of guide layers is that they do not appear in final animations, but enable you to position the elements on your stage just so. Though motion layers are so easily made in Flash CS4, guide layers are useful in ensuring your animation is precise. Motion layers enable to you specify the path of the animation exactly, but guide layers are important because they allow you to place objects on the stage precisely.

To create a guide layer, select the layer you wish to become a guide layer and right-click it then select Guide, as shown in Figure 3-29.

> *Control-clicking brings up the menu from which you choose Guide in Mac OS.*

Motion guide layers

Motion guide layers enable you to control the movement of objects in a classic tween animation. Simply dragging an existing normal layer onto a guide layer creates a motion guide layer. The normal layer will then be linked to the newly created layer.

> *When you are working with large Flash CS4 movies that contain multiple layers, try to arrange all guide layers at the bottom. This will ensure that you don't accidentally convert guide layers into motion guide layers.*

3

Importing artwork from Photoshop

Flash CS4 integrates well with other Adobe products. Gone are the Macromedia days when importing art from Adobe Photoshop would cause hours of headaches. You can now drag from one Adobe application, such as Photoshop, Illustrator, and Designer, to the other or go to File ➤ Import.

For example, you might work in an agency that has a number of departments, meaning print artwork is created in Adobe Photoshop and the print artwork needs to be translated to the online medium. This is where Flash CS4 shines. You can import layered files created in other Adobe Creative Suite programs directly in Flash CS4. This has two very positive effects: it saves a lot of time that you can now invest in producing amazing animations, and it protects the layout and integrity of the original file.

Though Flash CS4 has the ability to import images in many and varied formats, it's the native Photoshop PSD format that is most popular in importing still images. Flash CS4 is more compatible with Photoshop than ever; it can preserve the attributes and settings that were created in Photoshop.

Photoshop will allow you to export PSD files with layers. This is particularly beneficial if you need to create complicated visual layouts in Flash CS4. When you import a PSD file into Flash CS4 you can import each PSD layer as an individual Flash CS4 layer or individual keyframes, or you can import the entire PSD as a single flattened layer in Flash CS4.

Using the PSD importer

The following exercise will demonstrate how to import a layered PSD as a flattened bitmap:

1. Open a new blank document in Flash CS4.
2. Select File ➤ Import ➤ Import to Library as shown in Figure 3-30.

   The Import "layers.psd" to Library dialog box will appear (see Figure 3-31).

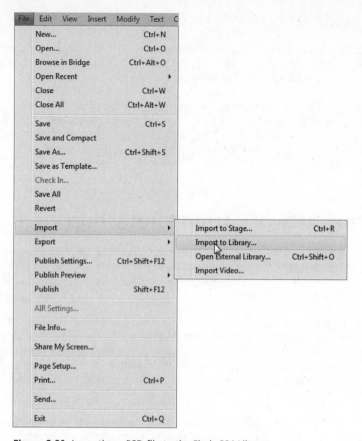

Figure 3-30. Importing a PSD file to the Flash CS4 Library

3. Select Flash Layers in the Convert Layers To field.

4. Click on square2 so that it is highlighted.

5. With square2 selected, press the Shift key on your keyboard and then click on the background layer. All layers will be highlighted as shown in Figure 3-31.

6. To import the PSD in layers, ensure that the Bitmap Image with Editable Layer Styles radio button is selected in the Import These Image Layers As section.

7. Click OK.

You will notice that the Library has been populated by assets from the layers.psd file, as shown in Figure 3-32. You can drag the flattened bitmap of layers.psd onto the stage or drag an individual asset that has been saved within a folder in the Library.

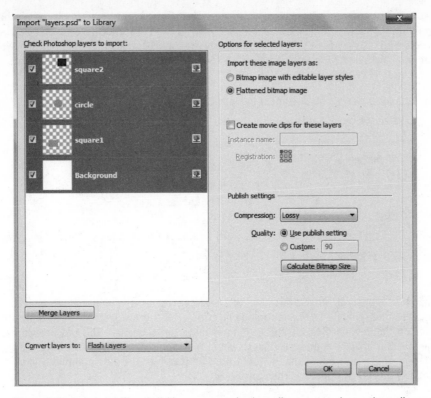

Figure 3-31. Pressing shift and clicking on your selections allows you to choose them all.

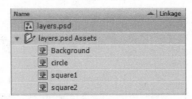

Figure 3-32. The Flash CS4 Library is populated from the layers.psd file.

We will pause here a moment to examine again the PSD importer. Follow steps 1 through 3 in the previous exercise to open the importer. The Convert to Layers field, shown in Figure 3-33, allows you to choose from keyframes or layers.

Figure 3-33. You can choose how to import a PSD into Flash CS4.

If you choose to import the PSD as Flash layers, all of the PSD layers are placed on their own individual layers, which are named the same as the Photoshop layers when they are placed in the Library folder. If you chose to import the PSD as keyframes, all of the layers that you have selected to import into Flash CS4 will be placed on individual keyframes on a new layer. Let's experiment with that now.

1. Open a new blank document in Flash CS4.

2. Select File ➤ Import ➤ Import to Stage.

> *Don't forget there are shortcuts to every action! The shortcut key sequence to import an object onto the stage is Control/Command+R.*

3. Select the layers.psd file and click OK.

4. Click on the square2 layer, press Shift, then click on the square1 layer.

5. At the Convert Layers To field, select Keyframes.

6. Click OK.

What has happened? The layers that you selected to import to the stage have been imported into separate keyframes on one layer. Select Control ➤ Test Movie or simply press Enter on the keyboard to see the keyframes played in sequence. This has been a basic example, but imagine the possibilities of importing sophisticated PSDs that have a slightly different image on each frame. It would then be possible to create complex animations relatively quickly by importing them into Flash CS4.

Flash CS4 and Photoshop compatibility

Though Flash CS4 has extensive compatibility with Photoshop, it's important to note that there are some attributes that can't be accurately imported, or that can't be edited in Flash CS4 after they have been imported.

While Flash CS4 can convert CMYK colors in images, it doesn't always preserve the color exactly. You will get a better result from converting CMYK images to RGB in Photoshop and then importing the images into Flash CS4. This approach ensures consistency across suites of ads, from offline print to online banners and sites. This also ensures that the colors of corporate collateral remain true to guidelines.

Not all Photoshop blend modes can be imported into Flash CS4; you may need to rasterize a layer in Photoshop previous to importing. Once you have rasterized a layer you will no longer be able to edit it. You can import the following Photoshop blend modes into Flash CS4 without having to rasterize them, which allows them to be edited in the Flash CS4 authoring environment:

- Darken
- Difference and Overlay
- Hard Light
- Lighten
- Multiply
- Normal
- Screen

Photoshop Smart Objects cannot be edited once they have been imported to Flash CS4, because they are automatically rasterized and imported to Flash as bitmaps. This is also true for Image and Fill layers.

When you are importing objects that contain transparent areas, the objects on the layers behind the transparent layers will be visible (providing they are also imported). If you do not want them to be visible, you can import the transparent object as a flattened bitmap in the PSD importer.

Summary

In this chapter you learned about Flash CS4's adaptability. You learned how diverse masks can be, and how beautiful illustrations that you have created in Photoshop can now be imported with little mess or fuss.

In Chapter 4 you will begin to pull design and technical knowledge together to create an artistic logo from a concept that was sketched by hand, and you'll learn more about using the drawing tools and different types of graphics in Flash CS4.

DRAW ME A PICTURE: USING THE DRAWING TOOLS

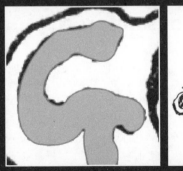  

Your life is inundated by branding, whether you realize it or not, regardless of what you are doing, whether it be listening to the radio, riding the subway, reading the newspaper, or surfing the Internet. Even advertisement-free television has branding in it in the form of product placement! You may have become so immune to it that it doesn't register consciously to you, but be assured, it is there. Every company has a logo that it uses to establish brand recognition, whether it is a tag line or a graphic that people immediately associate with their business. Think of the McDonald's golden arches, MSN's multicolored butterfly, and the Mercedes Benz three-pointed star. These logos all immediately indicate which company they represent.

All too often, the importance of the logo is lost in purely online marketing campaigns, or logos are hastily thrown together prior to the website launch. Though the beauty of online marketing is that it is relatively cost effective when it is compared to the price of producing equivalent campaigns in other media, the downside is that these campaigns are often thrown together with little thought about branding or positioning in the market place.

So how do you start to even conceive of a logo? To begin with, you need to consider a tagline or a graphic that demonstrates what service or product your company or website offers and begin to play with words and concepts that fit with your overall vision.

Whether a picture is drawn in sand or sculpted from empty beer cans, most of us can find a contextual relevance. The human brain is highly dedicated to pattern recognition, particularly visual pattern recognition.

Humans are visual creatures by nature and graphics underpin our psychology. Even when mating, our biological instincts are driven by the interpretation of point, line, and plane. From art to advertising, an understanding of visual attraction goes a long way.

In Chapter 2, we looked at design principles. In this chapter, we will look at the powerful drawing tools in Flash CS4 and the four important kinds of symbols. Then we will create an appealing logo by implementing the psychological concepts from the previous chapter via the Flash CS4 drawing tools.

A picture is worth a thousand words

Since the dawn of civilization, humans have sought ways to reconstruct and illustrate physical reality. Sand, stone, papyrus, canvas, or pixel, no matter where in time we are, humans want to draw. Today people are drawing in pixels. In the future, it may be the building blocks of mental imagery, but for now the question is this: Exactly what are pixels?

Not to be confused with pixies, which are tiny mythical creatures of Celtic origin, pixels are the tiny dots that create all the text, images, and backgrounds that your computer can display.

All about pixels

A pixel is the most basic piece of information used to transmit data from a computer's memory chip to the screen or display. Pixels are arranged in a rectangular grid pattern, and are also used to describe screen resolutions. 800×600 means 800 columns of 600 rows of pixels. That's 480,000 pixels! The more pixels you have, the better curves, photos, and nonlinear shapes will look on the screen.

Pixels get their name from the joining of two words, *picture* (*pix*) and *element* (*el*). Pixel colors are created using a mixture of the three primary colors; red, green, and blue. This is what the term *RGB* stands for.

You may recall from art class that the primary colors are red, blue, and yellow. Yellow and blue make green, remember? Well, in the digital realm, and also in the human eye, the primary colors are different: they are red, green, and blue. You make yellow using red and green. You make orange using red and half the amount of green that yellow is composed of.

On the Web, pixel colors are described by the intensity of the mix of red, green, and blue. The intensity is described using a 255-degree scale starting from 0; 255 equates to 100%, 127 equates to 50%, and 0 equates to 0%. To describe the color red to your browser, you would use RGB(255,0,0). This means 100% red, 0% green, 0% blue.

How would you describe bright purple? You may remember from finger painting that purple is a mix of red and blue (100% red and 100% blue). So this would translate to the RGB scale as RGB(255,0,255).

Notice that we are using 100% intensities. This creates bright and vivid colors. To instead create a dark purple, we would turn down the intensity of each value. A darker purple might be 20% red and 20% blue, which would translate to RGB(51,0,51). Why 51? Because 51 is 20% of 255.

Notice, however, that we retained the proportions of the color mix, which in turn retains the **hue**—that is, the quality—of purple, which is simply altering the intensity of light allowed to flow into the pixel. How then, would we create black? Actually, black is no colors. It's just 0% red, 0% green, and 0% blue. White is the opposite: 100% red, green, and blue.

Before the pixel, people didn't use displays when they output computer data, as there were no LCD or tube monitors, televisions, or calculator screens. People, mostly mathematicians, would receive their computer information from a series of flashing lights. Some would get their data from holes punched from pieces of card. Earlier still, this information was gleaned from the beads in abacas calculators (even earlier, from the shadow cast through the eyes of the Stonehenge computer!).

From a philosophical point of view, our eyes show us an interpretation of reality. In the same sense, pixels create a sample of reality and display it on the screen. If a photograph is scanned in at high resolution, it will look clearer and sharper. It will resemble the original source better. Digital cameras with a high megapixel rating will capture the image of physical reality better than their lower-rated counterparts.

In this chapter, we'll take the design principles covered in Chapter 2 and apply them to a real-life example. The final output of the chapter will be the logo for our gene-with-envy Flash CS4 site.

Types of image formats

I mentioned earlier that pixels sit in rectangular grids. Images are created on the screen by changing the color of the pixels in the grid. But where do the images come from in the first place? And how are they redrawn on screen?

Well, they actually come from many sources. The image may be created internally, hand-drawn using software like Adobe Photoshop, or from external sources such as a digital camera or a DVD screen grab. The source must be interpreted and stored in a uniform way that can be edited, shared, and redrawn on the screen or printed. The different ways of redrawing the graphics on the screen give rise to the various graphics formats.

But first, you need to understand exactly what image file formats are. In the digital sense, image formats are the standardized means of storing images. In it's most literal definition, an image file format is an image file that is composed of bitmap or vector data that is **rasterized** (converted) to pixels when it is rendered on the screen. The pixels are displayed on the image in a grid, with each pixel displayed as an RGB measure.

Bitmap or raster graphics

Images can be stored as a series of dots in a grid. Using an analogy of the beads on an abacus, the more beads you have, the more accurately the image represents reality. A **bit** is the smallest piece of data a computer deals with. A bit can either be **on** or **off**. Another way of saying this is that it can either be true or false, or represent a 1 or a 0. A map, as you know, is a relational guide to places. Likewise, a **bitmap** is literally a guide to the contents of visual memory in a computer. Bitmaps replicate exact details and color tones. Skin tones, in particular, replicate very well. The problem with bitmaps is that all that detail (especially in things like curved lines) needs lots of pixels to be reproduced accurately. This leads to bitmapped graphics having very large file sizes. As you know, large files don't move fast on the Net, so various methods of image compression were devised to try and solve this problem.

Image compression reduces the size of large bitmaps. One of the most well-known compression methods—the JPEG compression algorithm—looks for areas of similar color and groups those pixels, meaning it takes less information to describe the shape. At low compression levels, this can lead to big reductions in size with little visible difference, but as the level of compression is increased, you will notice **artifacts** appear on the image. These artifacts are visual corruption in the form of blockiness, blurring, color streaking, and halos caused by the compression algorithm being pushed to its limits. The upshot is you'll have smaller files, but worse image quality, and that's something that you'll have to balance individually across your images. Bitmap file formats that Flash CS4 can interpret are BMP, GIF, PNG, JPEG, TIFF, and TGA.

Vector graphics

Vector graphics are images that are described by geometry rather than by plotting each individual pixel. For example, to draw a simple line of 10 pixels in a bitmap, the computer would have to set the color information, brightness, and so on for each of those 10 pixels. For a vector, however, the computer just needs to say, "Draw a line between point A and point B." Much less information is required, and no matter how long the line is, the same amount of information is needed (whereas for a bitmap you have to keep adding information whenever you need more pixels). This also means that when you scale up a vector (e.g., if you're zooming in on an image, the vector will still be perfectly crisp because it is still just a mathematical line, whereas the bitmap shape will become blocky). The disadvantage of a vector is that it is inefficient for describing details. So if you have an image, such as a photograph, where the color information changes with each pixel, then it's preferable to use a bitmap than to mathematically describe every individual pixel using vectors.

The fact that vector graphics utilize both line and curve formulas to reproduce images makes vector files much smaller than bitmaps. Vector graphics also have the advantage of **scalability**. A vector graphic can be enlarged to fill a massive billboard using the same file created to display it on the screen. A bitmap file would have to be equally massive to allow for all the data used to describe such a large billboard.

Paths

In physics, a vector is a formula that describes an object's direction and magnitude. In graphics, a vector is a formula that describes a path of pixels. When you draw a line in Flash CS4, it is called a path. Paths are vector lines and can be composed of straight or curved segments. You can close up a path to create a shape.

Direction lines and points

Paths are made up of straight and curved lines. These lines are created using the Pen tool, which lets users place anchor points on the display that can be linked by straight lines or curves (called Bezier curves). Bezier curves are particularly useful in Flash CS4 as they do not follow the same constraints as rasterized images, since they are smooth curves that can be indefinitely scaled. This makes them ideal to use in graphics such as logos, as they can be scaled to fit the smallest banner and remain sharp, and increased in size with no degradation in line quality.

What can the drawing tools do?

Flash began life as an illustration and animation system for the Web, and has gradually had more tools and complex abilities added to it. At its heart, though, Flash CS4 still shows its illustration heritage in the form of its drawing tools.

The drawing tools are found on the Tools panel, as shown in Figure 4-1.

Flash CS4 offers not only the same the drawing tools as its predecessors, but also powerful new capabilities that allow you to bring your illustrations to life.

Before you draw and paint in Flash, it is important to understand how Flash creates artwork, and how drawing, painting, and modifying shapes can affect other shapes on the same layer.

Drawing objects

Like its predecessors, Flash CS4 allows you to draw shapes in two modes: **Merge Drawing mode** and **Object Drawing mode**. However, Flash CS4 comes with a new mode that allows you to manipulate shapes more easily: **Primitive Shape mode**. Let's take a look at the different methods of drawing shapes.

Using Merge Drawing mode

The Merge Drawing tool is displayed as the default, and it automatically merges shapes when you overlap them. We'll quickly investigate this in the following exercise.

1. Open a new blank document in Flash CS4 (ActionScript 3.0).

2. Using the Oval tool, draw a blue oval on the stage, as shown in Figure 4-2.

As discussed, Merge Drawing mode is the default for Flash CS4, but if you have changed the default settings, you can switch between Object Drawing mode and Merge Drawing mode by toggling the Object Drawing Mode button ◘ on the Tools panel.

Figure 4-1. The drawing tools are found on the Tools panel of Flash CS4.

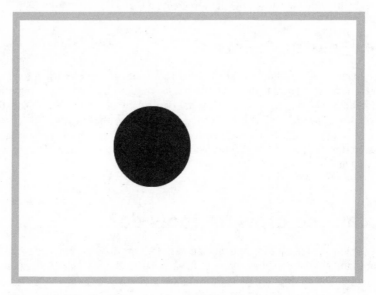

Figure 4-2. Using the Oval tool to draw an oval on the stage

3. Now, using the Rectangle tool, draw a green rectangle overlapping the blue oval, as shown in Figure 4-3.

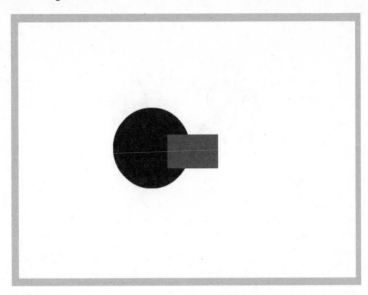

Figure 4-3. Using the Rectangle tool to create overlapping shapes

4. Change to the Selection tool and select the green rectangle.

5. Drag the green rectangle to the right of the stage.

6. You'll be using this same file to explore the different drawing modes, so save this as object_drawing.fla.

What happened? Where the shapes overlapped, they have merged, and when you dragged the rectangle to the right, part of the circle was cut out, as shown in Figure 4-4. This will occur anytime you draw shapes that overlap on the same layer in Merge Drawing mode.

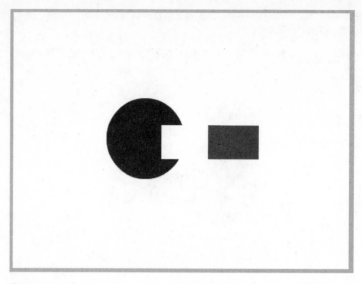

Figure 4-4. Merge Drawing mode causes overlapping objects to merge and change shape.

Using Object Drawing mode

Object Drawing mode enables you to specify that overlapping shapes that you draw on the same layer on the stage do not automatically merge. To use Object Drawing mode, you must enable it by selecting a drawing tool and clicking the Object Drawing Mode button on the Tools panel. We'll quickly investigate Object Drawing mode:

1. Open the object_drawing.fla file created in the previous exercise.

2. With the Oval tool, click the Object Drawing Mode button, as shown in Figure 4-5.

3. Draw a pink oval on the stage covering the other two shapes, as shown in Figure 4-6.

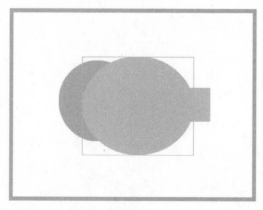

Figure 4-5. The Object Drawing Mode button appears at the bottom of the Tools panel when you have a drawing tool selected.

Figure 4-6. Drawing an object overlapping preexisting objects in Object Drawing mode

4. Change to the Selection tool and select the pink oval.

5. Drag the pink oval around the stage.

What happens? That's right, absolutely nothing! Enabling Object Drawing mode allows you to draw shapes as separate objects that don't automatically merge when you overlap them.

> *You can also toggle between Merge and Object Drawing modes by pressing J on the keyboard when you have a drawing tool selected.*

Using Primitive Shape mode

Flash CS4 allows you to extend Object Drawing mode by creating primitive shapes in Primitive Shape mode. Primitive Shape mode enables you to edit properties in the Properties Inspector that can customize your shapes. You are now going to see how easy it is to change an oval into a pie wedge using the Primitive tool.

1. Open a new blank Flash file (ActionScript 3.0) in Flash CS4.

2. Click and hold the Shape tool, and choose the Oval Primitive tool, as shown in Figure 4-7.

3. With the Primitive Oval tool selected, choose a black stroke and no fill.

4. Draw an oval on the stage, as shown in Figure 4-8.

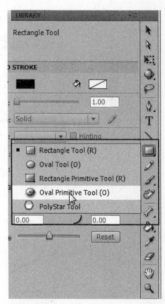

Figure 4-7. Clicking and holding the Shape tool allows you to choose the option you wish to use

Figure 4-8. Drawing a primitive oval on the stage

Notice that the Properties Inspector has changed—the Oval Options section has been added to it, as shown in Figure 4-9. This is where you adjust the angles of your circle to create a wedge.

5. Select the oval on the stage.

6. Drag the Start angle slider in the Oval Options section of the Properties Inspector to 180.00, as shown in Figure 4-9.

Your oval will now become a half oval. This is because you have specified an angle of 180°. Next, you'll manipulate the end angle to finish off your wedge.

7. Drag the End angle slider to 220°, as shown in Figure 4-10.

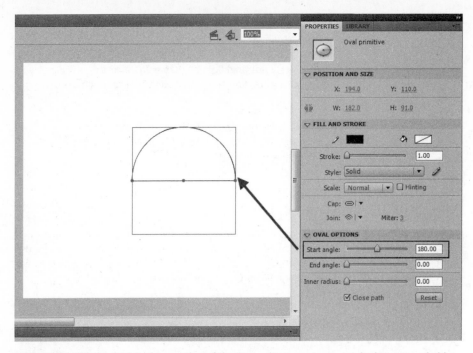

Figure 4-9. Using the Oval Options section of the Properties Inspector to manipulate your primitive shape on the stage

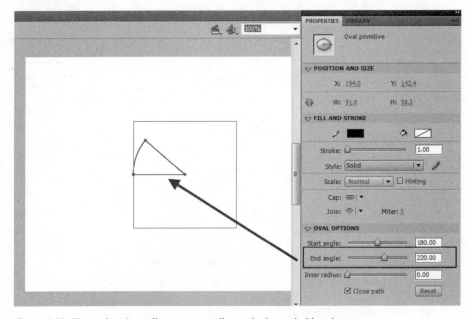

Figure 4-10. The oval options allow you to easily manipulate primitive shapes.

Using the 3D Rotation tool

The 3D Rotation tool allows you to rotate movie clip symbols in three dimensions. It's like grabbing a piece of paper and spinning it around. It is not a full 3D engine, but the 3D Rotation tool does allow you to emulate planar types of transformations, which previously would have taken hours to animate by hand.

In Chapter 1, you discovered how a 2D animation travels along an x-axis and a y-axis in the Motion Editor. In Flash, 3D animations are moved in 3D space along the z-axis.

The following exercise is a simple introduction to the 3D Rotation tool. We will be creating sophisticated 3D animations in Chapter 7.

To use the 3D Rotation tool, you must be using ActionScript 3.0.

1. Open a new Flash file (ActionScript 3.0) in Flash CS4.

2. Click the Rectangle tool to select it, and draw a square on the stage, as shown in Figure 4-11. Ensure that there is no stroke on the shape.

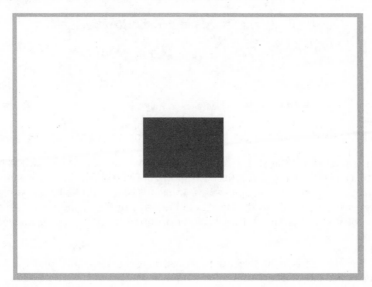

Figure 4-11. Draw a square on the stage using the Rectangle tool.

3. With the Selection tool selected, right-click the rectangle and choose Convert to Symbol.

4. On the Convert to Symbol dialog, name your symbol 3D_shape, ensure that Movie Clip is selected in the Type drop-down, and click OK, as shown in Figure 4-12.

Figure 4-12. Naming your movie clip in the Convert to Symbol dialog

Next, you're going to add a keyframe to the timeline of the animation.

5. Right-click frame 30 on the timeline and choose Insert Keyframe, as shown in Figure 4-13.

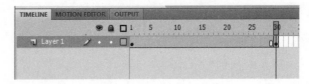

Figure 4-13. Inserting a keyframe on frame 30

6. Click the 3D Rotation tool from the Tools panel to select it.

What has happened on the stage? You will notice that the selection circle on the box changes to a colored circle and crosshairs, as shown in Figure 4-14. These crosshairs represent 3D movement on the x-, y-, and z-axes. The x-axis runs horizontally across the stage, the y-axis runs vertically across the stage, and the z-axis runs into and out of the stage—that is, to the viewer, the object appears closer or further away depending on where it is on the z-axis.

7. While still on frame 30, select the 3D Rotation tool and spin one of the circles. You will notice the square rotates to match the image shown in Figure 4-15.

This is a fantastic new feature that will help make Flash movies interesting and inviting. Imagine organizing products in a store that pop out at you. The possibilities are now only limited by your imagination.

> *To find out more about the 3D Rotation tool, flip to Chapter 7, where this component of Flash CS4 is thoroughly explained.*

Figure 4-14. When the 3D Rotation tool is selected, circles and crosshairs represent 3D movement along the axis

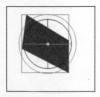

Figure 4-15. Rotating a 3D shape on the stage

Text madness! Using the Text tool

Flash CS4 allows you to integrate text into your Flash movie in a variety of ways. For example, you can create static text fields to display text that is not going to change in your movie, dynamic text fields that allow you the opportunity to update text on the fly, or input fields that will allow users to enter data into the text field.

You also have a number of ways in which text can be displayed. You can orient it horizontally or vertically, as well as set font, size, style, color, and line spacing attributes. You can run a spell check on your Flash CS4 document and transform the text by animating, rotating, flipping, and skewing it, and you can control font substitution.

This section will teach you numerous ways to use the Text tool in Flash CS4.

4

Implementing text fields

Text fields can be one of the following: static, dynamic, or input fields.

Static text fields are exactly that. They display text that is unable to dynamically update. **Dynamic text fields** enable you to display dynamically updating text, which allows you to optimize messages to get the best results from users. **Input text fields** enable you to create forms and capture data from users in your website or marketing campaign. We will be looking at text fields more closely further on in the book when you create a form to capture contact information from visitors to your website.

Anti-aliasing fonts

Anti-aliasing is a powerful design tool, as it allows you to smooth the edges of text online, which enables you to perfectly render small text on the screen. When you enable anti-aliasing, it affects all text in the current selection. It is equally effective with text of all sizes, regardless of whether that text is static, dynamic, or input text, providing the user has Flash Player 7 or later. If the user has an earlier version than Flash Player 7, only static text is anti-aliased.

When you are using a small-sized font, it's good to keep in mind that sans-serif fonts such as Arial and Helvetica appear clearer than serif fonts, and that some styles such as bold or italicized text can make small text less legible.

The Flash CS4 text rendering engine renders high-quality fonts in Flash CS4 SWF files and FLA files. Figure 4-16 shows the difference between the many anti-aliasing settings.

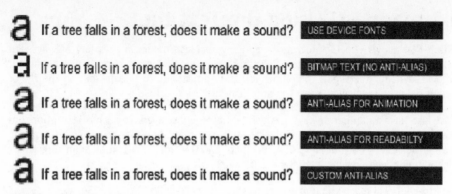

Figure 4-16. Different treatments of text affect the legibility of the copy.

Using device fonts

Device fonts are the standard default fonts that will work on every system, regardless of the type or OS of the machine. These are typically Arial, Times New Roman, and Verdana. Using device fonts greatly reduces a SWF file's final size. This is due to Flash not having to embed the extra font data into the final movie. Device fonts are very easy to read, and work well in most applications. The downside to device fonts is that they are very plain looking.

Flash CS4 includes three device fonts: _sans, which is akin to Helvetica or Arial; _serif, which is similar to Times New Roman; and _typewriter, a version of Courier. When you specify a device font in your Flash CS4 document, Flash Player will substitute the closest font available on the user's computer.

Using font outlines

By default, Flash CS4 will embed font outlines for all static text fields. If your design uses an input field or a dynamic text field, then you will have to be specific about how you embed your font outlines. If this is the case, a Character Embedding button will appear in the Properties Inspector, as shown in Figure 4-17.

Character Embedding...

Figure 4-17. The Character Embedding button enables you to specify the way that you embed font outlines into your Flash CS4 document.

If you click the Character Embedding button, a dialog box will appear, as shown in Figure 4-18.

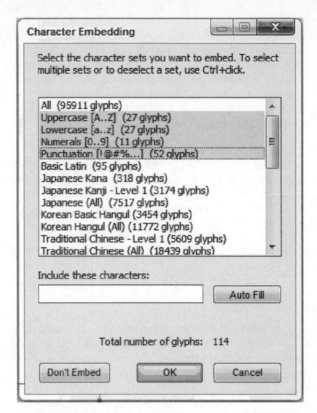

Figure 4-18. The Character Embedding dialog box allows you to choose which text option you would like embedded into your Flash CS4 movie.

This dialog box gives you the choice of which Unicode characters you would like to embed into your movie. **Unicode characters** are industry standard characters that allow computers to represent text used in most of the world's writing systems. For most English-based applications, I like to choose Basic Latin, which already includes uppercase, lowercase, numerals, and punctuation. You may need to include more or less depending on the application and end user.

Creating and working with symbols

Flash CS4 uses the concept of symbols to do all of its dirty work. Symbols are like baskets or containers. They can house anything that you create in Flash CS4. You can also nest symbols within symbols, a little like Matryoshka (Russian) dolls.

For example, you might have a symbol containing a drawing of a pig's face and head. You could then also have legs, a body, and a tail as individual symbols. You might then position all of the individual parts together into a complete pig and create another symbol containing all of those other symbols. You could then animate the legs walking and the tail twirling within the main pig symbol. If you then applied another animation to the main pig symbol, moving it across the screen, it would create the illusion of the pig walking across the screen. We will see an example of this in Chapter 6, when we create a banner campaign with a bug flying across the screen.

The beauty of symbols is that they are the equivalent of blueprints in Flash. You use the symbol blueprint to create an instance of something on the stage. An **instance** is a carbon copy of a symbol, but it can be individually customized. For example, you can change its color, opacity, proportions, and position. You can even name them different names. You could easily create an animation of an entire pig family by first drawing a pig, animating it, and then creating multiple instances of said pig.

There are four kinds of symbols: font symbols, movie clips, buttons, and graphics.

They each have their own particular properties and features.

Movie clips

Movie clips are used to build pieces of animation that you can reuse. They have their own timeline that works independently of the main timeline (called a **multiframe timeline**), and they can contain interactive functionality, sounds, video, and even other movie clips. They can also have ActionScript applied to them.

Buttons

Button symbols are used to create interactive buttons that respond to user actions such as clicks or mouseovers. To build a button symbol, you define the graphics or text that you wish to be associated with each of the button states, and then you assign the action to a button instance.

Button symbols will behave like buttons. This means they have the four button states common to graphical user interfaces. Buttons can either be hovered over, not hovered over, or clicked. Buttons also have a state you can define as the "over" area.

Graphic symbols

In Flash CS4, graphic symbols are used for static images and animations that are tied to the main timeline, with which they operate in sync. They are not compatible with interactive controls or sounds. As they have no independent timeline, they add less weight to the FLA file size, which can be particularly useful when you are developing banner campaigns for publishers that have strict file size restrictions.

Font symbols

Font symbols enable you to export a font from a Flash CS4 document to be used in other Flash CS4 documents.

Defining symbols and instances

To define a symbol, you simply select the object or group of objects on the stage. You can then right-click and select Convert to symbol on the context menu, as shown in Figure 4-19, or you can go to the Modify menu and select it there.

Figure 4-19. Right-click an element to display the menu.

Creating an empty symbol

Having too many elements on the stage can make it difficult to find space to create a new symbol. In this case, you would create an empty symbol. When you create an empty symbol, the stage opens up to give you lots of room to work with. To create an empty movie clip, go to the Insert menu and click New Symbol (Ctrl+F8), as shown in Figure 4-20.

Figure 4-20. Creating an empty movie clip

After you insert a new symbol, you will be prompted to complete the Create New Symbol dialog, as shown in Figure 4-21.

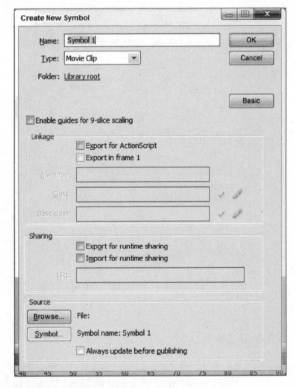

Figure 4-21. Creating a new symbol

After naming the symbol and choosing its Type, click OK to create the new symbol. The stage becomes blank as if you had just created a new Flash file. No need for fear, as this is not the case. The upper-left corner shows the stage hierarchy, as shown by the big black arrow in Figure 4-22. When you create an empty symbol, Flash CS4 clears some space on the workspace to build the symbol. Create a new symbol by quickly doodling something.

Figure 4-22. Blobby and the stage hierachy

Now click the Scene 1 icon, as shown in Figure 4-23. This will take you back to the main stage. Notice that your new symbol is missing from the stage. When you create an empty symbol, it gets stored in the library, waiting for you to throw it onto the stage. To edit the symbol, double-click its image in the library, as shown in Figure 4-24 (or on the stage if it appears there).

Figure 4-23. Scene 1 icon

Unless you have saved your FLA file, the drop-down list in the library will just appear as untitled-x.fla, not blobby. fla, which is the saved name of my document.

Editing symbols

You can edit symbols by double-clicking their images on the stage or in the Library. When you are editing a symbol, you will notice that the timeline changes. The title of the stage will change to match the symbol you are editing. To get back to the stage or the symbol you were just in, click its name or the back arrow in the movie clip navigation bar, as shown in Figure 4-25. If you have entered symbol editing mode from the stage, you will notice that the symbol you are editing retains it opacity, and the background loses it tone. This way of editing is perfect for viewing your symbol in its place. To return to the main stage, either click the Scene 1 icon as demonstrated previously, or double-click the opaque background.

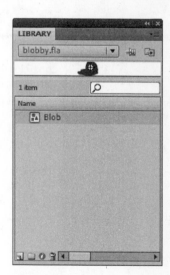

Figure 4-24. Drag your new symbol from the library and onto the stage.

Figure 4-25. Double-click a symbol to edit it.

4

Drawing a logo

Building a logo is a great way to learn the drawing tools. We will draw a logo for our online store, and define it as a symbol. But what is a logo, exactly?

A logo is a visual identity. It is a signature, characteristic, or marker. Logos have the power to evoke thoughts and feelings. What do you think of when you see the McDonald's, Apple, or Warner Bros. logos? Each of these logos are simple, powerful shapes that help consumers identify and relate to a product and service.

Keep this in mind when designing logos. The driving force behind a successful logo is brand recognition and identification. Research the competitor logos. Open your local phone book and see what colors other businesses are using. If you are producing a logo for a landscaping company, you may find many green logos. What color stands out against green? Looking back at the color theory discussed earlier, you will find that a red logo will pop out of a page full of green logos. Perhaps the landscaping logo could introduce a dash of red, or even be totally red. Making design decisions like this will ensure that your logo stands out against the competitors and makes a lasting impression on potential customers. There are a number of ways to classify logos, and the two most common are using logotype and pictograms (or you can even use a combination of both). **Logotype** is a typeface that has been modified to demonstrate a particular message or symbol. Some clever examples of good logotype are the FedEx logo and the Microsoft logo, as shown in Figure 4-26.

Figure 4-26. The Microsoft and FedEx logos

Look closely at the Microsoft logo. At first glance, it appears to be an ordinary italicized sans-serif typeface—nothing special. But if you look between the *o* and the *s*, you'll find a tiny pyramid: the symbol for power. The FedEx logotype also has a hidden message. Take a look at the design space between the capital *E* and the *x*. It is a forward-pointing arrow! This suggests motion, speed, and progress. When creating your logo, try to look for ways to manipulate the letterform to reveal symbols, or add to them.

The other popular way to design a logo to use a pictogram. Pictograms use simple shapes and imagery in interesting ways to conjure emotion, feeling, and meaning. Some well-known pictograms include the Apple logo and the Yamaha logo, as shown in Figure 4-27.

Figure 4-27. The Apple and Yamaha pictograms

The Apple pictogram is interesting because it has a bite missing. Knowing the good humor behind Apple's founders, this is most likely an inside joke paying reference to the byte, a small chunk of memory. The missing bite also helps the pictogram resemble an apple as opposed to a peach, plum, or other type of fruit. Yamaha is known for its finely tuned instruments and machines. The Yamaha pictogram carefully arranges three tuning forks to subconsciously spell out the letter Y.

So when should you use logotype, pictograms, or both? A logo has to communicate. So if the brand and its associated products are well known, like Mercedes and McDonald's, the logo can be extremely simple. The McDonald's logo is not clever or interesting. It works because it is used over and over, everywhere. If you are redesigning a well-known brand, you can afford to strip back on logo complexity. New brands and businesses are the opposite. They need to speak loud and clear about the products and services they represent. Usually a new business will need logotype and a pictogram to carry a message. As time passes and the business grows, the logo complexity can be refined in a process over time.

Again, remember that design is a process. Design is not a talent, skill, or set of rules. Design is like the growth of a tree. The design process is grounded by initial planning. A design will flourish under the right conditions. Although a design starts its life with a pre-determined end result, it may shift and change with its environment. For a tree to withstand harsh climatic conditions, it needs to have a strong set of deeply grounded roots. In design, we call this the **sketch**.

For our online store, I doodled the sketch with a pen on a napkin during a lunch. I then took a photo of the napkin using the camera on my phone, as shown in Figure 4-28. Phone cameras are much more accessible these days and the quality is good enough to replace the clunky old scanner.

Inspiration can strike at any time. When you feel an idea coming on, don't be afraid to draw it. If you are lying in bed trying to fall asleep, or if you are picking up diapers in a shopping center, it doesn't matter. Just get it down on paper, or onscreen if you have a touch-sensitive device. Even if you can't draw very well, the process will help you to iron out design problems early in the game. Use whatever medium is available. Keep the design simple. Just draw blobs if you aren't a confident artist. The premise of the process is to get the rough idea and concept from your mind to paper, and then from paper to the computer. Some people like to skip this step. They like to draw straight to computer. I have found if you fix a problem early on, then the entire building process is smoother further down the track. Imagine building a house without a set of plans.

Figure 4-28. A simple sketch is the basis for our logo.

We want our online store to convey a personal tone while remaining lighthearted and slightly amusing. The Gene with Envy logo consists of two main elements: the angry snail and the *Gene with Envy* lettering.

First we will begin with the lettering. There are many typefaces and fonts available on the Web, but nothing says "personal" like drawing the letters yourself. Remember that good design conjures emotion and feeling. If we were designing a logo for a financial institution, we would probably choose a serious and straighter-looking typeface like Garamond, Palatino, or Baskerville. Our shop, on the other hand, is organic. It is rounded, gooey, and messy. It sells a host of mutated plant and animal species. We would like the lettering to reflect this idea.

Importing the sketch

In Chapter 3, you learned about importing artwork. You again need to revisit this in the following exercise. Ensure that you have downloaded the source files for this book from the friends of ED website to get the most out of this exercise.

1. Open a new Flash File (ActionScript 3) document in Flash CS4.

> *You could also create an ActionScript 2.0 file, but we will be coding every website project in this book in ActionScript 3.0 standard. There are some marketing guidelines where ActionScript 2.0 is the standard, and for those we will be using ActionScript 2.0. Where publishers are not involved, we will be using ActionScript 3.0.*

2. Select File ➤ Import ➤ Import to Stage to import the gene-logo-sketch.jpg sketch, as shown in Figure 4-29.

Figure 4-29. The Import dialog box

3. Select and open the image file gene-logo-sketch.jpg.

4. The sketch will enter the stage oversized, so you'll need to zoom out to see the entire sketch. Select View ➤ Zoom Out.

5. Next, you need to make the graphic fit the stage size (or make the stage fit the graphic). Change the size of the graphic by clicking the Selection tool in the Tools panel and then clicking the image.

> *You are using a sketch as a guide to building a logo with the Flash CS4 set of drawing tools. If you wanted to, however, you could neatly draw and color your logo by hand, and then scan or photograph it to send it into Flash. Flash CS4 uses a fantastic tracing algorithm, called Trace Bitmap, to convert bitmap images into vectorized shapes.*
>
> *To use the Trace Bitmap command, select the image you like and then go to* Modify ➤ Bitmap ➤ Trace Bitmap. *You will be presented with the* Trace Bitmap *dialog box, as shown in Figure 4-30, which offers four values:*
>
> - Color threshold: Value from 1 to 500. Higher values attract fewer colors from the original image.
>
> - Minimum area: Value from 1 to 1000. Higher values create rougher shapes and lower values create finer shapes.
>
> - Curve fit: Allows you to specify the smoothness of the curve.
>
> - Corner threshold: Defines how far a single curve will bend before adding corners.

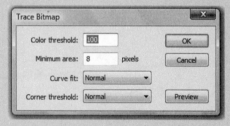

Figure 4-30. The Trace Bitmap dialog box

6. Use the Free Transform tool while holding down the Shift key, and drag the image down to a size that fits the canvas. Holding down Shift will keep the image in proportion.

7. Click the padlock icon in the timeline to lock the image, as shown in Figure 4-31.

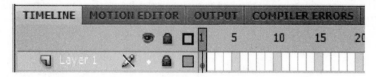

Figure 4-31. Click the padlock icon in the timeline to lock the image.

8. Double-click the Layer 1 label in the timeline and name the layer sketch.

Next, we will lay out construction graphics in accordance with the pen sketch. Due to the organic nature of the logo, we will use ovals. **Construction graphics** are like guidelines that you can trace to keep the logo looking consistent. In this exercise, we will be using light gray and dark gray to color the initial part of the logo.

9. Go to the Tools panel and select the Oval tool. If you don't see it, click and hold the Shape tool button, and a range of options will appear, as shown in Figure 4-32.

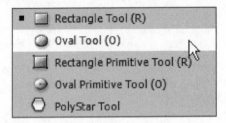

Figure 4-32. The Shape tool options

10. Click the New Layer button at the bottom of the timeline to make a new layer, as shown in Figure 4-33. The New Layer button looks like a page being turned.

Figure 4-33. Creating a new layer

11. Ensure that you're using Merge Drawing mode, and draw an oval over the top part of the G, as shown in Figure 4-34.

    You can toggle between the two drawing modes by pressing the keyboard shortcut (J), or by clicking its icon at the bottom of the Tools panel.

Figure 4-34. Using an oval to aid design

You may need to turn snapping off by toggling the snap icon to the off state. In the on state, the snap icon looks like this: [img]; and in the off state, it looks like this: [img].

12. Double-click the gray oval to select it.

> *Double-clicking objects in Flash selects both the shape and its outline.*

13. Copy and paste another oval, and place it further along the curve of the G. You can also hold down Alt as you drag the oval, as this will have the same effect as copy/paste.

14. Continue to place more ovals at major junctions in the letter shape, as shown in Figure 4-35. Try to use as few as possible while still keeping true to the letterform. Use the Transform tool [img] to shrink or grow the oval to fit the shape if you have to.

Figure 4-35. Placing ovals at major junctions on the G in the logo

15. Lock the oval layer and name it oval using the process described earlier.

16. As a final step, save the Flash CS4 document as gene-logo.fla.

With the ovals in place, we are now ready to construct the typography. The ovals are used as construction lines to keep the letters formed in correct proportion. This assures consistency and quality of the type.

Mastering the Pen tool

The Pen tool is one of the most important inventions for creating vector illustrations. It allows for fast and accurate line work. When you master the Pen tool, digital illustration becomes a whole lot easier. The Pen tool also has a counterpart, the Sub-selection tool. The Sub-selection tool allows you to move and manipulate pivot points created by the Pen tool.

The Pen tool can be used to draw two types of lines: straight lines and curves. Straight lines are plotted using a two-click process. Click the starting point. As you move the mouse outward, a line will follow the pointer. Click again to create an endpoint. To draw curves, you keep the mouse button held down when you click the second point. As you drag the mouse, the line will curve in response to the movement. Usually you will have to draw an initial point before making a curve. Sometimes the curve will not seem to fit, no matter which way you push or pull. If this happens, you can access the Convert Anchor Point tool from the Pen tool menu in the Tools panel. This tool will toggle between giving the line a sharp curve and a smooth curve.

Once you have drawn your outline most of the way around the first letter, you can close the shape by clicking back on the first point you made. The Pen tool icon changes to display a small o when you mouse over the initial point, indicating that you can close the shape by clicking that point . Figure 4-36 shows the Pen tool options.

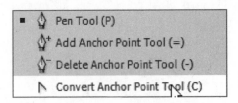

Figure 4-36. The Pen tool options

You can use the Pen tool to create crisp, hard-edged vector art.

Let's attempt to trace the letterform in the sketch, paying careful attention to following the outer shape of the ovals. Create a new layer and lock all the layers underneath. Ensure that snapping is on.

> In Flash, snapping helps you to align elements on the stage.

You can continue the exercise from its last save point if you wish, but if you haven't completed the exercise and you want to start from this point, load the file 4-3.fla, which is available for download from the friends of ED website.

1. Zoom in to the letter *G* so that it occupies most of your screen, as you did in the first exercise creating the logo.

2. Select the Pen tool. Starting from the uppermost oval, click a point on the top edge of the letter *G*.

3. Working clockwise, click and drag a curve along the oval to where the oval meets the sketch underneath. Try to use the fewest points possible while still keeping the integrity of the shape.

4. Click and drag curves along the entire outline of the letter. There should be no straight lines. Instead of using the scrollbars to move around the stage, try holding the space bar down to temporarily activate the Hand tool. The mouse will change into a hand. This hand will let you grab the stage and move it around.

5. The curves don't have to perfectly follow the sketch. Try to keep the curves fluid. Tracing around an oval will take four clicks.

During the tracing, you may have to convert the anchor point. To do so, mouse over the last point you made until you see the upside down *V*. When the icon changes, click again to convert the anchor point.

> **Anchor points** *are points that are stationary when you manipulate an object by stretching, skewing, scaling, or mirroring.*

At any time, you can stop and edit the path by choosing the Sub-selection tool. Use this tool to move the point around, and also to change the angles of curves. Observe that you can also select multiple points on the curve by either dragging a selection or holding down Shift and clicking.

To resume drawing the path you were working on, select the Pen tool and continue to draw.

6. Follow the outer edge all the way around until the Pen tool meets back up with the first point you drew. When you mouse over the initial point, the icon will change once again to display a small o . This will ensure that you complete the shape. If you don't complete the shape properly, you may not be able to fill it with color at a later stage.

Your completed *G* outline should look similar to Figure 4-37.

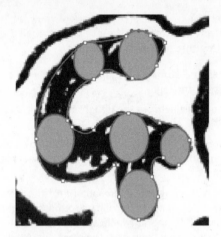

Figure 4-37. Outline of the gooey letter *G*

7. Select the Paint Bucket tool from the Tools panel, as shown in Figure 4-38, and fill the shape with color by clicking in the middle of the outline.

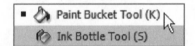

Figure 4-38. The fill tools

Your completed *G* should appear similar to Figure 4-39.

Figure 4-39. Your filled *G*

Now be brave and finish the rest of the words *Gene* and *Envy* using the same process. Notice that you will only have to create an outline for the *e*, *n*, *v*, and *y*. You can copy/paste and transform the *E* and the other *N*.

We'll start by temporarily hiding the current layer by clicking the hide dot in the timeline. Remember to turn snapping off.

1. Unlock the oval layer. Copy/paste more ovals in meaningful spots along the sketch, as shown in Figure 4-40.

Figure 4-40. Ovals used to construct the letters

2. Once the ovals are in place, lock the layer, turn snapping back on, and then start tracing.

3. Use the sketch as a round placement guide. Good-looking typography has an element of consistency. Remember this when positioning your ovals. The tops of the *n*, *v*, and *y* have the ovals placed the same distance apart.

> *If you copy/paste from one letter to another, you will end up with some uniformity, which is nice.*

When the letters are fully drawn, you will need to look at the proportion and placement. Obviously it is hard to get these two things perfect on a sketch, as sketches are only meant to be rough guides. Try to ensure that all the characters are the same height. To visually do this, activate the rulers by choosing Rulers from the View menu, as shown in Figure 4-41. A horizontal ruler will appear at the top of the stage, and a vertical ruler will appear to the left of the stage.

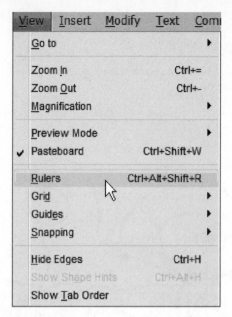

Figure 4-41. Activating the rulers from the
View menu

You can also use guides to visually align objects on the stage. You place guides on the stage
by clicking a ruler and dragging a guide outward and into an appropriate position. In this
case, drag two horizontal guides out to the bottom and top of the lettering. The *G* and the
E are almost 20% bigger than the other letters. This helps to improve readability and form.

> *When creating this sketch initially, I had a happy accident. As I drew over the y,
> the bottom of it reminded me of a tentacle. So, using the v shape I had just cre-
> ated, I copied another one and I added a descender to the letterform. Once the
> tail was drawn, I then added the little oval suckers.*

The finished *Gene* and *Envy* letters should look like Figure 4-42.

> *Remember to save your work regularly!*

Figure 4-42. Lettering with the Pen tool

In the Gene with Envy logo, you've reused the letters E and N. Also, the V has been reused and slightly manipulated to form the basis of the Y. Be aware of shortcuts such as this, as they are often time saving, which can be very important on jobs where a client is paying you by the hour to complete something.

We will continue with the type by drawing the *with* letters using the Rectangle and Oval tools. We will build the type up with modular pieces.

1. Start by locking the current shape layer and renaming it shape.

2. Click the New Layer button on the timeline and call it with.

3. While you are in the Merge Drawing mode, use the Rectangle tool, find some empty space, and draw a skinny rectangle, as shown in Figure 4-43.

4. Using copy/paste (or holding down Alt as you drag), arrange a series of seven rectangles, as shown in Figure 4-44. These will form the vertical pieces of the type.

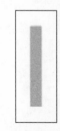

Figure 4-43. A skinny rectangle

Figure 4-44. Seven skinny rectangles

113

5. Copy another rectangle and rotate it 90°. Copy two additional rectangles. Place these rectangles along the bottom of the W, along the top of the T, and across the middle of the H. Trim any excess bits as you go.

The word *with* in the logo should look something like Figure 4-45.

Figure 4-45. The completed *with*

6. Now select the Ink Bottle tool in the Tools panel and create an outline around the rectangular type by clicking each of the shapes that make up the word. Move the letters left and right so that the gaps between them (the kerning) are in proportion. Try not to leave big holes between letters.

The final *with* should look like Figure 4-46.

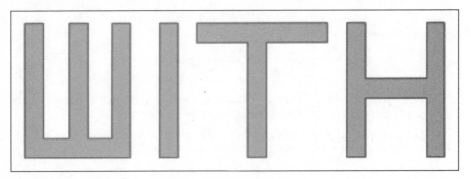

Figure 4-46. The final *with*

7. Select the whole word and move it down into place between the Gene and the Envy, as shown in Figure 4-47.

Figure 4-47. The final typography

> *A faster technique could have also been to use a text field and a font to generate the with vector art. Although this would not have looked as unique, it could have made the logo creation process faster.*
>
> *To create vector graphics from text fields, first select the Text tool. Type out the text you would like to use and then format it. After you have finished with the formatting, make sure it is selected, and then go to Modify ➤ Break Apart or press Ctrl+B (or Cmd+B on the Mac). This will pull the group of letters apart. These individual letters are not in an editable form. Use the Break Apart command once more to convert the font into an editable vector graphic.*

4

Finally, we will move on to the graphical element and the freehand tools. As a final exercise with the drawing tools, we will look at the Brush and Pencil tools. First, we'll paint the outline of the snail using the Brush tool.

1. Create a new layer and name it snail.

2. Select the Brush tool, as shown in Figure 4-48.

Figure 4-48. The Brush tool

3. Use the Zoom tool or the keyboard shortcuts (Ctrl/Cmd and +/-) so that you can fit the whole sketch vertically on the screen.

4. Choose a brush that is smaller than the line weight on the sketch.

> *Brush sizes can be changed via a drop-down menu in the Tools panel, which looks like Figure 4-49.*

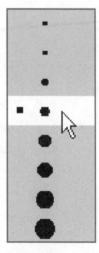

Figure 4-49. Choosing the correct brush size

5. Use the Brush tool to paint a fluid line over the top of the sketch, as shown in Figure 4-50. You use the Brush tool to draw the outlines of the snail, because the Brush tool gives you the option to paint what looks like a variable-width stroke. Variable-width strokes offer charm and character, while constant-width strokes can look flat and lifeless. It is impossible to achieve this style with the Pen or Pencil tools, which can only create constant-width strokes.

Figure 4-50. Choose a smaller brush size
to paint the linework.

When you have finished the outline of the snail, hide the sketch layer, and you will be presented with an image similar to Figure 4-51.

Figure 4-51. The final snail

The Eraser tool may come in handy along the way. You can rub out lines that don't feel right or line work that is spiky. When you have finished, double-click the snail to select it all. Smooth any wonky lines by clicking the Smooth button . The more you click the button, the smoother and simpler the shape becomes. When you are finished, change the color of the snail to the dark color of the text outline.

> *Another time saver is the Trace Bitmap command. If you can draw or find an image you are after, Trace Bitmap will convert the image into a vector shape for you. Once your image is highlighted, you can find the Trace Bitmap command in* Modify ➤ Bitmap ➤ Trace Bitmap.

Pulling it all together

Move the snail up from the type to give it some breathing space. It should now look similar to Figure 4-52.

Figure 4-52. Final snail with final type

Notice that the darker color of the snail dominates the logo. Return some balance to the type by using the Brush tool to paint shadow under the letters. Use the Paint Bucket tool to fill the snail's shell with a light gray. Fill the snail and its eye with white. The logo has been drawn on a white background. If the logo was moved over a colored background, the color would show through the eye. This is why you apply a white fill to the eye.

Create a new layer and name it shadows. We want the shadows to appear under the type, so drag the shadow layer to sit under the shape layer. Use the Brush tool with the darker color, similar to how you painted the snail. This time just use one thicker brush and follow the curve under the letters. The logo with shadows under the text should look like Figure 4-53.

Figure 4-53. Almost-final logo

Finally, you will add a ground plane line as a finishing touch. The Pencil tool 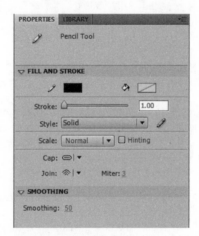 is used for drawing lines, and in particular, outlines for shapes. The Pencil tool properties are shown in Figure 4-54. Note that the Pencil tool could have been used to draw the snail, but doing so would have resulted in a constant-width stoke. A constant width can make your illustration look flat, computerized, and lifeless (not quite the feel we're trying to portray in the logo). This is why the Brush tool was used to draw the snail outlines.

The Brush tool is traditionally used to paint fills and splashes of color. However, using the Brush tool makes it easier to draw variable-width strokes, thus enhancing the hand-drawn style of illustration.

Figure 4-54. The Pencil tool options

We will now draw the ground line below the snail.

1. With the logo document opened, completed to the last exercise, create a new layer and name it ground. The ground line will be drawn using a very long, thin outline.

2. Starting from the left side, draw a line that roughly follows the tops of the lettering.

3. When you get to the right side, draw down and then head back to the start and close the loop. Fill the outline using the same dark green color.

Color me bad

The shop logo should convey a sense of life, a sense of bacterial infection. This has been done using fluid and organic forms. To continue with the "living" theme, you will need to splash around the color green—three yucky, stinky, slimy greens. First, choose a dark green for the outline of the snail—a good choice would be the hex RGB color #003300. You may need to apply color to the outline of the letters using the Ink Bottle tool. When using the Ink Bottle tool, you are also able to change stroke settings, but for this exercise we want to keep the default. Ensure you use the original settings of a 1.00 point stroke and a style of solid. I created a highlights layer and painted a few quick horizontal strokes of light green. This gave the type and shell a little added depth.

You will need to download the final 4-final.fla file to see the where to apply the three green colors, and to see an example of color choice. The logo is now complete, as shown in Figure 4-55.

Figure 4-55. The final logo

You have just witnessed how to make an idea come to life. The design process is a dynamic creature. The initial sketch looked quite different from the final logo. Some wise advice is to not spend too much time on the initial sketch, as the final outcome will most likely change (remember the design process from Chapter 2).

Not only have you just learned some practical uses of the Flash drawing tools, but you now have a funky piece of vector art to use throughout the remainder of the book.

Summary

Flash CS4 provides all of the drawing capabilities Flash designers need to bring their ideas to life. In this chapter, you have learned about the drawing tools and symbols, and have used them to create a logo that will form the basis of the site's design. Don't be afraid to experiment with the different tools until you find an effect that is right for you.

It's important not only to understand the techniques for building logos and graphics, but the commercial realities of why you build them. As the Internet becomes more and more an example of everyday advertising, it's important that you know how to achieve cut-through in the plethora of competing advertisements and websites out there. Understanding how to represent your company graphically via the creation of relevant and unique logos and marketing collateral is the first step in achieving commercial success.

In Chapter 5, you will be expanding upon this knowledge and learning how using these tools can really bring your Flash animations to life.

CHAPTER 5
FILTERS AND BLENDS

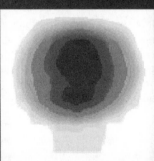

In Chapter 4 we explored how to create graphics with the drawing tools. In this chapter you will learn quick and effective ways to enhance your graphics using Flash's built-in filters and blends.

Filters and blends can be a blessing to Flash designers who are required to output high-quality Flash designs and movies in relatively short times. Using preset filters and blends enables you to produce quality designs without having to reinvent the wheel every time you want to use a particular effect.

They are particularly useful tools when you have clients that you create Flash movies for regularly. You can incorporate the blends and filters typically used for the client into their corporate guidelines. This then becomes a resource for the design team, and ensures that any creative assets produced are within specifications.

What are filters?

Filters are used to create special effects. In photography terms, filters are usually transparent attachments that screw into the top of a lens, varying the way light is captured by the camera. In Flash CS4, filters are used to enhance images, movie clips, buttons, and text objects by applying an effect to your artwork. The greatest feat of all is the ability to compose and animate filter effects without ActionScript!

There are two types of filters in Flash CS4, Pixel Bender and preset/animated. Preset/animated filters come standard with Flash CS4, while Pixel Bender filters are downloaded or coded.

Pixel Bender filters

Pixel Bender is the name Adobe gives to its bitmap shading language. The language and supporting IDE (Integrated Development Environment) allow Flash users to write their own customized filters to utilize and share with the world.

Pixel Bender allows you to write algorithms and processes to affect an image at the fundamental pixel level. Imagine you had a photography website and you wanted to make a Flash component that would allow a user to upload a color photo and then convert it to a black-and-white one. Pixel Bender allows you to dynamically assess images at a pixel level. The filter you write could grab all the red and green pixels and turn those white. It could then turn all the blue pixels black. The result would be a black-and-white variation of the original image.

Pixel Bender is also a versatile shading-language library that can be used in other motion-video software, such as Adobe After Effects. Its versatility also means that Flash users can share custom-created filters. The beauty of this open system is not only in the customization and personal reuse of filters, but also in the community. Many websites now host custom filters that other creative people have written for you. Adobe Exchange is a place where developers can share their custom-developed filters for Adobe products. Simply search *Adobe Exchange Pixel Bender* in your search engine, or visit www.adobe.com/cfusion/exchange/index.cfm?event=productHome&exc=26.

The filters are made accessible using ActionScript. You can write your own filters and functions or utilize the predefined Pixel Bender functions using the Library Import command. Writing your own filters is relatively ActionScript 3.0–intensive. ActionScript 3.0 will be covered in greater detail in Chapter 8.

> To download the Pixel Bender IDE, source files, and more tutorials, head to http://labs.adobe.com/downloads/pixelbender.html.

Preset/animated filters

The animated filters inherit their nature from the seven predefined graphical properties in Flash CS4: the Drop Shadow, Blur, Glow, Bevel, Gradient Glow, Gradient Bevel, and Adjust Color filters. These can be accessed in the same way as most other properties: using the Filter tab in the Properties Inspector.

Filters can be applied to movie clips, buttons and text objects, shapes, sprites, videos, and any other visible object on the stage. The filter properties for each object can be applied by using the Properties Inspector or using ActionScript. You can apply multiple filters on one object, too. The values of each filter can also be animated to produce flowing effects that draw users in. Note that filters should be used sparingly for the sake of performance on older, slower systems and also for aesthetics. Remember that less is usually more.

The preset filters have been designed for quick and easy operation. Filters can be applied on the fly or varied during animation or ActionScript. These properties are Blur, Bevel, Glow, Shadow, Color, and Gradient. For instance, you could apply Blur to a button. The farther away from the button the mouse moves, the greater the blur effect could be. Take a look at Figure 5-1. It shows a white square that has been affected by each different filter.

Figure 5-1. A simple white square affected by various filters. Square a has no filters applied. Square b has had a drop shadow applied to it, and square c has been blurred. Square d displays an outer glow, and square e has had a colored bevel. Square f has had a bevel filter applied to it, square g displays a gradient glow, and square h has been affected by applying multiple filters.

Figure 5-2 shows one of the characters developed for the exercises in this book, Tomtee. He will be the guinea pig that we'll apply filters to in this chapter. You can see in the figure the huge difference applying filters to a graphic can make.

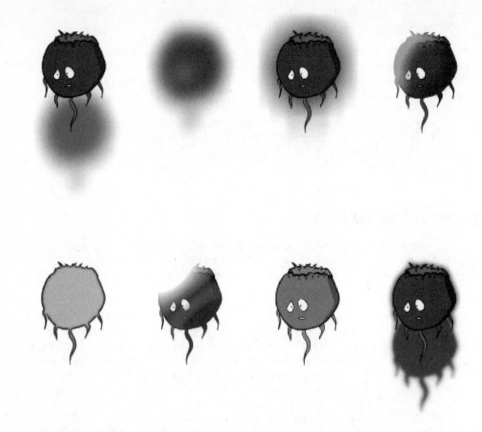

Figure 5-2. Tomtee affected by each of the filters. Top row: drop shadow, blur, outer glow, and colored bevel. Bottom row: beveled, gradient glow, adjusted color, and multiple filters.

Applying preset filters

Figure 5-3. Filters settings icons, from left to right: Add Filter, Save Filter Presets, Copy Filter, Enable or Disable Filter, Reset Filter, and Delete Filter.

Applying filters is easy. Select the movie clip, button, or text. Then open the Properties Inspector by either going to Window ➤ Properties or using the shortcut Control+F3. Click the Filters drop-down to display the Filters section. Notice the filter-settings icons at the bottom of the panel (shown in Figure 5-3).

These icons control how you apply, remove, copy, and paste all filter settings.

To apply a filter, click the Add Filter button, and select the filter you want to apply from the menu that appears. You are able to change all the values of the filter in the Properties tab. If you have more than one filter applied to an object, you will need to click on that filter's heading in the Properties tab, as shown in Figure 5-4. Once you've selected a filter, you can change all of its values. To remove the filter, click the Delete Filter icon at the bottom of the panel.

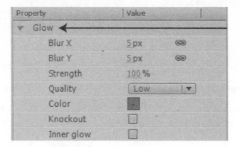

Figure 5-4. Selecting a filter

You can also copy and paste filter settings so that you can apply the same settings to multiple objects. Do this by clicking the clipboard icon, as shown in Figure 5-5.

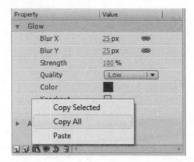

Figure 5-5. The clipboard icon allows you to copy and paste filter settings.

The Enable or Disable Filter icon, denoted by an eye, will toggle the filter on/off. The Reset Filter icon will return all the settings for the particular filter back to its original state.

We will now investigate each of the preset filters. To get the most out of the following exercises, ensure that you have downloaded the source files from the download page for this book at the friends of ED website, www.friendsofed.com.

> *The examples detailed in this chapter have been purposely exaggerated so that we can demonstrate in black-and-white print the effects of blends and filters. While the use of filters and blends is open to artistic interpretation, they are used to quickly and easily lend depth to objects on the stage. Manipulate the default filters and blends to produce custom ones to suit your client's needs. This enables you to streamline your production of Flash CS4 creative assets to meet your client's specifications in a timely and efficient manner.*

The Drop Shadow filter

Applying shadow to your designs can provide depth and a sense of added dimensionality. Let's investigate.

1. Open the exercises folder and open 5-01.fla in Flash CS4.

One of our loveable creatures, Tomtee, will load into the canvas. He is still line art at the moment, so we must convert him into a movie clip before we can apply filters to him.

2. Click on the Selection tool in the tools panel to select the whole character and right-click him to convert him to a movie clip symbol.

3. Give the movie clip the name of Tomtee, as shown in Figure 5-6.

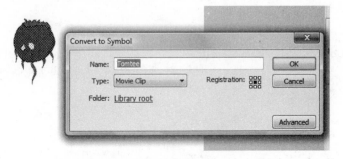

Figure 5-6. Converting Tomtee to a symbol

4. Next, find the Properties Inspector and expand the Filters drop-down menu as shown in Figure 5-7.

Figure 5-7. The Filter options live in the movie clip's Properties Inspector.

5. Select a drop shadow by clicking the Add Filter icon ⬛, then click on Drop Shadow as shown in Figure 5-8.

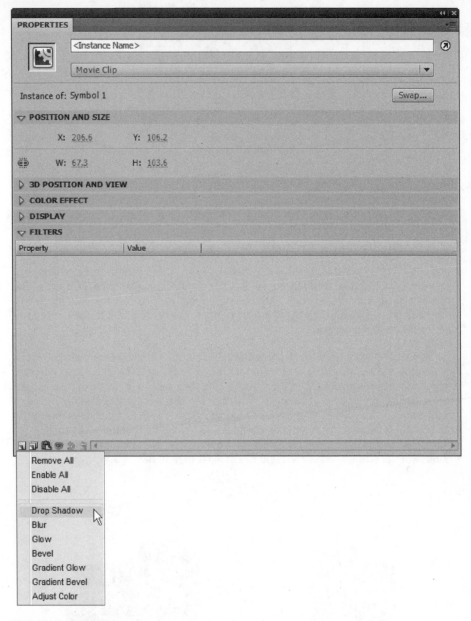

Figure 5-8. The Filter menu

Now that the Drop Shadow filter has been applied, you are able to alter the filter settings as shown in Figure 5-9.

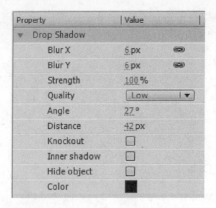

Figure 5-9. Drop Shadow options

We'll now take a moment to investigate the Drop Shadow options, as shown in Figure 5-9.

Blur X and Blur Y affect the edges of the shadow. Low settings yield a sharp outline, and high settings yield softer diffused edges. Strength defines how dark the shadow is. The Quality setting governs the accuracy of the rendered shadow. High settings look much better but add processing overhead, which adds to the resources required of the user's computer to display the published file.

Angle defines the angle from which the initial light source shines. Distance defines the distance of the shadow from the object that is casting it. Figure 5-10 shows two different Distance settings. Knockout takes the initial shape and deletes it from the scene and shadow, leaving an empty void where a body once lay. The Inner Shadow setting creates a negative shadow that can exist only in the object's space. Hide Object hides the movie clip from the scene, leaving only the shadow behind. Color is the basic color of the shadow. To emulate real shadows, this should be set to a dark color, as shown in Figure 5-10. Play around with the settings to get a good sense of what they all do.

Figure 5-10. Playing with the shadow settings

The Blur filter

Anything that is out of focus is said to be blurred. Take a look outside the window and notice how the distance blurs things far away. Like shadow, blur adds depth to designs. Let's explore this more.

1. Load the 5.02.fla file in Flash CS4.

You will notice that we have already made Tomtee into a movie clip symbol.

2. Select the movie clip character, then open the Properties Inspector, click the Add Filter button, and choose Blur from the filter drop-down, as shown in Figure 5-11.

> *Remember, the* Add Filter *button resides at the bottom of the* Filter *drop-down in the Properties Inspector.*

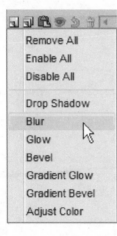

Figure 5-11. Choosing the Blur filter

Once the Blur filter has been applied, we can play with the Blur X and Blur Y settings, shown in Figure 5-12, to manipulate the extent of the blur.

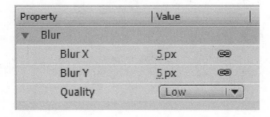

Figure 5-12. The Blur settings panel

Blur X and Blur Y control the intensity of the blurring effect. Higher values create more of a blurred look, while lower values retain a harder edge. Note the little chain links. These links keep both X and Y values the same, resulting in a consistent blur. If you needed an inconsistent blur, such as a motion blur, you would need to unlink the chains by clicking on them. You would then have the ability to blur the movie clip in one direction. The Quality setting controls how accurately the filter is calculated. Figure 5-13 demonstrates varying degrees of the Blur filter.

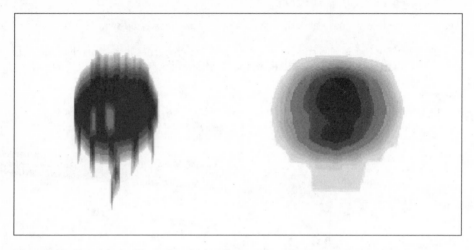

Figure 5-13. Changing the Blur settings in the Filters section of the Properties Inspector can have various results.

The Glow filter

Light-emitting objects glow. Think of the sun and moon, a mobile-phone display, or car headlights. Against a cold night sky, a glowing pale moon captures all attention. Glows in Flash CS4 have the same effect. Let's check these out.

> **1.** Load the 5-02.fla file in Flash CS4.

The by-now-familiar Tomtee returns to the canvas as a movie clip symbol. We are now going to add a new filter to the movie clip.

> **2.** Click on Tomtee to select him.

> **3.** Open the Properties Inspector and choose Glow from the Filter drop-down as shown in Figure 5-14.

When the Glow filter is applied, a faint outline surrounds the movie clip. Take a moment to play with the settings, shown in Figure 5-15, to get a handle on the filter.

Figure 5-14. Choosing the Glow filter

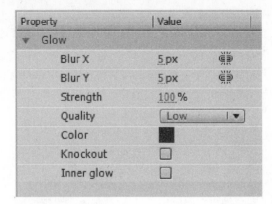

Figure 5-15. The Glow settings panel

The Blur X and Blur Y values control how sharp the edge of the glow appears. Strength controls the intensity of color. Notice that values greater than 100% can be entered. The maximum value here is 25500%. Knockout takes the shape of the movie clip and reverses it from the filtered effect. Inner Glow creates the glow effect from the inside of the movie clip shape as opposed to the outside.

Since glows are most frequently semitransparent shades, they often look best on contrasting backgrounds, like in Figure 5-16.

Figure 5-16. Our movie clip with the glow filter

The Bevel filter

Beveled edges have been borrowed from woodwork. A beveled edge usually has a highlighted edge and an edge in shadow. This style mimics buttons used offline, making it an important usability consideration.

Figure 5-17.
Choosing the Bevel
filter

1. Open 5.02.fla in Flash CS4.

2. Select the movie clip, then open the Properties Inspector and choose Bevel from the Filter drop-down as shown in Figure 5-17.

When you apply the Bevel filter, shown in Figure 5-18, you will notice that one side of the movie clip will appear light-colored and the opposing side will be darker.

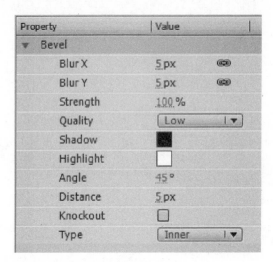

Figure 5-18. The Bevel filter settings

Again Blur X and Blur Y control the edges of the effect. Higher values produce softer edges while lower values are sharper. Strength controls the intensity of the beveled edges. Higher Strength values create a harder beveled edge. The Shadow color picker lets you choose the darker shade, while the highlight lets you choose the color of the lighter edges. The Angle option will rotate the bevel. Distance controls the size of the beveled edge. Note that you can use negative values for the distance. Again, Knockout removes the shape of the movie clip, leaving the effect behind it. There are three types of beveled edges: inner, outer, and full. Inner is the traditional bevel, with both light and shade occurring on the movie clip itself. Outer creates a beveled edge on the outside edges of the shape. Full combines both inner and outer beveled-edge effects as shown in Figure 5-19.

> *Try creating stereoscopic effects with this filter. Pick a red and a cyan that match your run-of-the-mill 3D glasses. The more offset the two edges, the farther away in 3D space your movie clips will appear to be.*

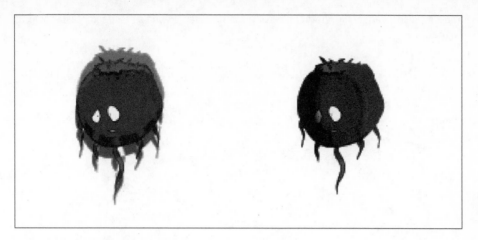

Figure 5-19. The Bevel filter effects

The Gradient Glow filter

Gradient Glow works the same way as Glow and allows you to add a string of color options to the effect.

1. Open 5-02.fla in Flash CS4.
2. Select the movie clip then open the Properties Inspector and choose Gradient Glow from the filter drop-down, as shown in Figure 5-20.

Now that the gradient glow has been applied, start to play with the settings, shown in Figure 5-21.

Figure 5-20. Choosing the Gradient Glow filter

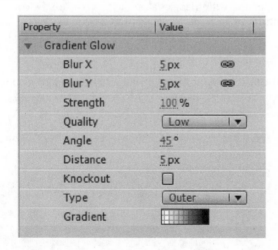

Figure 5-21. The Gradient Glow filter settings

Blur X and Blur Y control the edge of the glow. A greater blur yields a softer glow. Strength determines the intensity of the color.

135

You can also change the gradient setting in the Filter Properties Inspector, as shown in Figure 5-22.

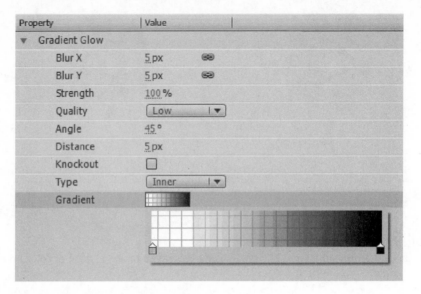

Figure 5-22. Gradient property expanded

The next exercise examines the gradient component more closely.

1. Click on the gradient component. The gradient options will expand, allowing you to configure the gradient.

You will see two color squares with triangles atop them. These are the colors that make up the gradient. Gradients must always have a least two colors.

2. Click on the colored square and pick a color. Note that the colors you choose can be opaque if you'd like.

3. To add more colors to the color sequence, click anywhere in the gradient box. Another square will appear, allowing you to add another color to the gradient. To change the depth of the gradient, click and drag the color.

Have a go at creating some crazy gradients, as shown in Figures 5-23, 5-24, and 5-25.

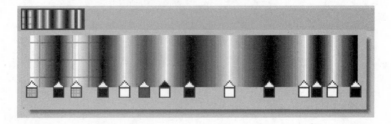

Figure 5-23. Experimental gradient

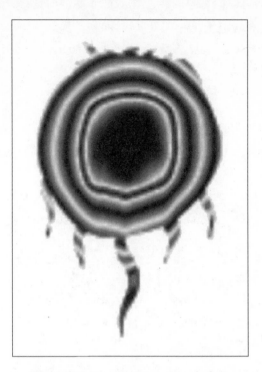

Figure 5-24. Experimental gradient applied

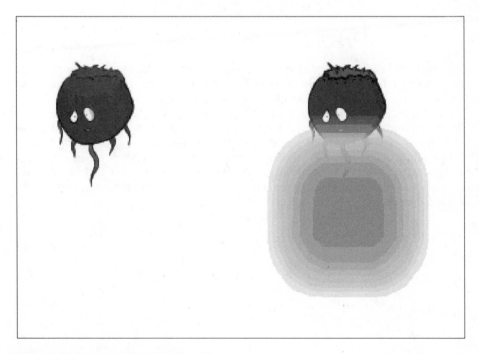

Figure 5-25. More examples of Gradient Glow

The Gradient Bevel filter

Gradient Bevel works the same way as a standard Bevel filter and allows you to add a string of color options to the edge.

1. Open a fresh copy of 5-02.fla, as downloaded from the friends of ED website.

2. Select the movie clip then open the Properties Inspector and choose Gradient Bevel from the filter drop-down, as shown in Figure 5-26.

Once you have applied the filter, you will be able to access its properties, shown in Figure 5-27.

Figure 5-26.
Choosing the
Gradient Bevel filter

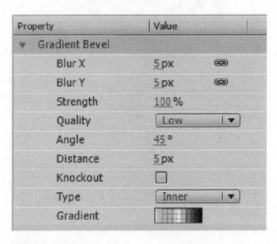

Figure 5-27. The Gradient Bevel filter settings

The Blur X and Blur Y settings allow you to control the edge of the bevel. Large values result in very soft edges, while lower values yield hard edges. The Strength option refers to the intensity of color output by the effect. Angle allows you to change the direction of the gradient string. The Distance setting varies how far away the highlight and the shadow sit from each other. Knockout removes the shape of the movie clip against the effect of the filter. There are three types of filters. Inner gives a traditional bevel, with shading appearing on either side of the movie clip. Outer adds shading to the exterior of the movie clip in an outward direction. Full combines both the inner and outer shading. To change the colors and position of color in the gradient, click on the gradient picker box, which works just like the color pickers discussed on the previous pages.

The Adjust Color filter

The Adjust Color filter applies a relative color change across the movie clip.

1. Once again, open 5.02.fla in Flash CS4.

2. Select the movie clip then open the Properties Inspector and choose Adjust Color from the filter drop-down, as shown in Figure 5-28.

The Adjust Color filter has four options. These options relate to the HSB (hue, saturation, brightness) color model, as shown in Figure 5-29.

Figure 5-29. The Adjust Color options

Figure 5-28. Choosing the Adjust Color filter

The Brightness option controls the energy of the pixels that constitute the movie clip. Higher values result in a brighter movie clip, and lower values result in a darker movie clip. The Contrast value represents the difference between light and dark. Higher values knock out the middle ranges, exposing the lighter and darker areas. Lower values eliminate the bright and dark regions, leaving the movie clip flat. The Saturation setting affects the richness of color. Higher values result in vibrant and energetic colors, while lower values render the movie clip gray and atonal. Hue refers to the position of color on the color wheel. The options range from –180 to 180. These values are the rotational movement around the color wheel. Remember from geometry that 360° represents a full rotation. 180° is a half circle, directly opposite the starting point. A red movie clip shifted 180 degrees will turn a cyan color. Any blue tinge in the movie clip would turn orange. Move the slider back and forth to understand how the colors shift; the extremes are shown in Figure 5-30.

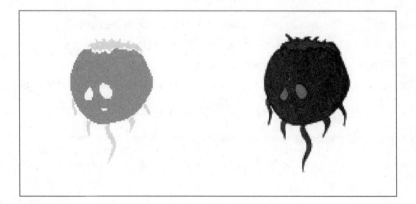

Figure 5-30. Examples of the Adjust Color filter

What are blends?

Blends are the visual effects produced by overlaying two or more objects while altering the way that their colors interact. Flash CS4 uses blending modes, in the Properties Inspector, to achieve this.

It may be difficult to digest blending concepts based on the grayscale images in the book, so open up Flash and have a play.

The blend modes

There are 14 blend modes: Normal, Layer, Darken, Multiply, Lighten, Screen, Overlay, Hard Light, Difference, Add, Subtract, Invert, Alpha, and Erase. These blend modes can act as operators in the following formula:

```
blend color (operator) base color  = Result color
```

A literal translation of this could be: Orange (Multiply) Blue = Black

Basically, the blend formula looks at the pixel color values for orange and multiplies them by the values for blue. This yields a black.

Formulas can be daunting. To put this into real-world terms, consider doing the following. Grab some colored food dye—opposite colors if possible. Red and green would work well. Add a drop of the green food coloring to one glass, and the red food coloring to another. The green water is the blend color, the red water is the base color. The operator will be Add. Add the green blend color to the red base color. The equivalent Flash CS4 operator is Darken. The result color? A murky brown.

Dissecting the blend modes

Blend modes enable you to vary the color interaction and transparency to create composite images that will interact with each other in different ways, depending upon the chosen Blend mode. Blend modes contain the following elements:

- Opacity is the amount of transparency that occurs between blends.
- Base color is the color of the movie clip directly under the movie clip being blended.
- Blend color is simply the color you apply to the blend mode.
- Result color is the color that remains after the blend formula has been applied.

Blends are based on one of 14 modes as defined in the following:

Normal Colors stay the same and have no blend modes applied to them.

Layer Movie clips can be layered and colors stay the same, as shown in Figure 5-31.

Figure 5-31. Layered movie clips stay true to their original settings.

Darken This blend mode replaces the areas that are lighter than the blend color with a darker mix of the two colors as shown in Figure 5-32.

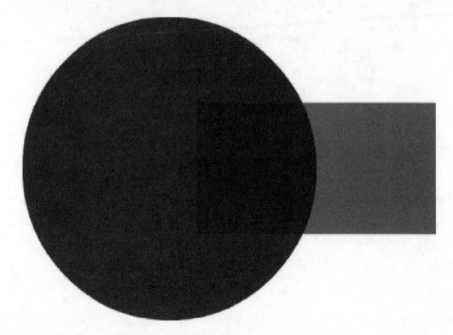

Figure 5-32. The darken blend mode mixes the two colors.

Multiply The base color values are multiplied by the blend color values. This results in very dark colors.

Lighten Removes pixels from the base color that are darker than the blend color.

Screen The blend color values are multiplied by inverse values of the base color. This yields a washed-out look.

Overlay Depending on the base color, the result color multiplies or screens the colors.

Hard Light Multiplies or screens the colors, depending on the blend-mode color (Figure 5-33).

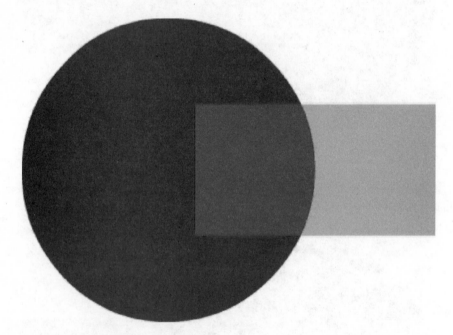

Figure 5-33. The Hard Light blend mode

Difference The blend color is subtracted from the base color, or the base color is subtracted from the blend color, depending on which has the greater brightness value.

Add Commonly used to create an animated lightening dissolve effect between two images.

Subtract Commonly used to create an animated darkening dissolve effect between two images, as shown in Figure 5-34.

Invert Inverts the base color, as shown in Figure 5-35.

Alpha Applies an alpha mask.

Erase Removes all base-color pixels, including those in the background image.

Figure 5-34. Subtract creates a darkening dissolve effect.

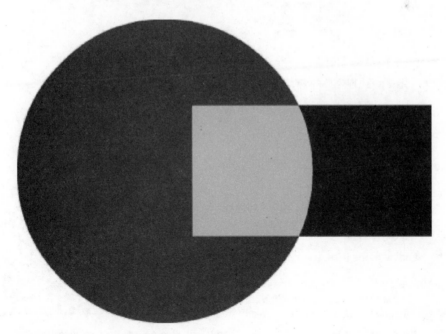

Figure 5-35. Invert changes the base color.

Applying a blend mode

1. Open the 5-03.fla file that you have downloaded from the friends of ED website. Two characters will appear on the stage as shown in Figure 5-36.

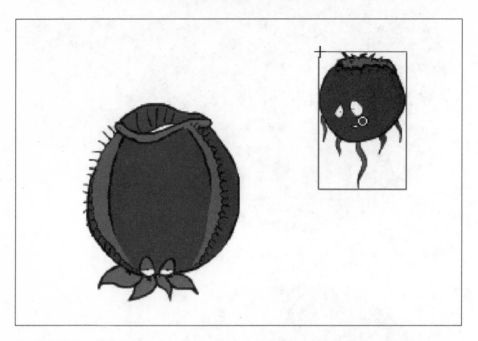

Figure 5-36. Two characters on stage

2. Select the movie clip Tomtee.

3. Move Tomtee so that he is positioned on top of the other character, Skwidge.

Notice nothing special happens. Tomtee overlaps Skwidge in an expected way.

4. Open the Properties Inspector and expand the Display drop-down section as shown in Figure 5-37.

The blending mode is set to Normal by default.

5. Set Blending to Multiply. The bright-orange character now turns dark as the colors from the underlying movie clip are manifested.

6. Now change the blending mode to something else. Notice the blend modes change as described earlier in the chapter.

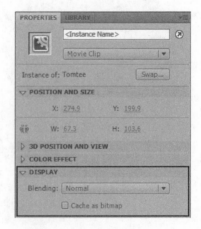

Figure 5-37. The Display section expanded in the Properties Inspector

Blend modes can generate useful and interesting effects, one of which will be a glass viewing jar used in our example website www.gene-envy.com, as shown in the following section.

Applying a filter and blend to simulate glass

Now that we have investigated all of the default filters and blends in Flash CS4, we are going to use that knowledge to create a glasslike effect on a movie clip by playing with the opacity of an object and creating a filter. Please ensure that you have downloaded the source files for this exercise from the friends of ED website.

1. Open glass-jar.fla, from the downloaded exercise files, in Flash CS4.

A glass container will appear on the stage, consisting of four layers, as seen in Figure 5-38: the glass outline layer, the glass layer, the glass fill layer, and the glass floor layer.

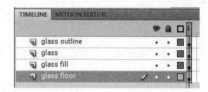

Figure 5-38. Four layers comprise the glass-jar.fla file.

In the next step, we are going to apply a blend to the glass and the glass fill layers.

2. Double-click on the Glass movie clip on the stage to enter the movie clip edit mode, as shown in Figure 5-39.

Figure 5-39. The Glass movie clip is editable after you double-click it.

Figure 5-40. Highlighting the fill in preparation to changing its opacity

We are now going to change the opacity of the fill within the Glass movie clip.

3. Click once on the fill of the Glass movie clip to highlight it as shown in Figure 5-40.

4. Click on the Fill button in the Properties Inspector to display the color picker as shown in Figure 5-41.

5. Click on the Alpha value and change it to 40% as shown in Figure 5-41.

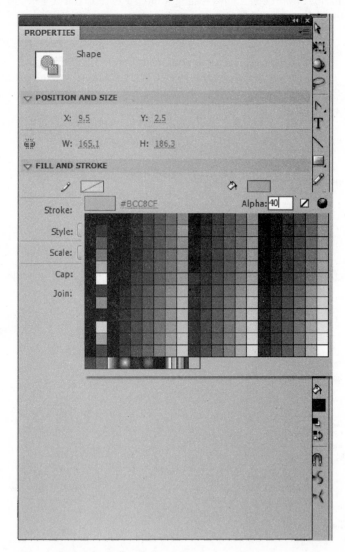

Figure 5-41. Change the fill to 40% opacity in the Alpha channel.

If you return to the main stage, the glass will appear less opaque than when you started. You will now be able to see our little character Tomtee. Changing the Alpha value made the material translucent.

In the following part of the exercise you'll see how blends can give your Flash CS4 movie depth.

6. Select the glass fill layer from the timeline.

7. Select the glass fill movie clip on the stage.

> *If you can't select the* glass fill *movie clip directly from the stage, remember that you can click on the* Library *panel and select it from the list of movie clips there.*

8. Click on the Properties tab to display the Properties Inspector if it is not already displayed.

9. Click on the Filter drop-down in the Properties Inspector to expand it if needed.

10. Select the Add Filter button from the Filters panel.

11. Apply a Gradient Glow filter. Apply the same settings as shown in Figure 5-42.

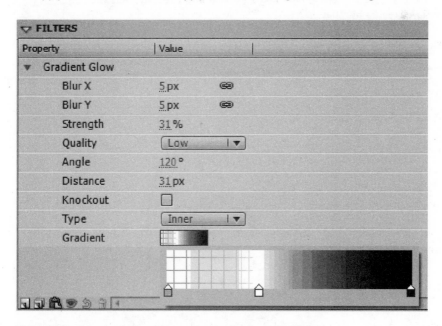

Figure 5-42. Glass simulation settings using the Gradient Glow filter

The result is shown in Figure 5-43. As it stands, it is hard to see any real difference, but we will see the changes when we create a new layer and place an object on it.

Figure 5-43.
The completed
glass jar

In the final exercise for this chapter, we are going to create a new layer that exists behind the glass and glass fill layers and drag an object into the layer. This will demonstrate how we have created transparency.

1. With the previous exercise completed, click the New Layer button on the timeline.

2. Call the new layer tomtee.

3. Drag the new tomtee layer to sit below the glass floor layer as shown in Figure 5-44.

Figure 5-44.
Glass viewing jar
rendered by
filters and the
blend mode

Summary

In this chapter you learned how filters and blends can make a huge difference when applied to graphics and movie clips. They give your Flash animation a depth that truly brings them to life. You have also seen how they can be a time-saving strategy when you need to apply effects to objects on your stage.

In the next chapter you will begin to learn about the commercial realities of the Flash developer when we build our first banner-ad campaign.

5

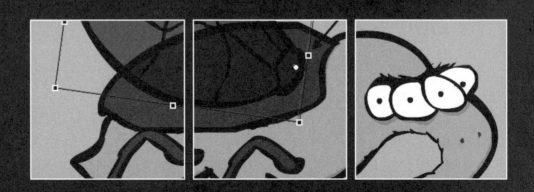

Pixar, Disney, and Looney Tunes—they make magic. Sometime in the mid-1980s I happened to visit my cousin Nick. He had just gotten his hands on an amazing piece of animation software for his Apple IIe. It was called Fantavision (see Figure 6-1). Once I had made an oval move, I was hooked. I had the power to make magic.

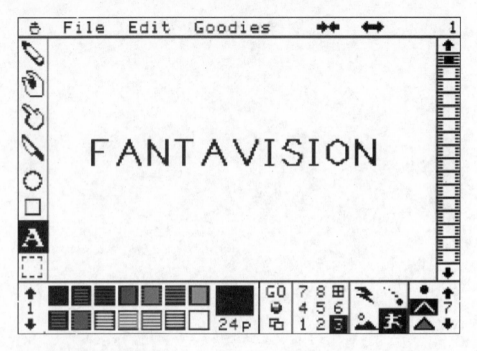

Figure 6-1. Early animation software

The word *animate* stems from the Latin word *anima*, meaning life, or for a more passionate word, *soul*. In Flash CS4 and most other screen-based media, *soul* is translated as "moving images." If seeing is believing, then movin' is groovin'. Film, movies, video, and television use the same process. Animations are basically a series of still frames changed so rapidly that you are fooled into thinking the image on the screen is moving. The picture is changed so fast that the viewer believes the motion. Animation is most believable when the sequence of images alternates faster than 18 images per second. 25 images per second and greater creates a flawless animation. This rate is also known as **frames per second (FPS)**. Film is usually shot at 24fps. NTSC video uses 30fps.

There are two ways to move images with Flash: using keyframe techniques and using ActionScript. It is also possible to use both at once.

Keyframe animation is very intuitive. Moving an object from point A to point B is as simple as dragging the object from A to B over a given timeframe. ActionScript, on the other hand, is slightly more complex, but allows for much more flexibility in the look and feel. ActionScript animations are on average much smaller than their nonscripted keyframed counterparts. This is of particular importance when faced with size restrictions.

This chapter will study fundamental animation techniques using the timeline, keyframes, and tweens.

Setting up the timeline appearance

When you first open Flash CS4, the timeline appears tabbed in the lower half of the screen. If you have used any previous versions of Flash, this will be one of the greatest interface changes you'll notice. You don't like the timeline at the bottom? Then move it. The timeline is completely dockable. Click the timeline tab and drag it out to the middle of the screen. Note that the timeline pops out into its very own window. This is fantastic for people like myself who work with dual screens. You can place the stage on one screen and the timeline on the other. You can also dock the timeline to other areas of the interface. To dock the timeline, drag the timeline header to the edges of the interface. As you get close to the edges, notice that a blue border highlights the edge you want to click onto. Almost all the tabs, windows, and elements are fully dockable. They allow a customized layout that suits personal workflow.

If you ever mess up the interface and want to return Flash to the way it looked when you first installed it, then you can reset the interface by going to the menu Window ➤ Workspace ➤ Reset 'Essentials', as shown in Figure 6-2.

6

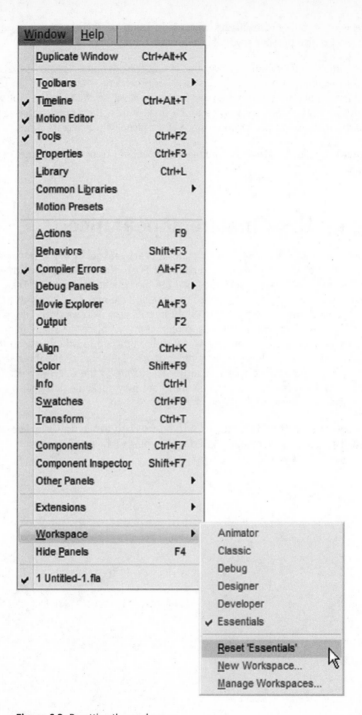

Figure 6-2. Resetting the workspace

The timeline consists of rectangular frames. To change the frame size and shape, click the drop-down menu on the upper-right side of the timeline, as shown in Figure 6-3.

Figure 6-3. Change the frame attributes by clicking the Frame View menu.

Menu options will appear allowing you to change sizes.

The first seven options change the width of the frames, as shown in Figure 6-4. The Short option controls the height of the frame.

Figure 6-4. Changing the width of the frames

Using the playhead

The playhead is the red line and rectangle that rules over the timeline. It can be moved left or right, frame by frame. The position of the playhead dictates what is shown on the stage at any given time. As a general rule, anything that lies in a layer under the red line of the playhead will appear on the stage, as shown in Figure 6-5. You can move the playhead by using the < and > keys or scrubbing it backward and forward with the mouse.

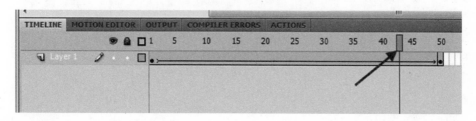

Figure 6-5. The playhead shows the frame you are currently displaying in Flash CS4.

Sailing the seven scenes

Flash has always been about objects and animating those objects. Using the theater analogy, the Flash stage is the platform where you view the performance. The cast and props live in the library. The playhead is the stage manager. It lets the cast and crew know when to appear on stage. Every actor and prop should live in its own layer. The scene icon lets you browse the different scenes of your movie.

Flash scenes are just like scenes in a movie or a play. A scene is a way of grouping a particular place, time, event, or notion.

> While it's important to understand what scenes are so that you can choose where to use them, as a general rule of thumb, animations should utilize ActionScript wherever possible, as it allows you greater control. Scenes are useful when you are working on full-scale cartoon animations.

Adding and deleting scenes

The stage defaults to scene 1 when you create a new Flash file. To add additional scenes, invoke the Scene panel. Access it by navigating to Window ➤ Other Panels ➤ Scenes, as shown in Figure 6-6, or by pressing Shift+F2.

The Scene panel lets you navigate between scenes by double-clicking their names. When you change scenes, notice that the name of the scene changes in the upper-left corner.

You add a scene by clicking the Add Scene button at the bottom-left corner of the Scene panel. It's a good idea to name your scenes. In Figure 6-7, the scenes have been labeled Scene 1, ZIGGY, CHINO, CHUB CHUB, and CHEWY.

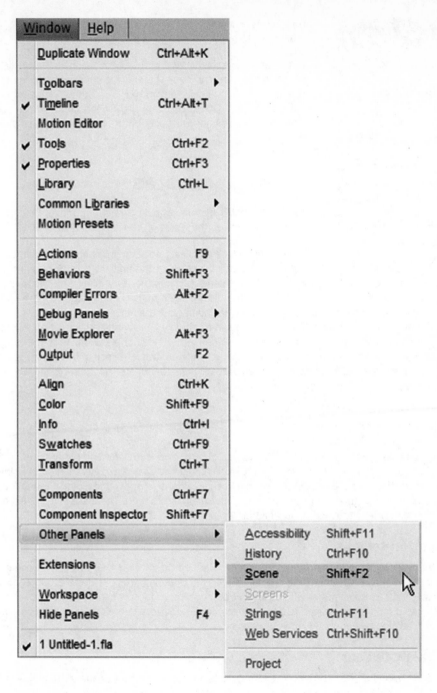

Figure 6-6. Displaying the Scene panel

6

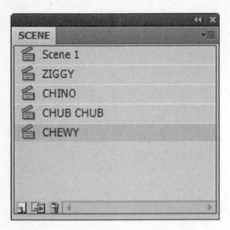

Figure 6-7. Labeling scenes enables you to organize your animation.

You can have as many scenes as you need. Just remember to use scenes to break your content into logical parts.

To delete a scene, highlight it in the Scene panel and then click the trash can. You can copy the entire contents of a scene by clicking the Duplicate Scene button. This is handy when using similar animations that vary slightly. Instead of rebuilding the entire scene again, you can duplicate it and make the minor changes.

Getting animated

You are probably itching to make something move. But first, we need to explore the world of keyframes and tweening.

Keyframing lies at the heart of all animation. The concept of keyframing is ancient; think of the brilliant stills of cave art or Bronze Age glyphs. A keyframe is a frame that is crucial in the storytelling. The frame may contain a change in sound, image, or video. Today, keyframing is not limited to Flash CS4, but also extends across many applications including sound editing, video editing, and 3D animation. Keyframe animation has its roots in traditional hand-rendered animation. A lead artist would draw the important images that defined a stanza or a notion. Then the lowly "tweeners" would draw in between each frame, filling out the sequence of images to create movement. Flash CS4 grants the power of lead animator to the user, leaving the boring tweening tasks to the computer processors.

Tween time!

Flash makes the job of animating characters, objects, and text faster and easier by using a technique known as **tweening**. Flash CS4 tweening looks at two keyframes, and using some mathematics, estimates the in-between positions, shapes, and colors. Instead of drawing each picture frame by frame, it is all calculated for you. There are three kinds of tweens, as briefly touched on in Chapter 1.

Motion tweens

Motion tweens are the latest addition to the Flash world. Motion tweening makes tweening even simpler by eliminating steps in the classic tweening process. There is no need to create your own keyframes when using motion tweens. Motion tweens also illustrate their animated path on the stage. This makes the animation process more intuitive. You can also apply motion tween presets to your objects.

Classic tweens

Classic tweening is the process of setting up two or more keyframes and getting Flash to draw in between each keyframe to create convincing animation.

Shape tweens

Shape tweens morph your object over time. You use keyframes to create a start shape and an end shape. You then right-click to apply a shape tween, and the object will transform! Shape tweens are great for animating organic motions, like breathing, crawling, and slime effects.

Frame-by-frame animation

There may come a time where tweening doesn't work for your situation. It may be that you are trying to achieve a certain style or look. In this case, you will have to resort to frame-by-frame animation. Frame-by-frame animation is exactly how it sounds: manually altering a picture frame by frame. Over a long animation, this process is extremely time-consuming. However, some of the greatest animation effects can be achieved this way. The most well-known frame-by-frame effect is rotoscoping. In this technique, images and motion are traced from an original life source like video or time-lapse photography. Each frame of the film motion is traced to provide lifelike movement in the animation. In the past, Disney has used this technique to capture life in its hand-drawn cartoons. Think back to Snow White dancing with the prince.

Inverse kinematic poses

Inverse kinematics is another name for bone animations. Imagine if you could put a set of bones that hinge and join, just like human joints, into a Flash object. Now you can. If you needed to create an animation of a crane from the side on, you would place a bone in the arm of the crane. You would find the motions you try to make with the crane restricted to the axis of normal crane arm motion. This restriction makes for more lifelike animation.

In Chapter 1, we created an arm using the Bone tool, and connected it in such a way that it has the ability to give a lifelike wave when it is animated. That was basic inverse kinematics. Inverse kinematics is simply the manner of determining the positions of the joints in a jointed flexible object, called a **kinematic chain**, that will enable the figure to achieve certain poses. You will find that inverse kinematics allows you to give animations a lifelike spin.

Creating a motion tween

We are going to quickly revisit creating a motion tween and then expand it.

1. Open a new Flash file (ActionScript 3.0) and draw a circle in the center of the stage.

2. Right-click the oval to convert it to a symbol.

3. Right-click the oval on the stage and select Create Motion Tween from the menu that appears upon the right-click.

Notice that the oval layer in the timeline changes color for 24 frames. The new Flash file you've created is set to 24fps. This means that the animation will run for 1 second. The oval isn't doing much, but it will very soon.

6

4. Slide the playhead along to the 24th frame, and then move the oval down to the bottom of the stage. Magically, a dotted line will appear. This dotted line tells you about the motion tween. Scrub the playhead back and forth to see the oval move.

5. Try positioning the playhead on the middle of the tween, around the 12th frame.

6. Move the oval to the top of the stage, as shown in Figure 6-8.

Observe that the dotted path illustrates the motion you've just defined for the animation!

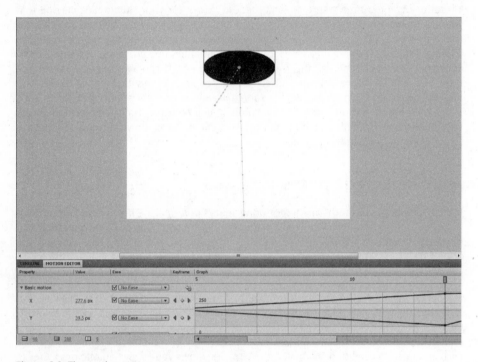

Figure 6-8. The motion tween

New to Flash CS4 is the Motion Editor. The Motion Editor gives you better control over how the objects on your stage move. It is accessible when you select a motion tween on the stage. The large black dots in the graph of the Motion Editor represent the keyframes on the timeline. The Motion Editor, for all purposes, is just the timeline shown in a different way.

If you have ever used After Effects or music recording software such as Logic or Cubase, you will be familiar with this method of interaction. Despite it's name, the Motion Editor isn't just about controlling motion within your Flash movie. Virtually any property of a movie clip, including transparency, color, and shape, can be tweened from the Motion Editor.

The Motion Editor makes tweens more powerful, as each keyframe on each property is independently editable, giving you better and more detailed control over your tween.

Let's examine this now. The Motion Editor is divided into three intuitive sections, as shown in Figure 6-9. The leftmost section (the properties section), includes property values, animation properties, easing options, and the keyframe navigator. The second section, Graph, is where the animation is graphically presented. The third section—the Motion Editor panel display settings—is located at the bottom of the Motion Editor. The three buttons in this section give you the ability to choose how the Motion Editor is displayed. Here you can change the height of the graphs, select the parameters of the graph you wish to view, and choose the number of frames that you can view without scrolling.

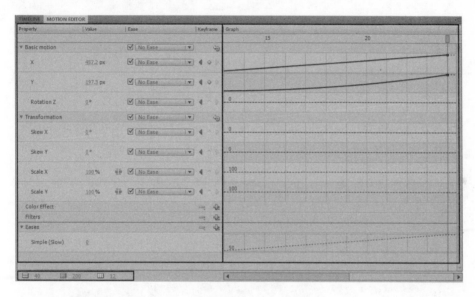

Figure 6-9. The Motion Editor is divided into three sections.

The following exercise will demonstrate how the Motion Editor can help you to better control your animation. Ensure that you have downloaded the source files for this chapter from the Downloads section of the friends of ED website (www.friendsofed.com) prior to beginning the exercise.

1. Create a new Flash file (ActionScript 3.0) in Flash CS4.
2. Select File ➤ Import to Library, and import Blobby.jpg from the source files.
3. Drag Blobby.jpg onto the left side of the stage, as shown in Figure 6-10.

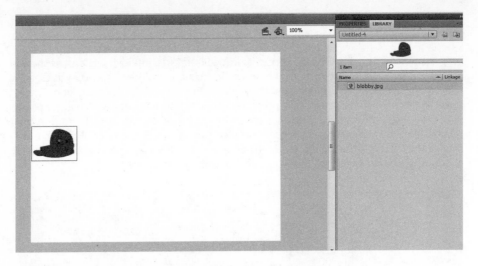

Figure 6-10. Dragging the image from the library to the left side of the stage

4. Right-click the image and select Convert to Symbol from the menu that appears.

5. Select Movie Clip from the Type drop-down in the Convert to Symbol dialog box, and give it the name Blobby.

We are now going to create a motion tween to see the effect of the animation in the Motion Editor.

6. Right-click the Blobby movie clip on the stage and select Create Motion Tween. The timeline will automatically expand.

> *The timeline automatically expands to create a 1-second film clip. If you have the frame rate set to 24fps, the animation will automatically expand to 24 frames. If the frame rate is set to 12fps, the animation will automatically expand to 12 frames. In the case of this exercise, my frames per second was set to 24.*

7. With the playhead still on frame 24 in the timeline, drag the pink creature to the right side of the stage, as shown in Figure 6-11.

Figure 6-11. Dragging the figure across the stage to create a motion path

You're now going to see how you can manipulate the animation in the Motion Editor. With the pink figure on the stage still selected, click the Motion Editor tab next to the Timeline tab above the timeline. You will see that the x graph in the Basic motion section has been changed to reflect the animation. Go ahead and play with it. What happens when you move the x-axis up? It changes the x value of the animation. You will see that the animation moves along the horizontal axis.

Move the y-axis in the Motion Editor, and you will see the animation move along the y-axis—that is, it moves up and down along the stage. We'll now take a closer look at how you can manipulate the y-axis to bring more to the animation. In the following exercise, you are going to see the effect that changing the y-axis in the Motion Editor has on your animation.

1. With the previous exercise completed, scrub the playhead along the graphical part of the Motion Editor until you reach frame 12, as shown in Figure 6-12.

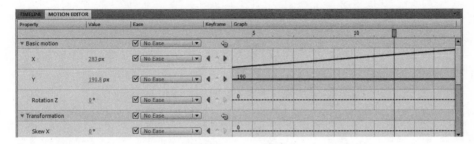

Figure 6-12. Scrub the playhead to frame 12.

2. Right-click the y-axis at frame 12 and select Add Keyframe.

3. Scrub the playhead back to frame 1, and move the y-axis up.

What happens? You will see that the motion path is no longer straight! There is an incline in the path now. You can use the Motion Editor to fine-tune animation paths.

As previously noted, there is more to the Motion Editor than simply editing straightforward animations. It also allows you to apply easing to animations to give them a more natural feel. The animations created with Flash CS4's default tweening feel very artificial because the frames are distributed at regular intervals along the timeline. Easing allows you to adjust that distribution for a more natural feel.

Applying easing to any axis is very easy, as you will find out in the next short exercise.

1. With the previous exercise completed, scroll down to the bottom of the Motion Editor until you see the Easing section, as shown in Figure 6-13.

> *You can leave the frames per second rate at 24 if you wish, but to better see the changes that the easing makes to this animation, I reduced my frames per second to 18.*

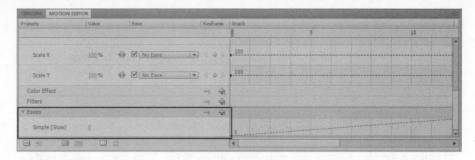

Figure 6-13. The Easing section of the Motion Editor enables you to make your animations lifelike.

2. Click the Add Color, Filter, or Ease button  in the Easing section, and choose Stop and Start (Slow) from the menu that is presented.

3. Scroll back up to the x-axis in the Basic Motion section.

4. From the Ease drop-down list in the x-axis part of the Basic Motion section, select Stop and Start (Slow) from the list, as shown in Figure 6-14.

Figure 6-14.
Selecting the Stop and Start (Slow) ease from the Ease drop-down list

Notice that an easing path has appeared on stage alongside the motion path, as shown in Figure 6-15. The dots on the easing path indicate the changes in time between each frame.

Figure 6-15. Easing on the motion path

5. Select Control ➤ Test Movie to test your movie.

You will see that the animation has a lull in movement as it hits the peak of the incline, and then increases in speed as it runs down the hill.

Using motion tween presets

Motion tween presets are a library of predefined motions that you can quickly and easily apply to your Flash CS4 animations. Not only can you select from a library of preexisting motion presets, but you can save your own customized motion presets to the library, and then apply them to future Flash animations.

In the following exercise, we will place a motion preset upon an object to see the impact that it has upon the animation.

1. Open the Motion Presets panel by choosing the Window ➤ Motion Presets. The Motion Presets panel will appear, as shown in Figure 6-16.

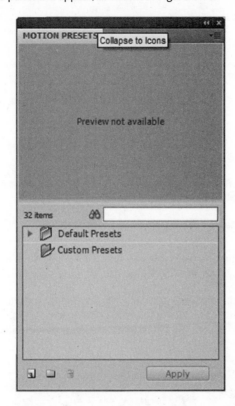

Figure 6-16. The Motion Presets panel

2. While you have the graphical path of the motion tween you just created selected, click Custom Presets. Then click the Save selection as preset icon found at the bottom left of the Motion Presets panel.

3. Call your motion UpDown.

The UpDown motion that you created is now saved in your custom preset library, which will save you time later if you need to construct something similar. If you open the Default Presets section of the Motion Presets panel, you will notice a large range of fun motions. To use the motion preset, you simply select the object you wish to apply the motion preset to, choose your preset, and click Apply.

If your object already has a motion preset, a dialog box will appear asking you to confirm whether you want to replace it, as shown in Figure 6-17. If the object doesn't have a motion preset already applied to it, it will inherit the new motion.

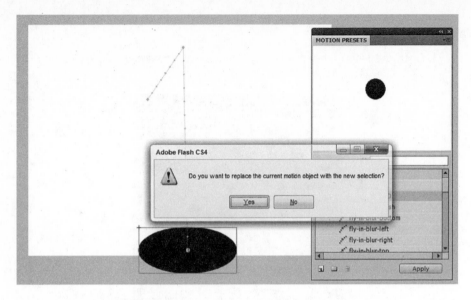

Figure 6-17. Dialog box asking if you want to replace the motion object

Moving an object in a motion tween creates a dotted line known as a **motion tween path**. Use this path as a guide and reference to predict how the object will animate.

To ease a motion tween, simply open the Motion Editor. The third column is the Ease column, as shown in Figure 6-18. It lists all the tween property changes, such as position, blur, and color. Checking the boxes controls whether the motion tween experiences easing for each checked property.

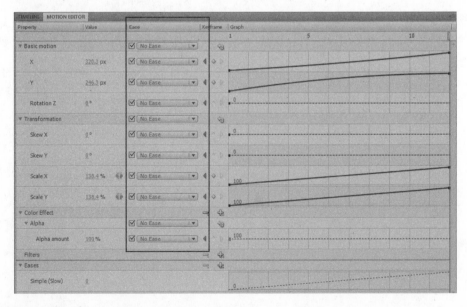

Figure 6-18. The Ease column of the Motion Editor allows you to fine-tune your tweens.

Creating a classic tween is easy, as the following exercise demonstrates.

1. Open a new blank document in Flash CS4.

2. While in Merge Drawing mode, select the Circle tool and draw a small circle on the left side of the stage.

3. Convert it to a movie clip symbol by right-clicking, pressing F8, or finding the menu option under the Modify menu.

4. Name the movie clip circle, as shown in Figure 6-19.

Figure 6-19. Renaming your movie clip in the Convert to Symbol dialog

When creating any animation, you should try to keep all symbols, especially movie clips, on their own layers. The general rule is that when you create a new object for animation, you should place it on a new layer.

The two other symbol types are graphic and button. Although we've touched upon them before, they're worth revisiting.

It's best to create a graphic symbol when the image is going to remain static, or when it should move with its parent container's timeline. A button symbol enables you to give your object a clickable state—that is, you can make buttons click through to other pages on your website, other sections in your animation, and much more.

5. Right-click the 50th frame in the timeline and convert the frame to a keyframe, or press F6.

Notice that a long gray bar extends out from the first frame and continues all the way to the 49th frame, where it meets a white rectangle. This long gray bar represents the circle movie clip remaining in the same place for 49 frames. The black circles are keyframes.

6. With the playhead running through the keyframe on the 50th frame, select the circle movie clip and drag it to the right side of the stage.

7. Move the playhead black and forth. Notice that the circle on the stage only moves when you're viewing the 50th frame.

8. Insert a classic tween by right-clicking anywhere on the timeline between the two keyframes. Your timeline should look like Figure 6-20.

167

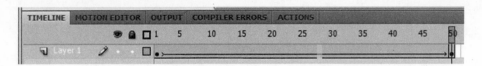

Figure 6-20. The timeline

Now move the playhead back and forth. Notice that the circle moves relative to the playhead! Doing this is a quick way to preview animations.

To view the animation in full SWF glory, you need to publish it. To publish a movie, select Control ➤ Test Movie, which will enable you to watch your Flash CS4 animation, as shown in Figure 6-21. You should see the circle loop from left to right across the screen.

> *If you don't see an animation, make sure your circle is a movie clip and ensure that a tween arrow stretches the two keyframes on the same layer.*

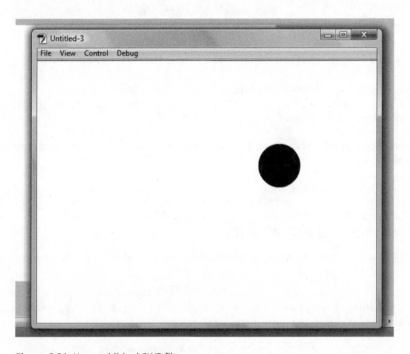

Figure 6-21. Your published SWF file

Creating pathed tween motion

Instead of animating an object from point A to B, B to C, C to D, and so on, you can use a path. A path lets your object drive along a predetermined road. For example, if you wanted a circle to trace your business's logo, you could use the logo outline as a path and assign the Flash object to this path. Let's see how this works in Flash CS4.

1. Open a new Flash file and draw an oval. Convert the oval to a movie clip symbol.

2. Create a new keyframe at frame 30.

3. Right-click layer 1 and click Add Classic Motion Guide.

4. On the motion guide layer, use the Pencil tool to draw a squiggle from left to right on the stage.

5. Drag the center of the oval till it is positioned perfectly at the end of the pencil line on the first frame.

6. Right-click between frames 1 and 30 on the oval's timeline, and click Create Classic Tween.

7. Move the playhead to the 30th frame, and move the oval so that it clicks to the right end of the pencil line.

Move the playhead. Notice how the oval follows the line, just like a roller coaster!

Customizing easing on classic tweens

Easing controls the acceleration or deceleration of moving symbols. An **ease out** is a positive number and will make an object come to a smooth end. An **ease in**, which is a negative number, as shown in Figure 6-22, will start the motion off smooth and end abruptly.

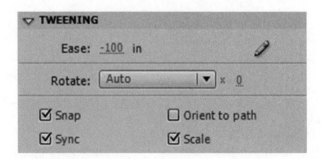

Figure 6-22. Easing controls the speed of moving symbols.

Shape tweens

Shape tweens animate a morph from one shape to another. Imagine you wanted six blobs to form the word *Spotty*. You would first draw a blob shape in the first keyframe. You would then find the last frame and create an *S* shape. Apply the shape tween, and then watch the blob mutate as depicted in Figure 6-23!

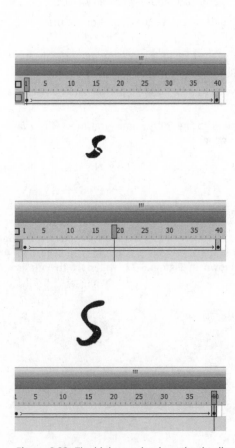

Figure 6-23. The blob morphs along the timeline to become an *S*.

Creating a shape tween

Remember that symbols cannot be shape tweened. A movie clip has to be broken apart in order for it to shape-tweened. Let's check this out.

1. Open a new file in Flash CS4.
2. Using the oval tool, draw a perfect circle on the stage.
3. Insert a keyframe on frame 30.
4. Using the eraser tool and paint tool, turn the circle into something more—like an *S*, perhaps.
5. Right-click between frames 1 and 30 and create a shape tween.

When the playhead is scrubbed, the circle festers. Flash CS4 provides this alternative way to create a shape tween, as opposed to the usual onion skinning method (discussed further on in the chapter).

Creating a frame-by-frame animation

Frame-by-frame animations can be tricky; however, don't be discouraged. Time and patience can yield great results. Let's make one.

1. Create a new Flash File (ActionScript 3.0) document in Flash CS4.
2. Draw a rectangle on the stage.
3. Go to frame 2 of the timeline and insert a keyframe.
4. Move the rectangle right a few pixels.
5. Repeat another eight times, moving the rectangle further and further right along the stage.

This is the general gist of frame-by-frame animation. If there was a person walking, then each frame of the walk cycle would have to be drawn.

Using onion skinning in frame-by-frame animations

"Onion skinning" is an old animation term to describe being able to see previous or future frames transparently composed with the current frame. This is shown in Figure 6-24.

6

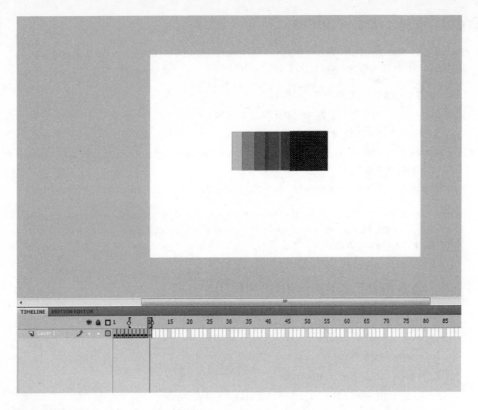

Figure 6-24. An example of onion skinning

To see onion skinning in Flash, click the Onion Skin icon ⬚ at the base of the timeline. Notice the transparent copies of the rectangle. The amount that you can see backward and forward is controlled by the onion skin handles that sit in the upper parts of the timeline, as indicated in Figure 6-25.

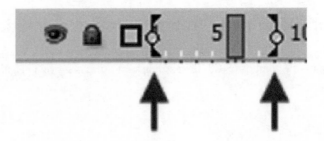

Figure 6-25. The handles that control the length of the onion skinning

Creating an animated leaderboard

This section will help you apply what you have learned in this chapter and extend it to real life. A banner ad animation will be used to promote the online store project. The banner will feature a curious bug, a sinister plant, and some motion-tweened text.

The first step it to scope the keyframes out on paper. Draw up the dimensions, as shown in Figure 6-26. In the first frame, the bug enters and makes its way to the pretty-smelling flower. The bug is weird looking, but playful. In the second frame, the bug investigates the flower before deciding to take a piece of it. The final frame comes to a finish as the plant snaps down to engulf the bug. Some promotional text for the store animates over the design space.

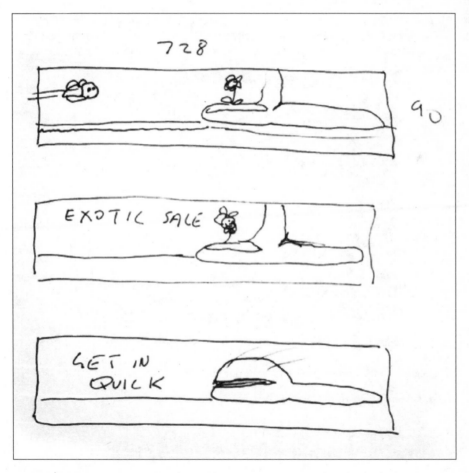

Figure 6-26. Sketching the rough idea for the banner

Let's make our ad!

1. Begin the banner by creating a new Flash file (ActionScript 3.0).

2. Set the stage size to the standard leaderboard dimensions of 728×90. Ensure that the FPS is set 24.00, as shown in Figure 6-27.

Figure 6-27. A blank 728×90 banner

Next, we will import the assets to the stage.

3. Go to File ➤ Import ➤ Import to Library. Browse to the Chapter 6 assets folder, as shown in Figure 6-28, and import all seven SWF files. You may find this quicker if you use the Select All shortcut—Ctrl+A or Cmd+A (on the Mac).

Figure 6-28. Locating the correct file

Let's begin with the ground layer and work our way up.

4. Rename the current layer Ground.

5. Go to the library and drag the ground graphic to the stage. Position it so that it hangs over the edge of the stage, as shown in Figure 6-29.

Figure 6-29. Placing the ground on the banner

Next, we will arrange the hungry plant, which is made up of two different graphics on separate layers.

6. Create a new layer called Plant body.

7. Drag the graphic labeled Plant body from the library and position it so that it sits on the right side of the banner, as in Figure 6-30.

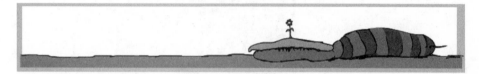

Figure 6-30. Placing the plant body onto the banner

8. Now create a new layer for the head, and call the layer Plant head.

9. Position the head so that the corners of the lips touch, like in Figure 6-31.

Figure 6-31. Placing the top jaw onto the plant body

10. Currently, the pivot point of the plant's head is set at the center. You need to make the head hinge from the lips. Select the plant's head, and then select the Free Transform tool. Move the pivot point (the white circle) to the bottom-left corner of the head, as illustrated in Figure 6-32.

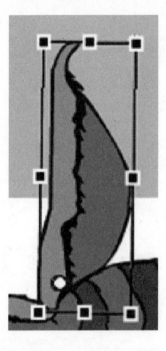

Figure 6-32. Hinging the jaw onto the plant body

11. Next, create a new bug layer called Flying Bug.

12. Drag the flying bug graphic from the library and place him off the stage, like in Figure 6-33.

Figure 6-33. The flying bug should be positioned off the stage

At the moment, the bug is a static graphic. You need to make his wings flutter like any respectably annoying insect.

13. Double-click the bug to edit him in his timeline.

14. Select the wing and then select the Free Transform tool. Note that the anchor point is positioned in the center of the graphic, but you need it at the tip of the wing. Placing the anchor at the tip of the wing will yield a convincing flap, rather than the rocking motion you will observe if you keep the anchor point in the center. The wing's anchor point should be positioned like in Figure 6-34.

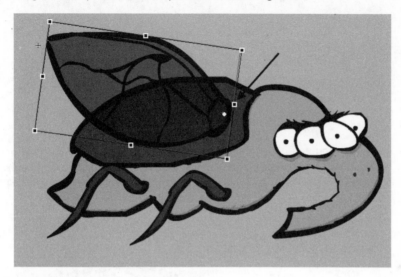

Figure 6-34. Moving the bug off the stage

15. Right-click the 5th frame and insert a keyframe.

16. Rotate the wing slightly upward so that the wing angle looks like the wing in Figure 6-35.

Figure 6-35. Positioning the wings to flap convincingly on the bug

Now the wings should be ready to fly across the banner, and your stage should be similar to Figure 6-36.

Figure 6-36. Your bug is now ready to fly.

17. Select the 300th frame of the Flying Bug layer. Click and drag the mouse downward to select every layer of the 300th frame. Right-click the now highlighted frames and click Insert Frame. The stage will now populate with every element, and the timeline will display frames up to frame 300 on every layer, as shown in Figure 6-37.

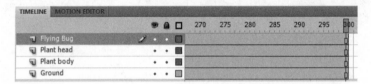

Figure 6-37. Inserting keyframes on every layer of the 300th frame

The bug is to fly in a fun, erratic pattern. He could be animated frame by frame, or he could be keyframed. In this case, it will be fun to animate him on a motion guide.

18. Select frame 80 of the Flying Bug layer and create a new keyframe.

19. Go back to the first frame and select the Flying Bug layer. Right-click the Flying Bug label in the timeline and click Add Classic Motion Guide, as shown in Figure 6-38. A new layer will stretch out directly above the Flying Bug layer.

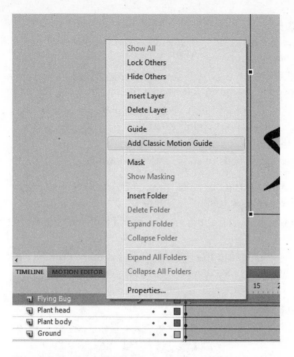

Figure 6-38. Right-click the layer names in the timeline to show the layer context menu.

20. Select the first frame of the motion guide layer.

21. Select the Pencil tool and draw a buggy-looking line toward the flower, like the one shown in Figure 6-39.

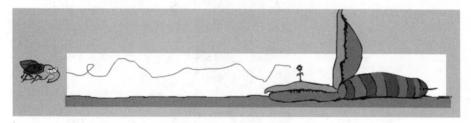

Figure 6-39. Creating the motion guide on which the bug will fly

6

22. Select the bug and snap him to the left tip of the line.

23. Now move the playhead to frame 80. Move the bug and snap him to the right tip of the pencil line.

24. Right-click the Flying Bug layer between frames 1 and 80, and create a classic tween. If you move the playhead, you will see the bug fly along the path!

25. The bug will hover for a short while over the flower before descending upon it. So put another keyframe on frame 90 of the Flying Bug layer. Move the bug down and over the flower.

The hungry flower head needs to come crashing down.

26. Go to frame 95 of the Plant head layer and right-click it to insert a keyframe. Insert another keyframe on frame 99.

27. While on frame 99, select the Free Transform tool and rotate the head down to eat the bug.

Notice that the head hinges in the right spot. This is due to the fact that you moved the anchor point earlier in the exercise. This is shown in Figure 6-40.

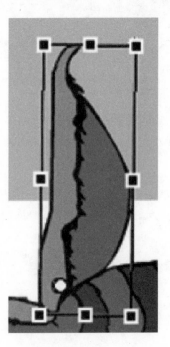

Figure 6-40. The rotation point is the white circle in the bottom-left corner.

You may notice that the bug is actually sitting above the plant's head and in front of its mouth, not in it—as shown in Figure 6-41. We'll need to fix this.

Figure 6-41. Positioning the bug

28. Select the motion guide and pull the path down to meet the base of the flower perched on the plant's tongue.

29. Select the 80th frame of the Flying Bug layer and reattach the bug to the tip of the motion guide. The bug will refuse to follow the path unless he is soundly snapped from end to end.

30. Reposition the Plant head layer so that it sits on top of the Flying Bug layer.

31. Now scrub your animation back and forth to check that the plant's head actually consumes the bug, as shown in Figure 6-42.

6

Figure 6-42. Move the playhead up and down your animation to ensure it is lifelike.

32. Right-click between frames 95 and 99 of the Plant head layer, and create a classic tween.

33. Make sure you delete the bug from the plant's mouth by inserting a blank keyframe on the 99th frame of the Flying Bug layer.

34. Save your file as 6-09a.fla.

35. Test your movie by pressing Ctrl+Enter (or Cmd+Enter on the Mac).

Now the character animation is complete. Next comes the copy tweening.

Animating text on the banner

The next exercise will complete the text component of the banner. The text will fly from the left, pause, and fly out the right.

The first block of text will read, "Get in quick."

1. Open the saved file 6-09a.fla in Flash CS4 if it isn't already open.

2. Create a new layer called Get in quick and drag the movie clip GetInQuick_txt from the library to the center of the stage.

Take a moment to preview your movie by pressing Ctrl+Enter. Notice that the text appears throughout the entire animation, but is only needed after the head slams down.

3. Select frame 99 and insert a keyframe on the Get in quick layer.

4. Go to the first frame and delete the keyframe.

Let's preview again. What happens now? The text should now appear as the head comes down, as shown in Figure 6-43, but it still needs some action!

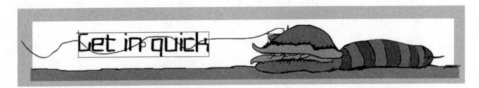

Figure 6-43. The text now appears in the correct place in the sequence of the animation.

5. Select the text on the stage.

6. Move the text so that it originates off the left side of the banner.

7. Insert a blank keyframe at the 160th frame of the current layer.

8. Create a new layer called Exotic life and insert a keyframe on the 160th frame of the new layer.

9. Drag the movie clip titled ExoticLife_txt from the library into a similar spot as the previous text.

10. Insert a blank keyframe at the 220th frame of the current layer.

11. Create a final layer called Gene Envy and insert a keyframe on the 220th frame of the new layer.

12. Drag the movie clip titled GeneEnvy_txt from the library into a similar spot as the previous text.

13. Preview the movie clip.

Notice how the character animation is lively, but the text is missing something. Add a transition to the text to give it some energy.

14. Go back to the 99th frame of the Get in quick layer. Select the text and go to Window ➤ Motion Presets.

The Motion Presets panel will appear, as shown in Figure 6-44.

15. Select the fly-in-blur-left preset, and click Apply.

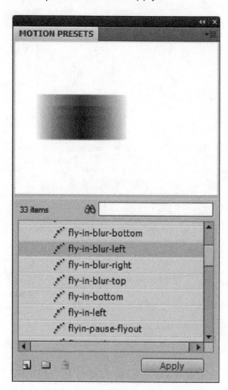

Figure 6-44. The Motion Presets panel

The motion tween needs to be adjusted so that the text flies from beyond the left of the stage and lands in the middle.

16. Bring the playhead to the 99th frame. Drag the text so that it sits outside the stage, as shown in Figure 6-45.

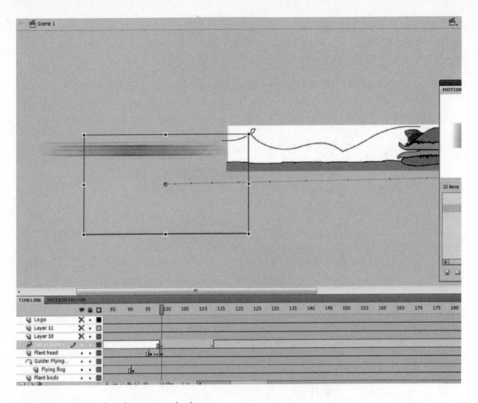

Figure 6-45. Animating the text on the banner

17. Position the playhead to where the motion tween ends on the 113th frame.

18. Now position the text neatly on the design space, as shown in Figure 6-46.

19. Stretch the motion tween out to the 160th frame.

Preview the movie again. As you can see, the text does not stay still. We'll fix that now.

20. Ensure that the exercise is still open (or open the 6-03.fla file).

21. Select the blank keyframe on the 114th frame of the Get in quick layer.

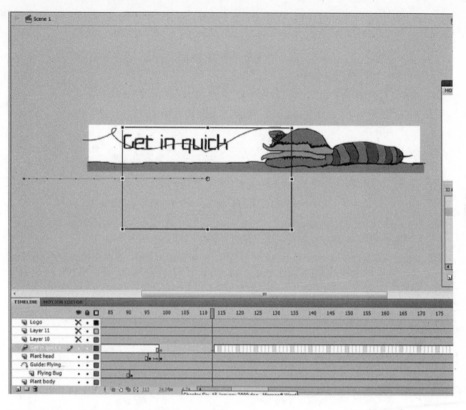

Figure 6-46. Positioning the text on the stage

22. Drag it along and position it on the 160th layer, as shown in Figure 6-47.

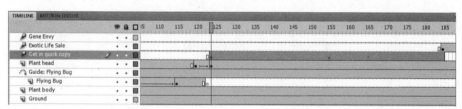

Figure 6-47. The timeline

The text should now fly in, stop for a while, and then disappear. It would be great if the same treatment could be applied to the rest of the copy. We'll do that next.

23. Save this motion tween by selecting it and selecting Save selection as preset. Name the tween fly-left-banner.

24. Apply the same treatment to the next layer, the Exotic life text.

25. Apply the fly-in-blur-left preset by selecting it in the Motion Presets panel, and then click apply.

26. Again, you will need to reposition the text so that it begins off the stage. You will then have to position the text so that it sits neatly in the design space.

27. Grab the blank keyframe and drag it along to the 220th frame.

28. Lastly, apply the same preset to the Gene Envy text on the upper layer.

29. You will need to reposition the text outside of the stage on the 220th frame, and then in the design space on the 234th frame.

30. Grab the blank keyframe on the 235th frame and slide it out to the edge of the timeline, to the 300th frame. You may need to actually go to the 300th frame and insert a frame there for the final text layer.

The banner is now complete! Press Ctrl+Enter (or Cmd+Enter on the Mac) to publish the leaderboard banner. Voilà! Your first piece of marketing collateral.

Summary

In this chapter, you discovered the powerful animation tools in Flash CS4 and the aspects of the program that allow you to control the animation. We discussed scenes, tweens, and onion skinning, and we used selected animations to create an industry standard 728×90 banner advertisement.

The next chapter will see us taking animation into the future! Inverse kinematics will enable you to create amazing and lifelike animations in Flash CS4.

CHAPTER 7

ACHIEVING LIFELIKE MOTION WITH INVERSE KINEMATICS

Inverse kinematics will revolutionize your Flash CS4 movies. It allows you to animation Flash CS4 movies in a way approximating lifelike movement. When you animate with Flash CS4, as we have in the previous chapters of this book, the motion is fairly limited due to the animation techniques that are employed. While the standard approach to animation is effective for certain things—for example, the bug flying in the final exercise in Chapter 6—when it comes to lifelike animation, such as a person walking or running, the animation can feel stilted. This is where inverse kinematics (IK) can make your Flash CS4 animations *great* as opposed to *good*. To create convincing motion, you need to study how objects move.

Kinematics is the branch of motion study that considers all aspects of the motion of an object, without considering the causes that led to that motion. Inverse kinematics is the study of determining the parameters of a flexible jointed model to reflect desired poses. When you combine physics and Flash, you have a system for creating fairly accurate animations without a pure math degree. Usually, to take full advantage of kinematics you would utilize a mathematical formula to impose motion restrictions. Take for instance the centripetal force in the orbit of the planets around the sun. These orbital velocities aren't erratic or random, they are elliptical and can be calculated precisely. Kinematics is not restricted to the heavenly bodies, though; it can be applied to everyday objects. Flash CS4 has some tools to help create convincing motion without the need of calculus, an abacus, or a sundial.

You see inverse kinematics daily around you. It uses a system of bones to impose a limitation to object movement. Think about how the bones and tendons in your arms restrict your arms' motion. The same thing goes for your legs and other parts of your body. Bones aren't limited to living creatures or characters, either. Mechanical devices like cranes and pulleys all use motion restrictions. The "bones" employed in these machines restrict movement and help to anchor or move the object in accordance with our sense of the real world.

Inverse kinematics has been employed by 3D artists and character animators for a long time, because it helps us achieve lifelike movement in animations by relying on algorithms designed to assist in the movement of joints. Cast your mind back to Chapter 1, where we designed a basic arm structure consisting of an upper arm, a forearm, and a hand. Once we had placed the joints in the correct positions, we were able to move the hand, and rely on inverse kinematics to move the rest of the arm in a way that appeared natural but was in fact reliant on these algorithms. Once the bones have been rigged to the character, inverse kinematics allows the animator to move a character model's limbs to a desired position and not have to worry about the accurate positioning of the rest of the body. Inverse kinematics, once set up, provides a no-brainer solution for the problem of achieving realistic animation.

Learning about armatures and bones

Armatures are also known as *rigs*. They are the kinetic chains used in character animation to give them lifelike movement. Think of the system of bones and tendons that moves animals, or the pulleys and levers in machinery. The motion of puppets and marionettes is also controlled using armatures. In Flash CS4, a chain of bones is defined as an armature. The bones are connected to one another in a defined hierarchy.

Armatures can be branched or linear, and are connected to one another in a parent-child hierarchy. Branches of an armature that generate from the same bone are called *siblings*.

So what are bones? Bones, as you already know, structure your limbs. They also structure movement. In Flash CS4 you create a system of bones by selecting the Bone tool and dragging the bone in a straight line through the middle of the object you wish to rig. You can also place a restriction on the rotation of bones. For instance, in a leg joint, you know the knee cannot bend forward. Therefore, when placing bones through the leg, you would need to restrict the rotation of the bone. We'll look at an example of all of this in a moment. First we'll discuss a little more about bones.

Bones can be added to simple shapes to create organic motions. To add bones to a shape, select the shape, then select the Bone tool and drag a number of bones into the shape. The shape will deform in accordance with the bone motion.

Bones can also be added to a symbol. When you set up bones within a symbol, the symbol is oriented by the bone structure, but retains its own shape. This is great for character animation and for animating machinery.

Understanding inverse-kinematic shapes

The easiest way to understand inverse kinematics in Flash CS4 is to use it. You will now apply inverse kinematics to a shape. The shape will deform everywhere a bone has been placed. You will start with a basic rectangle and make it bend and coil organically.

1. Open a new Flash (ActionScript 3.0) document in Flash CS4.

2. Draw a long, thin rectangle like the one in Figure 7-1.

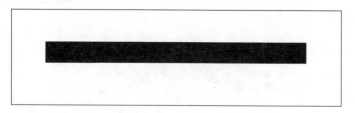

Figure 7-1. Drawing a long, thin rectangle on the stage

3. Select the Bone tool, as shown in Figure 7-2.

4. Starting from the left side, place six bones within the rectangle by clicking the left edge and dragging a short distance, as shown in Figure 7-3.

Figure 7-3. Adding the bones

Figure 7-2.
Selecting the
Bone tool

As you drag the mouse from left to right, a bone will form. The rounded base is the bone's pivot point. To attach one bone to another, you need to begin each child bone from its parent bone's end pivot point. Bones can be moved and stretched just like any other object in Flash CS4—use the Selection tool then drag the bone to match the underlying shape or symbol. Use the Transform tool to adjust the bone's pivot point. The pivot point is important to restricting the motion of the armature.

When a bone is applied to the stage, a new layer appears on the timeline; it's called Armature as shown in Figure 7-4. The Armature layer is where all of the information about a chain of bones is stored in the timeline.

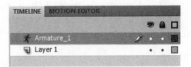

Figure 7-4. The Armature layer appears on the timeline when a bone is placed on it.

The rectangle can be now be deformed by manipulating the bone joints. Notice how this is similar to moving the bones of an arm to create a pose.

5. Click the Selection tool and hover it over a bone pivot point.

Notice how it changes its icon to include a bone. This indicates that the bone can be manipulated.

6. Click and drag a bone.

Watch how the whole rectangle becomes fluid and responds to the bone manipulation, as illustrated in Figure 7-5.

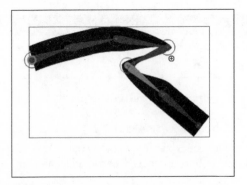

Figure 7-5. Bone deformation

7. Save the file; you will use it in the next exercise.

We are going to animate this shape in the next exercise, so let's get it ready to move! The next exercise begins with a coiled-up version of the boned rectangle from Figure 7-5. Drag the sixth bone, ikBoneName6, until you have coiled the rectangle into a spiral approximating Figure 7-6.

Figure 7-6. Coiling the boned rectangle in preparation for animation

Inverse-kinematic poses

Inverse-kinematic poses behave just like real-life poses and enable you to bend and stretch objects to move them in lifelike ways. By grouping symbol instances together, you can position them in different ways on different frames, and Flash CS4 will estimate the positions in the intervening frames.

1. Open the completed FLA document from the previous exercise, or if you have not completed that exercise, open 7-01.fla in Flash CS4.
2. Move the playhead to the 20th frame.
3. Right-click and select Insert Keyframe from the context menu.
4. Choose the main spiral shape using the Selection tool.
5. Select the first bone at its joint, as shown in Figure 7-7. This bone has the label ikBoneName1. The label is shown in the Properties Inspector.

You will notice a number of sections in the inverse kinematics Properties Inspector. Later in this section we'll investigate how manipulating those sections affects your animation.

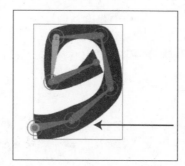

Figure 7-7. Select the first bone, as indicated by the arrow.

6. Drag this bone downward so that the spiral begins to flatten.
7. Move the playhead to the 40th frame on the timeline.

8. Select the second bone, as shown in Figure 7-8. This bone has the label ikBoneName2.

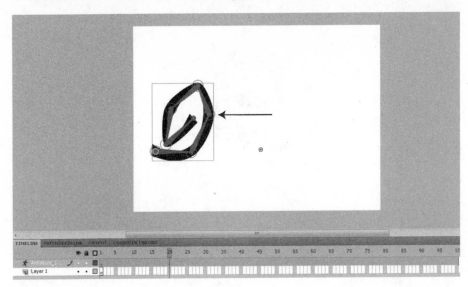

Figure 7-8. Select the third bone, as indicated by the arrow.

9. Drag this bone downward and across to the right so that the spiral flattens out more.

10. Move the playhead to the 60th frame on the timeline and insert a keyframe.

11. Select the fourth bone, as shown in Figure 7-9. This bone has the label ikBoneName3.

12. Drag this bone downward and across to the right so that the spiral flattens out more.

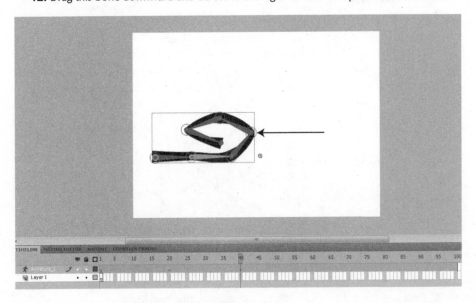

Figure 7-9. Select the fourth bone, as indicated by the arrow.

13. Move the fifth bone, as shown in Figure 7-10. This bone has the label ikBoneName4.

14. Drag this bone downward and across to the right so that the spiral flattens out more.

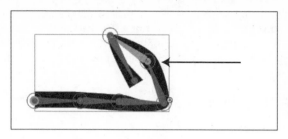

Figure 7-10. Select the fifth bone as indicated by the arrow.

15. Move the playhead to the 100th frame.

16. Select the sixth bone, as shown in Figure 7-11. This bone has the label ikBoneName6.

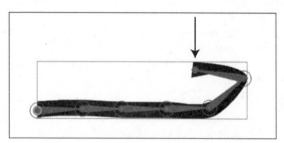

Figure 7-11. Select the sixth (and final) bone, as indicated by the arrow.

17. Drag this bone downward and across to the right so that the spiral flattens out completely to a relatively straight line, as shown in Figure 7-12.

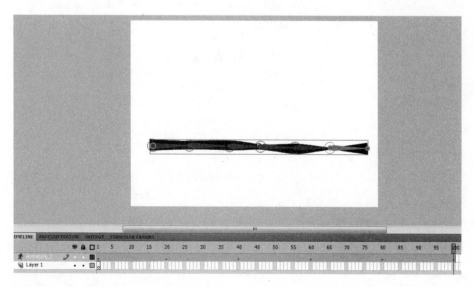

Figure 7-12. Spiral no more

7

Watch your animation by pressing Control+Enter on your keyboard (Windows), or Command+Enter on your Mac keyboard.

As the playhead travels along the timeline, the animation will unravel from pose to pose. We have set a new pose every 20 keyframes over a 100-keyframe animation. When the animation is played, Flash ensures that in each of the 20 frames, the pose has been achieved, and while it is traveling between poses it calculates the position it should be in for a smooth animation.

Now that you have mastered applying bones, we'll investigate the inverse kinematics Properties Inspector.

Using the inverse kinematics Properties Inspector

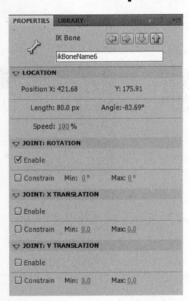

When you click on a bone on the stage, the inverse kinematics Properties Inspector is displayed, as shown in Figure 7-13. The inverse kinematics Properties Inspector allows you to quickly and easily add depth to your animations.

The inverse kinematics Properties Inspector is divided into five sections: the bone information, Location, Joint: Rotation, Joint: X Translation, and Joint: Y Translation. We'll investigate each of these sections now.

The topmost section of the Properties Inspector, shown in Figure 7-14, displays the name of the currently selected bone. By default, the bones are named ikBoneName1, ikBoneName2, ikBoneName3, and so on, sequentially. Every bone on the stage is assigned a name. You can rename bones by simply changing the name in the Name field.

Figure 7-14. The bone-information section of the inverse kinematics Properties Inspector

Figure 7-13. The inverse kinematics Properties Inspector

While the names are not used in keyframe animation, they are used when you combine ActionScript 3.0 with inverse kinematics. The name of the bone is referenced in the ActionScript.

Also in the bone information section is a series of four arrows. The left and right arrows allow you to move from the previous to the next sibling bone, and the up and down arrows allow you to scroll between parent and child bones. Let's try this now.

1. Open the previous completed exercise (or you can download 7_Properties.fla from the friends of ED website, http://friendsofed.com).

2. Click on the first bone, ikBoneName1.

3. Click on the down arrow .

Note that the stage will highlight the parent's child bone.

The Location section of the Properties Inspector, shown in Figure 7-15, contains the location information of the selected bone. As well as displaying the position of the bone on the x- and y-axis on the stage, it gives details about the length of the bone and the angle at which the bone is currently positioned.

Figure 7-15. The Location section of the inverse kinematics Properties Inspector

The final component of the Location section allows you to give your animations the illusion of weight by adjusting the Speed value. By default it is set at unlimited speed; that is, 100%. To give the illusion of weight in the bone, simply slow the speed to less than 100%.

The Joint: Rotation section, shown in Figure 7-16, is where you can inhibit movement. By default, Joint: Rotation is enabled; that is, by default all joints can move 360° on the pivot point.

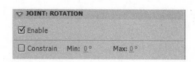

Figure 7-16. Joint: Rotation is enabled by default.

In the next exercise you will see the impact that disabling a joint has on your bone's animation. For this exercise, use the 7_Properties.fla exercise downloaded from the friends of ED website.

1. Open 7_Properties.fla as it was downloaded from the friends of ED website.

2. With the Selection tool enabled on the Tools panel, click on the fifth bone, ikBoneName5, of the chain of bones on the stage (see Figure 7-17).

Figure 7-17. Selecting the fifth bone on the stage

3. Uncheck the Enable box in the Joint: Rotation section in the Properties Inspector, as shown in Figure 7-18.

Figure 7-18. Disabling rotation in the Properties Inspector

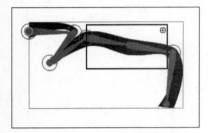

Now play with the animation. What has happened? The rotation has been disabled on the fifth bone, and it is now rigid and no longer about to be rotated at its pivot point on its parent bone, as shown in Figure 7-19. Because we haven't done this on every other bone, the other bones are still malleable.

Close this exercise without saving; we will be using the same file for the following exercise.

Figure 7-19. Disabling rotation on a bone causes it to be rigid.

The second part of the Joint: Rotation section of the Properties Inspector is the Constrain section. Here you can limit the amount of movement in rotation without making the bones completely rigid. This enables you to create lifelike effects—for example, a leaf unfurling wouldn't have the same kind of rotation as a snake moving.

Let's investigate this effect now.

1. Open 7_Properties.fla in Flash CS4.

2. Click on the first bone, ikBoneName1, to select it

3. Click on the Constrain check box in the Joint: Rotation section of the Properties Inspector.

4. Set the Minimum value to –45° and the Maximum to 45° in the Constrain section, shown in Figure 7-20.

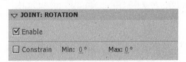

Figure 7-20. Setting the Minimum and Maximum values

5. Repeat steps 3 and 4 for all of the bones in the chain.

Now play with your animation. You'll notice that you can no longer rotate joints 360°.

We'll now move on to the Joint: X Translation and Joint: Y Translation sections of the Properties Inspector, shown in Figure 7-21.

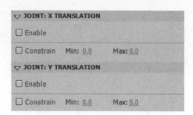

Figure 7-21. The Joint: X Translation and Joint: Y Translation sections

These sections enable the selected bone to move along the chosen axis, which also allows the parent bone to stretch to accommodate the movement of the child bone, as shown in Figure 7-22.

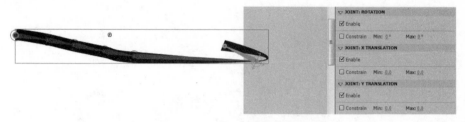

Figure 7-22. Changing the X and Y translation allows the parent bone to stretch to accommodate the movement of the child.

Making a monster!

Now that we have delved into the way that you can bring your animation to life using inverse kinematics, let's apply it to an animation. In Chapter 4 you learned how to bring a sketch to life in Flash CS4. The assets in the following exercise were developed in the same way, and are now ready to animate with inverse kinematics. Please ensure that you have downloaded the exercise files from the friends of ED website to complete the following exercises.

1. Open the exercise file Creature01.fla in Flash CS4.

You will see a strange polyeyed creature load onto the stage. It has a number of body parts ready to rig and animate. We have converted each body part into a movie-clip symbol for you so that you can concentrate on animating the creature. Each of these movie clips is on a separate layer—don't be daunted by the number of layers; they simply make it easier for the animator to separate movie clips.

As many bones are added to an armature, the movie clips that have been added most recently sometimes overlay the whole stack of rigged movie clips. You may encounter this during this exercise; we will step through how to fix that in this section.

> *Remember:* to convert an object into a movie clip, you simply right-click the object and select *Convert to Symbol. You then select* Movie Clip *from the* Type drop-down list in the *Convert to Symbol dialog box.*

2. Using the Zoom tool, enlarge the view so the green creature occupies the entire screen.

3. Select the Bone tool and connect the abdomen to the mouth by dragging the bone from the base of the abdomen up to where the mouth opens, as shown in Figure 7-23.

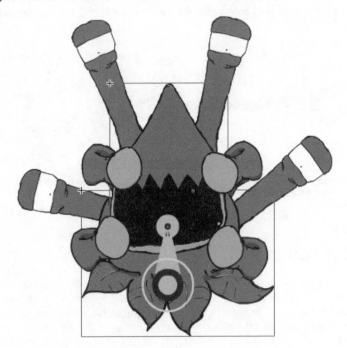

Figure 7-23. Placing the base bone

Notice that the two movie clips are highlighted, connected by a bone. The Armature layer has appeared in the timeline. This layer holds all the bone information used for animation.

4. With the Bone tool still selected, drag out another bone from the tip of the previous one and up to one of the eyes, as shown in Figure 7-24.

5. Using the Bone tool, click on the base of the second bone and drag a bone out to the other eye.

The second bone starts in the middle of the mouth as shown in Figure 7-25.

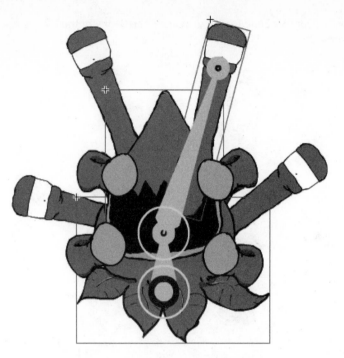

Figure 7-24. Drag a new bone from the mouth to the eye.

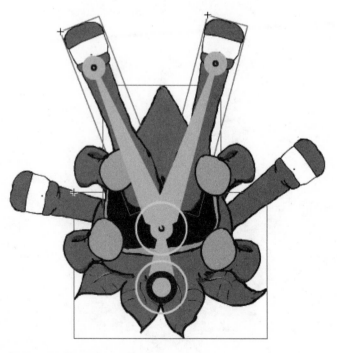

Figure 7-25. Attaching another eye to the rig

6. Drag out another bone from the second bone to one of the arm joints, as shown in Figure 7-26.

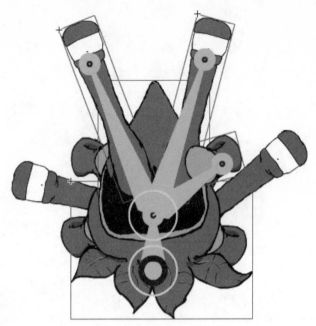

Figure 7-26.
Attaching the
first arm

7. Drag another bone up and out from the central second bone and up the remaining arm, as in Figure 7-27.

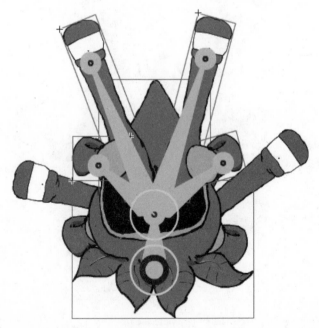

Figure 7-27.
Attaching the
second arm

8. Connect another eye to the rig. Drag a bone from the second bone across to a remaining eye, as in Figure 7-28.

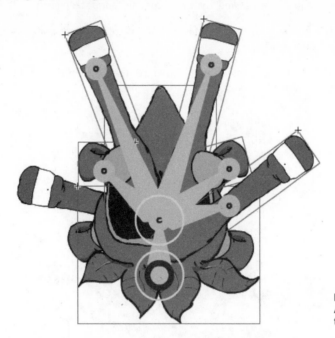

Figure 7-28.
Attaching the
third eye

7

9. Connect the remaining eye to the rig. Using the Bone tool, drag a bone out from the base of the second bone across to the last eye, as shown in Figure 7-29.

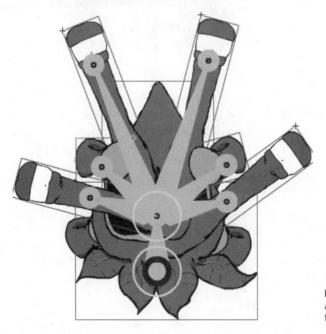

Figure 7-29.
Attaching the
final eye

As the bones crowd the armature, placing new ones can become daunting. The Bone icon will dictate if a bone can be created. The icon will change from a white bone and + symbol to a black bone and a "not allowed" symbol if a bone cannot be placed.

The armature is almost complete. The last two items to add are the inferior arms, which will be added to the first bone.

10. With the Bone tool selected, drag a bone from the base of the first bone up to one of the rear arms; see Figure 7-30.

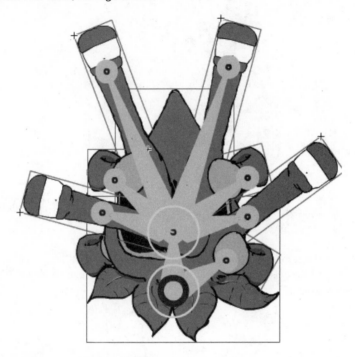

Figure 7-30. Adding the inferior arms

11. Save your file; we will be starting from this point in the next exercise.

12. Drag a bone from the base of the first bone across to the final arm, as shown in Figure 7-31.

You have now created the structure of your animation; however, it's not perfect. In the next exercise we will fine-tune it.

As we have mentioned previously, when bones are added to an armature, the most recently added movie clips have a tendency to sit over the entire stack of rigged movie clips. Look at Figure 7-32 for reference. Notice that it looks as if the creature is eating its own eye parts, as opposed to the eyes stemming from the rear of the creature. Don't panic—we'll now step through rearranging the limb layers to correct this.

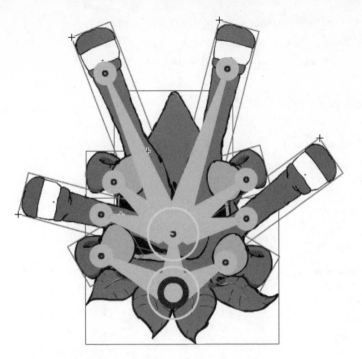

Figure 7-31. All limbs attached

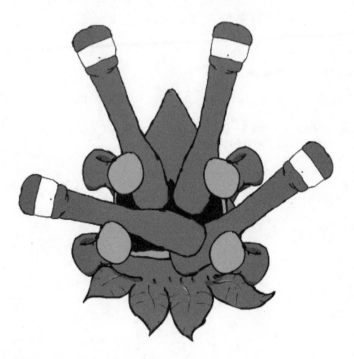

Figure 7-32. The limbs need layer arrangement.

1. Using the Selection tool, select one of the eye limbs.

2. Hold down Shift on your keyboard and select the other three eye limbs.

3. Choose Modify ➤ Arrange ➤ Send to Back (see Figure 7-33).

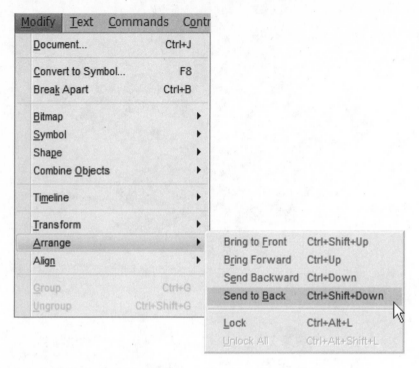

Figure 7-33. The Arrange menu

The selected eye limbs are placed behind the other body parts.

Now that all the limbs are attached to the creature and the limbs are layered in the proper order, the armature can be fine-tuned.

If the limbs are moved, they will behave strangely. This is due to their registration points being initialized in the wrong spot. By default, a registration point is located in the center of a movie clip. Fix this by moving each pivot to a better location.

1. Select the Free Transform tool and click on one of the eye limbs.

Notice the white circle that appears in the middle of the Free Transform cage, as illustrated in Figure 7-34.

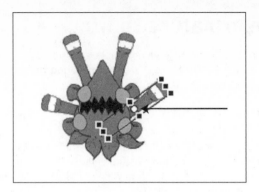

Figure 7-34. Use the Free Transform tool to move the bone pivot.

2. Use the Free Transform tool to move the pivot point—the white circle—close to the base of the creature, as shown in Figure 7-35.

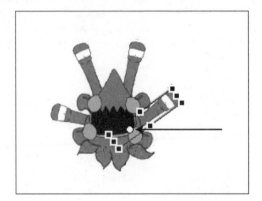

Figure 7-35. The pivot point moved to a better location

> *Moving the pivot point to the center of the creature makes the limb movement more natural. If the pivot point were left in the middle of the limb, the limb would hinge from the center, and would appear to spin in midair!*

3. Repeat step 2 for the remaining limbs.

We now have all of our structure in place to create a convincing animation. The next section allows you to bring your creature to life via animation.

Bringing the armature to life

In the following exercise you will observe how an IK armature can be manipulated to create a character animation. You will create a short animation that portrays the creature a little drowsy, perhaps ready to fall asleep.

1. Open the file `creature-rigged.fla` in Flash CS4, or continue working from the previous exercise.

You will see the green polylimbed creature staring at you from the middle of the screen. You need to extend the timeline to allow for some animation. There are again many layers in this animation, as per the previous iteration you were working on. Again, this is because each movie clip is housed on a different layer.

2. Select all the layers under the 100th frame by clicking the top layer and dragging down in a straight line, as shown in Figure 7-36.

> *There are layers outside of the timeline's viewable area. You can stretch the timeline panel to see all of the layers, or you can scroll up and down to see them all. To select all of the layers, scroll to where the top layer is visible, click on the 100th frame of that layer, and drag the mouse to the bottom layer.*

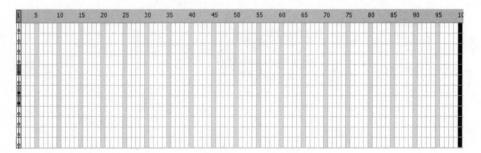

Figure 7-36. Select all the layers.

3. Right-click and insert frames, or go to Menu ➤ Insert ➤ Timeline ➤ Frame.

The final frame will show the creature at rest. (Because the creature doesn't really have legs and a torso, *lying down* isn't the right terminology.) To put the creature to rest, you'll move and rotate the limbs on the final frame.

4. Click on the Selection tool in the Tools panel while you are on the 100th frame,

5. Select the creature's base and rotate it clockwise as shown in Figure 7-37.

6. Using the Selection tool, choose the creature's mouth area and drag it down to the right as shown in Figure 7-38. Picture the head hitting an imaginary floor.

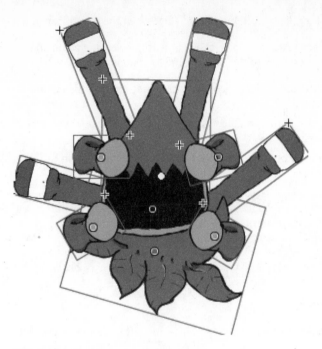

Figure 7-37. The base rotated clockwise

Figure 7-38. The creature's head tipped to one side

The rightmost eye limb has tipped to the floor when the mouth part is tipped clockwise.

Scrub the timeline back and forth at any time to preview the animation. Just remember to move the playhead back to the 100th frame to continue the animation.

7. Select the upper-right "hand." Position it so that it rests comfortably on the other right hand.

8. Select the third eye limb from the left. Move it down so that it rests atop the hands.

9. Grab the second eye limb from the left and drag it down to rest against the creature's head.

> Note that even though IK motion would allow the limb to touch the ground, this doesn't represent a physically believable motion for the creature. Avoid using unrealistic motion when employing IK, unless you are going for that effect. Unrealistic motions defy physics and the space-time continuum, so they're best used to animate things like the physical bending of UFOs and interdimensional body deformations.

The first eye limb from the left could fall to the left or to the right. Make the limb fall to the right.

10. Drag the leftmost eye limb down to the left to look like Figure 7-39.

Figure 7-39. Did someone say "Pan-Galactic Gargle Blaster"?

11. Preview the animation by selecting Control ➤ Test Movie.

When you preview the animation, you see the creature slowly arc its limbs to rest. This animation lacks character, however. Character can come from timing, and timing is crucial to conveying a concept. This can be fixed easily in Flash CS4 with armature easing.

1. Select the Armature layer.

2. In the Properties tab, roll out Ease and set the Strength to 100 and the type to Stop and Start (Fast).

3. Preview the animation again.

Now notice the peak in the motion, then the sudden fall. The creature now seems sleepier.

Summary

This chapter introduced the wonderful world of inverse kinematics! You have used the Bone tool to help create a lifelike animation of a cute little creature who is for sale on the gene-with-envy website.

Chapter 8 will walk you through basic ActionScript 3.0 functions and exercises, and show you how to build some useful applications using ActionScript 3.0.

7

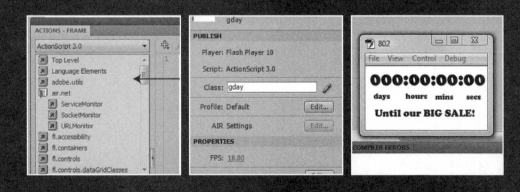

The ActionScript programming language dates back to 1996 when it was introduced to designers and programmers as part of FutureSplash Animator, a vector-based animation application that was also Flash's predecessor. Developed by SuperWave Software after it decided that its vector-based drawing program, SmartSketch, should be deployable over the Web, FutureSplash changed the face of the Internet forever. Until then, animations were created using Java only. This radical new program was used on the sites of many well-known companies, including Fox, Disney, and MSN.

Shortly after its 1996 release, FutureSplash was purchased by Macromedia, and with the next version of FutureSplash, the world was introduced to Macromedia Flash 1.0. Eleven versions of Flash later, ActionScript is a more important factor than ever. ActionScript has enabled Flash to evolve beyond pretty animations to allow Flash developers to produce fully interactive applications for both the Internet and desktop applications.

You've dabbled a little bit with ActionScript throughout this book, but this is the chapter where you'll really get your hands dirty and use it to make your Flash CS4 files do some cool things. In the pioneer versions of Flash, ActionScript was used only for basic functions such as stop() and play(). In this chapter, you'll learn how to do a whole lot more!

Using the Actions panel

Though for many Flash CS4 applications it's better practice to use an external file to execute your ActionScript 3.0, there are still many kinds of applications, such as banners and smaller files, where it is acceptable to enter the ActionScript on the timeline. It's time now to get thoroughly acquainted with the Actions panel. As you have done many times previously, open a new Flash file (ActionScript 3.0) in Flash CS4. Right-click frame 1 of the timeline and select Actions from the context menu, as shown in Figure 8-1.

> *Remember that you can also open the Actions panel by pressing F9 on your keyboard or selecting Window ➤ Actions from the main menu.*

The Actions panel will display, as shown in Figure 8-2. We'll now investigate each section.

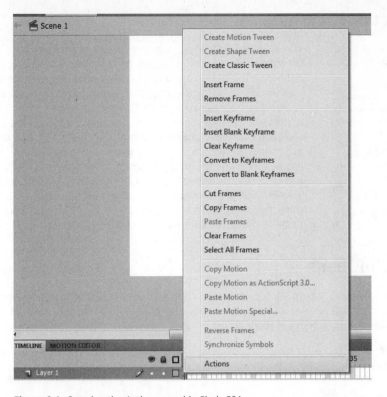

Figure 8-1. Opening the Actions panel in Flash CS4

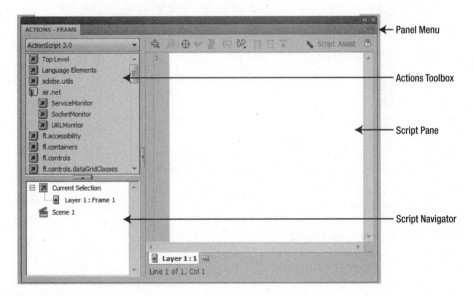

Figure 8-2. The sections of the Actions panel

The Actions toolbox

Figure 8-3. The Actions toolbox enables you to drill down to specific ActionScript functionality.

The Actions toolbox provides you with comprehensive access to the complete realm of scripting functionality available to you in ActionScript 3.0. It is divided into intuitive categories that enable you to drill down to the singular functionalities. For example, to access the click functionality of a button, you would click the fl.control entry in the index of the toolbox, then click the button, and then click the Events drop-down. You could then drag the click event into the Actions panel, as shown in Figure 8-3. The Actions toolbox gives you the ability to access many functions without having to memorize them. However, as you learn ActionScript, you may find it easier and quicker to simply type the information into the Script pane, rather than manually clicking through to drill down to the desired functionality in the Actions toolbox.

The Script pane

The Script pane, shown in Figure 8-4, not only provides you a place to type your ActionScript, but it also provides you with shortcuts to access assistance in coding ActionScript from a series of icons across the top.

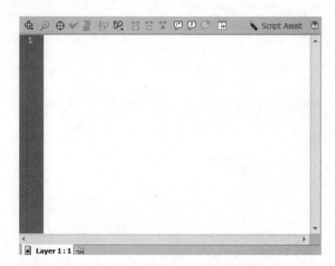

Figure 8-4. The Script pane allows you to easily access coding assistance.

Table 8-1 lists each of these functions.

Table 8-1. The Buttons in the Script Pane

Icon	Button Name	Function
	Add a new item to the script	This button enables you to add a new item to the script. Clicking this button gives you an alternative way to access functions available in the Actions toolbox.
	Find	Particularly useful in long lines of code, the Find button allows you to find and replace text in your ActionScript.
	Insert a target path	This button allows you to create interactions within your FLA file that send messages from one timeline to another by choosing whether to set a relative target path or an absolute target path. A relative target path targets only documents loaded into their level within the document, while an absolute target path allows you to create interactions between documents throughout the levels existing in your FLA.
	Check syntax	This handy shortcut allows you to check your ActionScript for syntax errors. Results will be displayed in the Output window.
	Auto format	When you are typing long lines of code, using this function will format your code, allowing you to read it more easily.
	Code hint	If automatic code hinting is turned off, you can use this button to provide you with a code hint for the line of code that you are currently working on.
	Debug options	This allows you to set breakpoints in your ActionScript files for easier debugging.
	Collapse between braces and Collapse section	These buttons are very handy when you are dealing with lengthy pieces of code, as they allow you to collapse the content between braces ({ }) and sections, respectively.
	Expand all	This button allows you to once again expand your collapsed section to view the piece of code in its entirety.
	Apply block comment, Apply line comment, and Remove comment	In ActionScript, placing // in front of your code comments it out. A comment in ActionScript is a piece of code or text within the file that is not executed. Coders often use comments to leave instructive notes in large pieces of code that multiple people may be working on. These buttons respectively allow you to write a block comment (consisting of more than one line), write a single-line comment, and remove the comment.
	Show/Hide toolbox	This button allows you to show or hide the Actions toolbox, allowing you to take advantage of more screen space for larger blocks of ActionScript.
	Script assist	This button allows you to build code with the assistance of the ActionScript 3.0 Script Assistance.
	Help	When you require it, you can click this button to access the official Adobe Flash CS4 help documents (Internet access required).

8

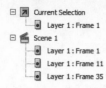

Figure 8-5. The Script Navigator allows you to navigate quickly through scripts within your FLA file.

The Script Navigator

The Script Navigator, shown in Figure 8-5, allows you to navigate quickly between the scripts in your FLA document. A single FLA file may have many occurrences of ActionScript along its timeline, and the Script Navigator allows you to jump to each instantly.

The Panel menu

The Panel menu ▦ provides shortcuts for many of the features of the Actions panel, as shown in Figure 8-6, such as autoformat. It also allows you to access features such as pinning scripts, which allow you to keep the script in the Script pane even after you have clicked away from it.

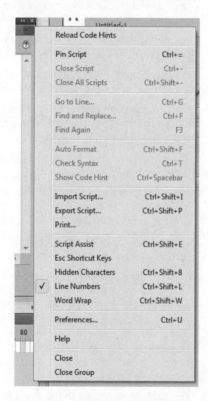

Figure 8-6. The Panel menu provides shortcuts for Actions panel features.

This has given you an overview of the Actions panel. Now that you have this knowledge, you can begin to use it to code ActionScript. The next section is designed to give you a basic overview of ActionScript 3.0 before delving into some more complicated uses.

Object-oriented programming and ActionScript 3.0

ActionScript is an **object-oriented programming (OOP)** language that was designed especially for website animations, and was modeled on the ECMA-262 standard, an international standard for the JavaScript language. OOP is a programming method that uses objects, defined as data structures, and the interaction of those data structures to design functional and interactive Internet and software applications. ActionScript was originally released with Flash 4 and has been evolving ever since. ActionScript 3.0 was introduced in Flash CS3, but with the new capabilities of Flash CS4, you can take your animations to new levels of interactivity.

Programming ActionScript 3.0 is not magic, it is simply the art of breaking down a complex task or problem into a series of simple steps. Programming is a lot like writing a cooking recipe. You write the recipe—the steps to making the meal—and the computer cooks the dish every time the recipe is read.

Imagine explaining the process of making a cup of tea to a robot. You would need to break this process down into simple steps:

1. Get a teacup from the cupboard.
2. Get a saucer from the cupboard.
3. Place the saucer on the bench.
4. Place the teacup on the saucer.
5. Fill a kettle with water.
6. Use the kettle to bring the water to a boil.
7. Add boiling water to the teacup.
8. Add a tea bag to the teacup.
9. Serve the cup of tea.

The trick to being a good coder is being able to laterally solve problems logically. Lateral problem solving involves thinking outside the usual or regular course of action.

For example, the previous tea making process could be executed as follows:

1. Get a teacup from the cupboard.
2. Fill the teacup with water.
3. Heat the teacup in the microwave.
4. Add a tea bag to the teacup.
5. Serve the cup of tea.

8

> *Both programs instruct the robot how to make a cup of tea, but using a microwave cuts the number of steps involved. This is a little like ActionScript 3.0. ActionScript 3.0 has many advantages over previous ActionScript versions. For example, it offers superior XML processing and it executes commands incredibly quickly. Note, though, if your FLA file uses ActionScript 3.0, you may not include earlier versions of ActionScript within the same file.*

Programming uses language to describe the problem solving steps. The ActionScript language is written using keywords and user-generated names. **Keywords** form a group of 50 or so commands that are reserved for the basic ActionScript vocabulary. These keywords, when mixed with user-generated names, are arranged to form short, meaningful sentences. These are also known as **statements** or **expressions**. ActionScript programs can be filled with thousands of statements—however many it takes to solve the problem at hand.

When programming, try to think about the different ways to solve a problem, and then attempt to break down the solution into simple steps. Sometimes the solution is so simple; there is only one step involved in the process. Other times the solution can become tricky and involve you having to follow a range of different steps based on decisions and looping.

An example statement would be

```
trace("G'day World");
```

This expression tells Flash to output the greeting "G'day World" to the Output window. The command trace tells Flash to write whatever is within the quotation marks. The semicolon at the end (;) marks the end of a statement in Flash. It's the equivalent of a period at the end of a sentence.

ActionScript can be written in the timeline, in an external file, or in the **document class**. Writing complex code in the timeline can have drawbacks. It can be hard to parse and navigate, and as it becomes more intricate, code in the timeline can become harder to organize. The document class helps to eliminate this, as it is in an external file that is easier to parse. ActionScript written in the external document class can also enable your designers and developers to work in parallel on a project—the designer can design within Flash CS4, and your developer can create ActionScript in an external editor to implement the Flash animation.

"G'day World"

An introduction to ActionScript would not be complete without a classic "Hello World" implementation. For those of you who are new to programming, a "Hello World" application is a simple application that prints "Hello World" on the screen, and has been used as the standard introduction to programming languages for many years.

You will write your first piece of ActionScript using timeline scripting:

1. Create a new Flash File (ActionScript 3.0) file.

2. Select the first frame on the timeline.

3. Open the Actions panel by selecting Window ➤ Actions, as shown in Figure 8-7 (or by pressing F9 on the keyboard or right-clicking a frame on the timeline and selecting Actions from the context menu).

As you know well, the Actions panel is where you write code. If you click an object, the Actions panel displays the ActionScript for that specific object. In this example, we are placing code on the first frame.

4. Type the following into the Actions panel, as shown in Figure 8-8:

```
trace("G'day World");
```

The first thing you'll notice is that different parts of the code in the Actions panel are colored differently. This is called **syntax highlighting**, and it shows you which parts Flash recognizes as keywords. It's also a great way to spot errors in your typing. If a keyword isn't colored correctly in Flash, it means that you've spelled it wrong.

Figure 8-7. Opening the Actions panel

8

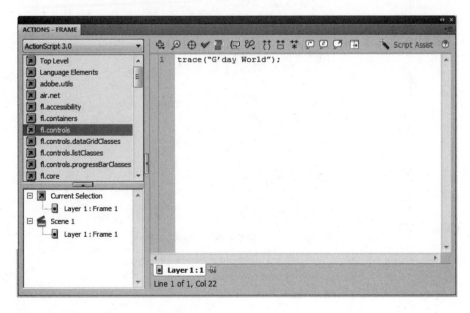

Figure 8-8. Entering code into the Actions panel

So, in our first line of code, there are three different colors shown. Blue indicates a Flash keyword, so trace is in blue; green means a string (basically some text enclosed in quote marks), so "G'day World" is in green; and black is used for any code that doesn't need to be specially colored. You'll notice that the parentheses and the semicolon in our line are in black. You'll usually stick with the default colors, but if you want to change any of them, you can do so from the ActionScript category of the Preferences dialog (see Figure 8-9) by selecting Edit ➤ Preferences.

> Remember, you can also check your syntax by clicking the Check Syntax icon at the top of the Actions panel.

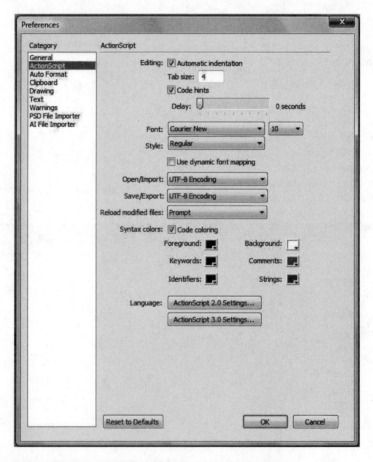

Figure 8-9. Syntax highlighting options in the Preferences dialog

5. Publish the movie by pressing Ctrl+Enter on your keyboard.

You will notice an antipodean greeting in the Output window, as shown in Figure 8-10.

Figure 8-10. Your first programmed application

External ActionScript files

You can also write your ActionScript in an external AS file. There are many advantages to separating your code from your design. Some of these include code that is easier to manage, debug, and reuse. Also, having a separate AS file allows one person to work on the design while another can work on the code. All in all, even though it may seem like extra work at first, organizing your code in external files can save you time in the long run.

To write your Flash File (ActionScript 3.0) in an external file, start Flash CS4.

1. Create a new Flash File (ActionScript 3.0) file, as shown in Figure 8-11.

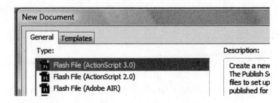

Figure 8-11. Create a new ActionScript file.

2. Enter the same code as the previous exercise, as shown in Figure 8-12:

```
trace("G'day World");
```

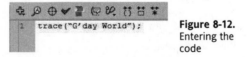

Figure 8-12. Entering the code

3. Save the file as external.as.

4. Go to File ➤ New and create a new Flash (ActionScript 3.0) file.

5. Save the file as external.fla.

> *Make sure you save the AS and FLA files in the same directory.*

6. Select the first frame of the timeline.

7. Open the Actions panel and enter the following code:

```
include "external.as";
```

The include command tells Flash to run the external.as file, as shown in Figure 8-13.

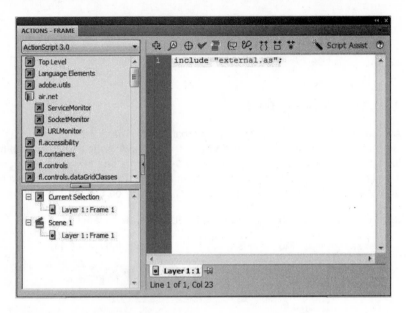

Figure 8-13. Commanding Flash to run an external ActionScript file

8. Publish the movie by pressing Ctrl+Enter, and the Output window will display the greeting!

Using a document class

The final and most elegant way to code ActionScript 3.0 is by using a document class. A document class is an external ActionScript file that is called automatically by your FLA file.

1. Create a new ActionScript 3.0 file in Flash CS4.

2. Save the file as gday.as.

3. Enter the following code, as shown in Figure 8-14:

```
package {
import flash.display.*;
        public class gday extends MovieClip {
                public function gday() {
                        trace("Gday World!");
                }
        }
}
```

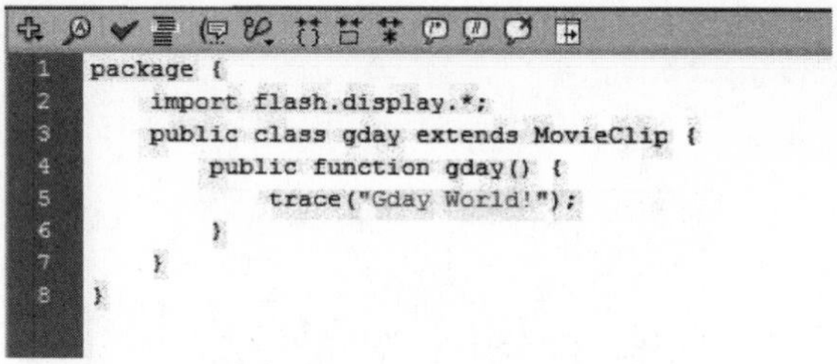

```
1   package {
2       import flash.display.*;
3       public class gday extends MovieClip {
4           public function gday() {
5               trace("Gday World!");
6           }
7       }
8   }
```

Figure 8-14. Entering code into the gday document class

The important thing to note right now is the familiar statement:

```
trace("G'day World");
```

Recall that the trace command displays messages to the Output window.

The rest of the ActionScript should be treated as a container you can use to write code in the document class. You can replace the trace ("G'day World"); statement with your own code.

If you are itching to understand the nuts and bolts, then read on.

The package command tells Flash that everything grouped between the outer braces (i.e., the { } symbols) belongs to the FLA file you are planning to create. For this reason, you should save the AS file with the same name you plan to use for the FLA file. The braces act as visual aids to help group similar blocks of code.

The line import flash.display.* tells Flash that it needs to load more information—in this case the display library—in order for the program to run. The flash.display library handles all the tricky bits that Flash needs to know in order to draw things on the screen.

The line public class gday extends MovieClip is the heading that says "start the program here." Everything that follows this statement is the programmatic logic. The keywords public class tell Flash that this program is part of the document class. It is a mandatory statement, like the package statement. The next word must be the exact same word you used to save the file you are currently writing. In this case, the file is saved as gday.as, so the word gday must follow the keywords public class. Make sure that both uses of the word are lowercase. The last two words, extends MovieClip, tell Flash that the program you are writing is to behave just like a movie clip. Finally, the code that displays "G'day World" is enclosed in a public function called gday. Notice that this function shares the same name as the document class. Functions provide a simple method to group and execute tasks, which makes it easy to amend your code. They are generally placed at the end of your code. This means that anything within this part of the program is run first.

4. Save the gday.as file.

5. Create a new Flash ActionScript 3.0 file.

6. Save the file as gday.fla, remembering to use the same name and lowercase lettering.

8

7. Locate the Properties Inspector in the gday.fla file. Expand the Publish section and find the Class input box.

8. Type gday into the Class input box, as shown in Figure 8-15.

Figure 8-15. Setting the document class and entering gday in the class field

9. Save the file.

10. Publish the gday.fla file by pressing Ctrl+Enter, and the message "G'day World" will be displayed in the Output window.

You should now understand how to add ActionScript to your projects using the document class. This is the preferred way to code using ActionScript 3.0 and Flash CS4 for larger website projects and Flash animations. Not only does this offer the flexibility for developers to work alongside designers on the same project, but it allows developers to modify code in external editors without having to open the FLA file. For advertising banners, you are required to place the ActionScript on the timeline of your Flash CS4 animation.

Now we'll dive a bit deeper into coding and demonstrate how to write some simple code that will help you immensely with your projects. There isn't room to go into the full extent of ActionScript 3.0 here, so for more information, I suggest you read *Foundation ActionScript 3.0 for Flash and Flex*, by Darren Richardson (friends of ED, 2007).

Variables and data types

A variable is a keyword that is linked to information stored in the computer's memory, or can be used to determine a particular value. In Flash CS4, variables are the containers that hold different values or data. You write variable statements to manipulate these values, assigning a name to the value. You declare variables using a statement. Each variable begins with var, which declares it as a variable. For example, consider the following statement that we have created to define the height of a video player in pixels:

```
var playerHeight:Number = 203.67;
```

The var command declares the next word as a variable and gives the variable a name. The variable name in this case is playerHeight. Try to give your variables descriptive names, as it will help when you or others try to make sense of the code later. If you are working in an agency with many Flash developers, making your variable names transparent and intuitive will cut down on precious development time, and ultimately make your Flash projects more cost effective.

> *Variable names can only contain letters, numbers, and the underscore symbol (_). A variable name cannot start with a number and it cannot be a keyword that Flash CS4 uses as a command. A variable name must be unique and meaningful. The first character must be an uppercase or lowercase letter or underscore, and the remaining characters must be letters, digits, or underscores. Variable names are case sensitive. In our example, were we going to refer to the playerHeight variable later in the code, we would need to be sure to capitalize it exactly the way we wrote it first in the code.*

In ActionScript 3.0, you must specify the type of the variable. In this case, the variable playerHeight is a number, so you define it as one using the colon operator (:). Once you have declared a variable and defined its data type, you can then assign a value to it. In this case, the value of the playerHeight variable is 203.67.

Flash variables can be any of a number of data types. You can even create your own type. The Number type, as you have just seen, means that only a number can be assigned to the variable. The Number type allows for any number, positive or negative, with a floating point (decimal point).

The Int data type, on the other hand, represents only whole numbers. *Int* is short for *integer*, a counting number. Integers cannot contain decimal points. For example:

```
var myFingers:Int = 8;
```

If you tried to write myFingers = 8.5, Flash would give you an error message.

The Number and Int types can only store numbers. This means that you could not assign myFingers to cat, because clearly, a cat is not a number.

If you did want to store a word in a variable, you would need to use the String data type. Strings can be made up of letters, words, and sentences. A string must be enclosed by quotation marks. For example:

```
var myPet:String = "Cat";
```

One other data type you may come across is Boolean. This data type can only be in one of two states, either "on" or "off," "true" or "false." Think of it as a switch. For example:

```
var brownEyes:Boolean = false;
```

This statement is saying that the variable brownEyes is false. Boolean data types have a great practical use, as you can use them to test for things like, "Is the user's mouse hovering over the movie clip?" This could be coded as follows:

```
mouseOver = true;
```

We're now going to investigate the previous in an exercise.

1. Open the gday.as file from the previous exercise.
2. Replace the line

```
trace("G'day World");
```

with

```
var myName:String = 'Jon';
trace(myName);
```

so that the whole body of code looks like this (see Figure 8-16):

```
package {
import flash.display.*;

        public class gday extends MovieClip {

                public function gday() {
                                var myName:String='Jon';
                                trace(myName);
                }
        }
}
```

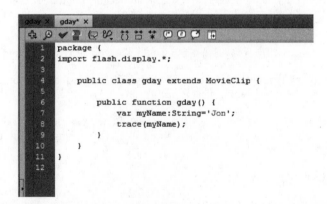

Figure 8-16. Enter the string variable code.

3. Make sure the target is set to gday.fla, as in Figure 8-17.

4. Save gday.fla, and then publish the movie by pressing Ctrl+Enter.

Figure 8-17. Setting the document class. Enter gday in the class field.

What has happened? As shown in Figure 8-16, my name, Jon, appears in the Output window of the published gday.fla movie. The information from the ActionScript file, gday. as, has been pulled into the gday.fla file. This is because we have linked the public class, gday, from the FLA to the AS file.

Operators

Statements and expressions are evaluated using operators. Operators work by taking single values and returning a total value based on the type of operator. To make this clear, let's consider the most universally understood operators—mathematical operators:

- **Addition**: +
- **Subtraction**: -
- **Multiplication**: *
- **Division**: /

Mathematical operators take two inputs, and apply a mathematical function to them. For example:

```
trace(87*3);
```

ActionScript also makes use of the unary operators:

- **Increment**: ++
- **Decrement**: --

Unary operators take one input and apply an incremental or decremental function to it. In the following line of code, we are taking a number, myInventory, and applying a decremental function to it:

```
trace(myInventory--);
```

This will have the effect of decreasing myInventory.

There are also equality operators. These are usually put to the test during the decision making process:

- **Less than**: <
- **Greater than**: >
- **Greater than or equal to**: >=
- **Less than or equal to**: <=
- **Equal to**: ==
- **Not equal to**: !=

For example:

```
trace(myInventory==yourInventory);
```

Finally, there are logical operators. These are also used during the decision making process:

- **And**: &&
- **Or**: ||
- **Not**: !

These operators combine with two inputs to join or separate logical statements.

Decisions

A program cannot think unless it can make logical decisions. The best way to make these is by using the if statement. The if statement uses Boolean logic to make its decisions. Firstly, an expression is evaluated. If the expression returns true, then a block of code is executed.

```
if (expression){
```

Then, if the expression is true, the code is executed.

```
}
```

For example:

```
if(sunIsOut){
                            goPlayOutside();
}
doSomethingElse();
```

or

```
if(a+b<6){
                    a=0;
b++;
}
```

Sometimes you may need to let your code do one thing if the expression is true and another if it is false. In this case, you would use the else statement. For example:

```
if(sunIsOut){
            goPlayOutside=1;
} else{
            stayInside=1;
}
doSomethingElse();
```

or

```
if(a+b<6){
            a=0;
b++;
```

```
    } else{
            if(a+b>3){
                    a=5
                    b--;
            }
    }
```

Loops

The whole point to programming is to make tasks automatic for the people. This is where loops shine like stars. Say you wanted to trace the following multiplication tables to the Output window. You could go about it like this:

```
trace("5 x 1 =",5*1);
trace("5 x 2 =",5*2);
trace("5 x 3 =",5*3);
trace("5 x 4 =",5*4);
trace("5 x 5 =",5*5);
trace("5 x 6 =",5*6);
trace("5 x 7 =",5*1);
trace("5 x 8 =",5*8);
trace("5 x 9 =",5*9);
trace("5 x 10 =",5*10);
```

The preceding statements would print out the multiplication tables up to 10. In the previous example, the trace statement is being used to concatenate the string and the result of each expression.

> Remember from earlier in this chapter that the trace function outputs whatever is written between the quotation marks. In this case, Flash would write each line, including the information in the quotation marks and the value of the calculation. Therefore, the first line, trace("5 x 1 =",5*1);, would output 5 x 1 = 5.

The process is arduous and open to error. Look carefully at the seventh trace statement and you will find a typo (5*1 when it should read 5*7).

ActionScript loops can help better the speed and accuracy of repetitive processes. The most used iterative construct is the for loop. The for loop works like this:

```
for ( set initial variable;
evaluate expression; alter initial variable){
        doSomething;
        somethingElse;
        etc;
}
```

8

The general rule of thumb of a for loop is that while the expression remains true, the code block is executed. Using the preceding multiplication tables, the for loop would look like this:

```
for (var i:int=1; i<=10;i++){
        trace("5 x ",i," =",5*i);
}
```

The for statement contains three elements. The first element defines the initial variable, i. The variable i is typed as an integer. The second element in the statement tests whether the variable i is less than or equal to 10. If the expression returns true, then the code in the block is executed. If the expression returns false, then the code block is broken. The third element iterates the loop—that is, it brings it to an end. When i becomes equal to 11, the value is greater than 10, and the loop comes to an end. So, in this example, what was ten lines has now become three.

There are two other types of loops: the while loop and the do...while loop. The while loop works like this:

```
while(evaluate expression){
        do stuff;
}
```

For example:

```
var i:int=1;
while(i<=10){
trace("5 x ",i," =",5*i);
        i++;
}
```

Clearly in this example, the trace code is executed while the variable i is less than or equal to 10. After that, the loop ends.

The do...while loop works in a very similar way to the while loop. Using the do...while loop, the expression is tested last, as opposed to first.

For example:

```
var i:int=1;
do{
trace("5 x ",i," =",5*i);
        i++;
} while(i<=10);
```

Functions

Programming is all about dividing and conquering. A large problem in code is tackled by cutting it down into many smaller chunks. Functions are the way to do this using ActionScript. Functions provide a way to group and manage problem solving tasks. Writing code with functions also makes it easy to modify and maintain your code, and it makes code reuse possible, meaning that you only have to program something once rather than every time you want to use it. It is common practice to place all functions toward the end of your code.

Functions work like this:

```
function functionName():type{
            doStuff;
doMoreStuff;
}
```

For example:

```
function display5Timetables():void{
            trace("The 5 times tables:");
            for (var i:int=1; i<=10;i++){
             trace("5 x ",i," =",5*i);
    }
    }
```

The first word, function, tells Flash CS4 to expect a function. This function is called display5Timetables. You must place two parentheses (one open and the next closed) directly after your function name. At the moment, there is nothing between the parentheses, as this function does not accept any arguments (an **argument** is the name for a value that is passed into a function). As it does not pass arguments, the function is typed void. **Void**, by the way, means "null" or "nothing." The next thing that you need to know is that a function doesn't do anything on its own. You need to call the function first to bring it to life. To call this function in the body of your code, you simply type the function name, as shown in bold in the following example:

```
package {
import flash.display.*;
    public class gday extends MovieClip {
                    public function gday() {
                            trace('Times Tables:');
                            display5Timetables();
        }
                            function display5Timetables():void{
                            trace('The 5 times tables are:');
                            for (var i:int=1; i<=10;i++){
                                    trace("5 x ",i," =",5*i);
                             }
        }                     }
    }
```

The previous function type was void. This means that the function returned nothing. Imagine if you wanted to create a function for adding two numbers. You would type the function as a Number because it would be returning a number as its output, and then set up the function to pass the two values as arguments. For example:

8

```
package {
import flash.display.*;
        public class gday extends MovieClip {

                public function gday() {
                        trace('Add two numbers');
                        trace(addNumbers(3,4));
                }
                function addNumbers(a:Number, b:Number):Number{
                        return (a+b);
                }

        }
}
```

Notice that when you call the addNumbers function, you include the two numbers to be added within the parentheses. In the actual addNumbers function definition, notice that there are two variable declarations—one for a and one for b, both of which are typed as Number. Also note the keyword return. This sends the answer back to where it was initially called. This is why it is crucial to data-type your function as Number. If there were no value to return, then the function would be a void type.

Now that you have a basic understanding of the components of ActionScript 3, we are going to do some really cool things with it!

If I could turn back time: Dates, times, and ActionScript 3.0

In ActionScript 3.0, dates and times are important information types, as Flash CS4 applications often rely on them to function correctly. For example, you might want to place some tracking code in your application that records for you the length of time and date of visits, or you might want to build a countdown timer to a date important to your website. There are many reasons why understanding dates and times in ActionScript 3.0 is beneficial to Flash developers.

Date and time basics

As noted previously, date and time are very common kinds of information used in Flash CS4 applications. The Date class displays the way that ActionScript 3.0 represents dates and times. ActionScript 3.0 defines every object by a **class**. Think of a class as a template for a kind of object, which you define by using the new operator in the code. Objects in turn are basic elements that describe data and its operations. In this exercise, we are going to define a Date class. Once you understand how to display dates and times, you'll be able to obtain the current system date and time from end users' computers and use that information to manipulate it. Later in this chapter, you will see the effects of this when we create a countdown timer.

Controlling time

This is the section where you get to be the person who controls time! We are going to use ActionScript 3.0 to create a countdown timer to our hypothetical store's once-a-year sale.

1. Open a new Flash File (ActionScript 3.0) document in Flash CS4 and set its dimensions to 200×100 pixels in the Modify section of the Properties Inspector.

To begin with, we need to create text fields that will display the time left until our big sale begins in days, hours, minutes, and seconds. Let's do that now.

2. Click the Text tool to select it, and draw a text field on the stage, as shown in Figure 8-18.

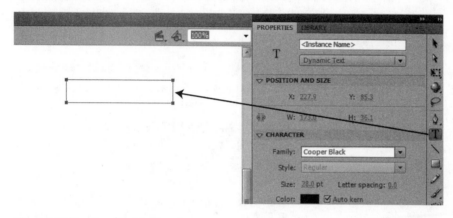

Figure 8-18. Drawing a text field on the stage

3. Convert the text field to a dynamic text field in the Properties Inspector. Right-align the text by clicking the Right Align button in the Paragraph section on the Properties Inspector.

> **Dynamic text fields** *are text fields that display text that automatically updates, such as RSS feeds, stock quotes, or countdown timers.*

We're now going to add placeholder numbers to the text field for the days, hours, minutes, and seconds. This will be where the time counts down until it is time for the sale. Since there are 365 days in a year, we will give the timer a days placeholder of three digits each. As hours, minutes, and seconds can all be expressed in two digits, we'll give these placeholders only two characters.

4. Double-click the text field on the stage to allow you to edit it, and type in the following, as shown in Figure 8-19:

000:00:00:00

As it doesn't look very impactful, let's edit the font.

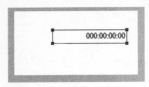

Figure 8-19. The baby countdown timer about to be functional

Figure 8-20. Designing your countdown timer

Figure 8-21. The template for your countdown timer

5. Choose stark bold Cooper Black font at 30 points, as shown in Figure 8-20.

Now we need to give our viewers a context for the countdown timer. It's pointless to put anything on your site that doesn't give users information or a reason to come back.

6. Create separate static text fields for the following: days, hours, minutes, and seconds, and the phrase "Until our BIG SALE!" Position them intuitively, as shown in Figure 8-21.

Now that we have our template set up, it's time to get serious about controlling time. The first thing we need to do is give our dynamic text field an instance name. **Instance names** allow you to refer to your objects in ActionScript, which enables you to manipulate them. In this case, we are giving our dynamic text field an instance name that we can refer to in our ActionScript to get the numbers to count down to an end date.

7. Click the Selection Tool , and then click your dynamic text field.

8. In the Properties Inspector, give the dynamic text the instance name Countdown, as shown in Figure 8-22.

Figure 8-22. Giving your dynamic text an instance name

For your Flash CS4 animation to display correctly, you need to embed the fonts. Embedding the fonts adds to the file size of your overall animation; therefore, embedding fonts into an animation where size matters, such as banner ads, needs to be done with caution.

> *If you are worried about the weight of your animation, due to file specifications or the addition of other large elements such as photographs, you always have the option of using system fonts. **System fonts** are the basic fonts installed on a computer's operating system, and as such add little to no weight to your Flash file, as there is no need to embed them—your system will be able to display them from its memory with no embedding.*

9. Select the dynamic text element and click the Character Embedding button from the Properties Inspector.

10. Select Numerals to display the numbers that you require in the dynamic text field. However, you are not only displaying numerals, but also a punctuation mark—the colon (:). Add this into the Include these characters field, as shown in Figure 8-23.

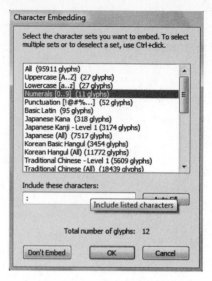

Figure 8-23. Embedding dynamic text

11. Click OK.

12. Save your Flash CS4 document as Countdown.fla.

Our countdown timer is ready for ActionScript 3.0 to be applied to it! We're going to give it an end date—in this particular example, it is the date the sale is going to start. First of all, we'll rename the existing layer.

13. Open the Countdown.fla document and rename the existing layer Timer by double-clicking the layer's title.

14. Create a new layer on the timeline and call it Actions, as shown in Figure 8-24.

Figure 8-24. Creating the Actions layer for your ActionScript

15. Select Windows ➤ Actions to open the Actions panel.

16. Enter the following code into the Script pane (as shown in Figure 8-25):

```
var endDate:Date = new Date (2010,1,1);
trace(endDate);
```

```
1  var endDate:Date = new Date(2010,1,1)
2  trace(endDate);
```

Figure 8-25. Setting the finish date for your countdown timer

You created a variable called endDate in the second line of code. This variable is where the new Date object will count down to for the sale date January 1, 2010. Notice in the code that we have entered 0 for the month, even though January is the first month. This is because months start with 0 in ActionScript. Refer to Table 8-2 for the months and ActionScript equivalents.

8

Table 8-2. Months and Their ActionScript 3.0 Equivalents

Month	ActionScript Equivalent
January	0
February	1
March	2
April	3
May	4
June	5
July	6
August	7
September	8
October	9
November	10
December	11

We have inserted a temporary trace statement into the third line of code. When the frame is played, the trace statement will send the information contained within it—in this case the date January 1, 2010—to the Output window. (Refer back to the "Loops" section of the chapter if you need a refresher on the trace statement.)

Publish your movie by selecting Control ➤ Publish Movie. You should see the Output window pop up with the information contained in your trace statement, as shown in Figure 8-26. The trace statement has been added to the code for testing purposes only.

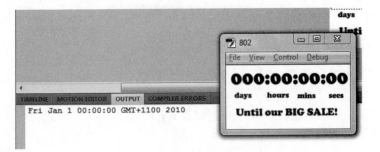

Figure 8-26. The trace statement sends information to the Output window.

The output has shown us the destination date for our countdown timer, January 1, 2010, which was described in the var endDate:Date = new Date (2010,0, 1); code.

Now that we have tested the code and we know it works, we are going to create a Timer object. Timer objects are new to Flash CS4, and they exist solely to assist you in creating time-based applications. The function of the Timer object that we are about to create is to update the countdown time every second.

1. Type the following code into the Script pane of the countdown.fla file, as shown in Figure 8-27:

```
var endDate:Date = new Date (2010,0,30)

var countdownTimer:Timer = new Timer(1000);
countdownTimer.addEventListener(TimerEvent.TIMER, updateTime);
countdownTimer.start();

function updateTime(e:TimerEvent):void
```

The third line of code creates a Timer object and stores it within the variable countdownTimer, which is defined in milliseconds by the code newTimer(1000). We then introduce an event listener. Event listeners are often also called **event handlers**, and they are functions that are executed in Flash Player in reaction to specific events defined in ActionScript.

In this case, our event listener is listening for the portion of the TimerEvent class that we have specified as Timer, which occurs every 1000 milliseconds. As this occurs, it initiates another function, defined as the updateTime function in the line function updateTime(e:TimerEvent):void.

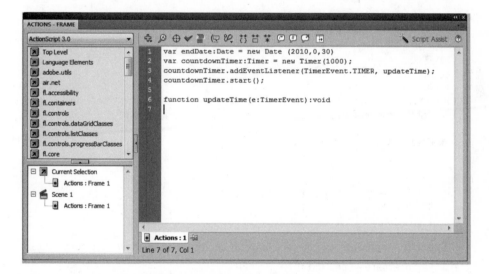

Figure 8-27. Adding the countdown timer object via ActionScript

We're now going to compare the current date and time with our target date, which is essentially a basic mathematical equation.

2. Add the following code under the existing last line of code:

```
{
var now:Date=new Date ();
var timeLeft =endDate.getTime() - now.getTime();
trace(timeLeft);
}
```

3. Test your movie again.

What happens? Though the countdown timer isn't yet working on the front end, we can see something happening on the back end. The Output window once again pops up, and it changes every second, as shown in Figure 8-28. It is displaying the total milliseconds until the sale date is reached.

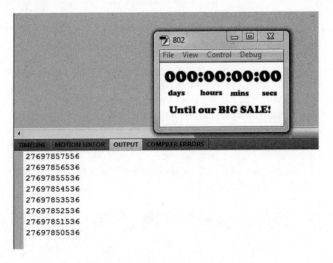

Figure 8-28. The Output window updates every second.

But it's not very intuitive to countdown in milliseconds, is it? In the next step, we are going to transform those milliseconds into days, hours, minutes, and seconds.

4. Delete the following code from your script:

```
{
var now:Date=new Date ();
var timeLeft =endDate.getTime() - now.getTime();
trace(timeLeft);
}
```

5. Add the following code at the end of the ActionScript, as shown in Figure 8-29:

```
var now:date = new Date();
var timeLeft:Number = endDate.getTime() - now.getTime();
var seconds:Number = Math.floor (timeleft / 1000);
var minutes:number = Math.floor(seconds / 60);
var hours:Number = Math.floor (minutes / 60);
var days:Number = Math.floor (hours/ 24);

seconds %= 60;
minutes %= 60;
hours %= 24;
```

```
var sec:String = seconds.toString();
var min:String = minutes.toString();
var hrs:String = hours.toString();
var d:String = days.toString();

if (Sec.length < 2){
sec = "0" + sec;
}
if (min.length <2){
min = "0" + min;
}
if (hrs.length < 2){
hrs = "0" + hrs;
}
var time:String = d + ":" + min + ":" + sec;
Countdown.text = time;
}
```

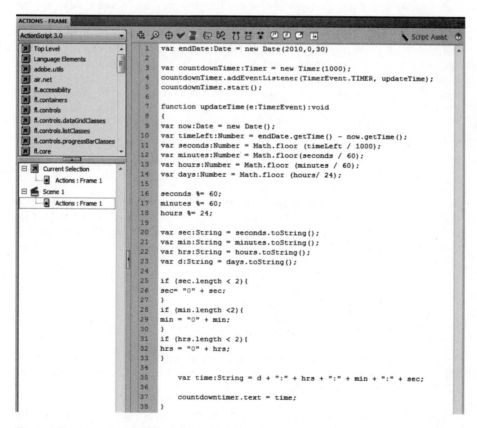

Figure 8-29. Completing the code for the countdown timer

Examine the code that you have just added to your ActionScript panel. Doesn't it seem like a familiar, everyday mathematical equation? If it seems familiar, that is because it is breaking down the time that is left into sections of time that we are more familiar with (i.e., day, hours, minutes, and seconds).

The following code creates variables that stores the end date and the time left in total seconds, minutes, and hours until January 1, 2010:

```
var now:date = new Date();
var timeLeft:Number = endDate.getTime() - now.getTime();
var seconds:Number = Math.floor (timeleft / 1000);
var minutes:number = Math.floor(seconds / 60);
var hours:Number = Math.floor (minutes / 60);
var days:Number = Math.floor (hours/ 24);
```

However, this is not exactly what we want to display. We want to display the time until the sale as it applies to the current hour.

That is, we want the hours displayed as 23 and under, as there are 24 hours in a day, and the 24th hour should be displayed as 0. Likewise, we want the minutes displayed as 59 and under, with the 60th minute displayed as 0, since there are 60 minutes in an hour. And of course we want the seconds to be displayed the same way as the minutes. Applying this logic will ensure that days, hours, minutes, and seconds will be displayed as per our text fields: 000:00:00:00. For example, if there were 100 days, 11 hours, 12 minutes, and 25 seconds left until our destination date, it would be displayed on our timer as 100:11:12:25.

Enabling this display of time is accomplished by the following piece of code:

```
seconds %= 60;
minutes %= 60;
hours %= 24;
```

Essentially, this code takes the total of the remaining time left and divides it by each denominator of time to calculate the days, hours, minutes, and seconds left. Now that we have calculated the time remaining in terms that we can immediately understand, the following code converts these numbers into strings that will be displayed in our dynamic countdown:

```
var sec:String = seconds.toString();
var min:String = minutes.toString();
var hrs:String = hours.toString();
var d:String = days.toString();
```

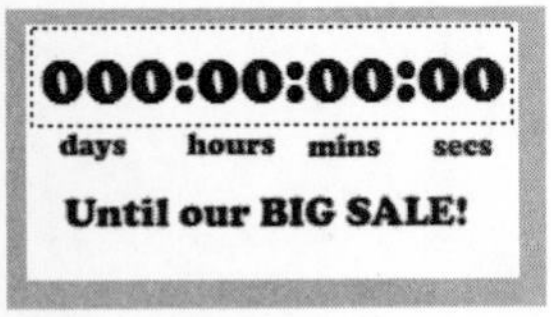

000:00:00:00
days   hours   mins   secs
Until our BIG SALE!

Figure 8-30. The number of digits defined for each time unit

Finally, we define the number of digits we want to display for each unit of time. Remember that when we created our countdown timer, we displayed on the stage the fields shown in Figure 8-30.

The following code ensures that our seconds, hours, and minutes each display no more than two digits, and where the number remaining is singular (e.g., 1), the number is displayed as two digits (i.e., 01):

```
if (Sec.length < 2){
sec= "0" + sec;
}
if (min.length <2){
min = "0" + min;
}
if (hrs.length < 2){
hrs = "0" + hrs;
}
```

The code is literally telling the Flash animation that if the number of seconds, minutes, or hours is less than two digits, a 0 should be displayed in front of it.

Now that we have specified the number of digits for each time unit, we simply create a variable called time that strings the numbers together to coherently display the countdown timer:

```
var time:String = d + ":" + min + ":" + sec;
Countdown.text = time;
}
```

Your countdown timer is almost complete! Test your movie by selecting Control ➤ Test Movie.

For the final step, we'll just tidy up the code so that it doesn't flash 000:00:00:00 before the timer kicks in. The original static information, 000:00:00:00, was placed there to ensure that the spacing was correct and that the countdown timer fit into the space that we assigned it at the beginning of the exercise.

6. Double-click the dynamic text to select it and delete it, as shown in Figure 8-31.

Your timer now counts down to January 1, 2010! Of course, you can easily tailor this timer to count down to your own special date by changing the date value in the first line of code:

```
var endDate:Date = new Date (2010,0,30)
```

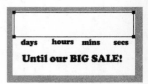

Figure 8-31. Deleting the placeholder text

ActionScript 3.0 and XML

You can harness the power of ActionScript 3.0 and XML to create dynamic Flash CS4 sites and applications. **XML** stands for **Extensible Markup Language**, and it's a common way of sharing information over the World Wide Web. Its main function is to store data, and this is reflected in your XML document.

Using XML in combination with Flash CS4 allows you to quickly and easily change the content of a Flash application without having to modify the FLA file. Consider the following example:

```
<genewithenvy>
        <product> Cute and fun genetically modified pets </product>
        <emailaddress> genie@genewithenvy.com </emailaddress>
        <telephonenumber> 555 1234 </telephonenumber>
</genewithenvy>
```

This example demonstrates markup and text within an XML document, albeit a very simple one. There are two different kinds of information in it: **tags**, which are <genewithenvy>, <product>, <email address>, and <telephone number>; and **elements**, which include all of the information that occurs within the markup tags. XML documents combine tags and text into a single file. Tags declare the start and end of elements, which are the logical units of information within your XML document.

We are now going to create a Flash CS4 application that pulls this information into the Output window using the trace command. Ensure that you have downloaded the chapter8.xml document from the source files of this book.

1. Open a new blank document in Flash CS4.

2. Save the Flash document as chapter8.fla in the same directory that you have saved the downloaded chapter8.xml file, as shown in Figure 8-32.

Name	Date modified	Type	Size
chapter8	16/03/2009 9:31 PM	Flash Document	32 KB
chapter8	16/03/2009 9:31 PM	XML Document	1 KB

Figure 8-32. The XML file must be saved in the same directory as your FLA file.

3. Open the Actions panel by selecting Window ➤ Actions.

4. Type the following code on frame 1 of layer 1 of chapter8.fla:

```
var myXML:XML;
var myLoader:URLLoader = new URLLoader();
```

The first line of code creates a variable to hold the instance of the XML class. The second line of code creates an instance of a URLLoader class, which will load the XML file into the Flash CS4 document.

5. Type the following code under the first two lines of code:

```
myLoader.load(new URLRequest("chapter8.xml"));
```

The third line of code calls the appropriate XML file—in this case chapter8.xml—into the Flash CS4 file.

Now we need to create an event listener, which will ensure that the XML file is processed correctly. As noted in previous exercises, an event listener is a function that is executed in Flash Player in reaction to specific ActionScript events. The event listener is attached to the URLLoader class instance in this case.

6. Type the following code under the existing three lines of code:

```
myLoader.addEventListener(Event.COMPLETE, processXML);
```

We're almost done! In the previous line of code, the event listener also serves to trigger the function processXML after the loading of the chapter8.xml file has completed. The next lines of code will assign the chapter8.xml file's contents as the XML data of our XML variable.

7. Now type the remaining lines of code under the existing code in the Actions panel, as shown in Figure 8-33.

```
function processXML(e:Event):void {
myXML = new XML(e.target.data);
trace(myXML.*);
}
```

Remember the trace function from previously in this chapter. In this case, the trace function will cause the information in the chapter8.xml file to be displayed in the Output window.

```
1   var myMXL:XML;
2   var myLoader:URLLoader = new URLLoader();
3   myLoader.load(new URLRequest("chapter8.xml"));
4   myLoader.addEventListener(Event.COMPLETE, processXML);
5   function processXML(e:Event):void {
6   myMXL = new XML(e.target.data);
7   trace(myMXL.*);
8   }
9
```

Figure 8-33. The ActionScript 3.0 code to call the XML file

8. Save your chapter8.fla file and publish it.

The information should be displayed in the Output window, as shown in Figure 8-34.

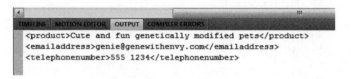

```
TIMELINE  MOTION EDITOR  OUTPUT  COMPILER ERRORS
<product>Cute and fun genetically modified pets</product>
<emailaddress>genie@genewithenvy.com</emailaddress>
<telephonenumber>555 1234</telephonenumber>
```

Figure 8-34. The Output window displays the information in the XML file.

If you were to change details such as the telephone number or the e-mail address in the XML file, when you published the Flash document, you would see these details change.

This is a very brief demonstration of how easy it is to update Flash CS4 documents using XML files. Basically, as you have seen, there are three steps:

1. Create a variable to hold the instance of the XML class.

2. Create the URLLoader class instance that loads the XML file.

3. Communicate the XML file's content to the XML instance variable when the file has completed loading.

This is but a very basic example of what you can accomplish when you combine XML and Flash CS4. Immediately, you can see how easy it is to update details from an external XML file. In Chapter 9, we'll take this exercise one step further when we use this powerful tool to build a 3D carousel that calls the information from an external source using XML.

ActionScript 3.0 and buttons

Buttons are ubiquitous in web design. They are a classic and widely recognized call to action in websites, banners, widgets, and animations. We use them to control videos, to submit information via forms, to trigger interaction, and for countless other uses.

Learning how to implement buttons is crucial in creating engaging interactive design. The simplest ActionScript 3.0 buttons need two things in order to behave correctly: an event listener and a function to reciprocate calls made by said event. Buttons are used in many instances in Flash animations, from calls to action in advertising banners, to buttons in forms.

This section will give you a brief understanding of event listeners on buttons.

Understanding mouse events

In the following exercise, you are going to learn how to apply ActionScript 3.0 to a button.

1. Open exercise file 801.fla in Flash CS4.

You will be greeted with a gray square. Double-click it to see how it expands to the four-state timeline that is common to all buttons, as shown in Figure 8-35.

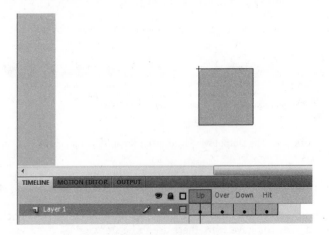

Figure 8-35. The button's four-state timeline

2. Return to the main stage by clicking the Scene 1 button at the top-left corner of the stage.

*Buttons are four-frame movies clips. Each frame has a specific function. The **Up** state reflects the button when it has no interaction applied to it (i.e., the mouse is neither hovering over it nor clicking it). The **Over** state defines how the button will appear on the stage when the mouse cursor hovers over it. The **Down** state defines the button's appearance as it is being clicked, and the **Hit** state defines the area of the button that responds to the mouse click.*

We are going to give the button an instance name, which will allow us to refer to the button within the ActionScript.

3. Click the button.

4. Give the button the instance name of myBut in the Properties Inspector, as shown in Figure 8-36.

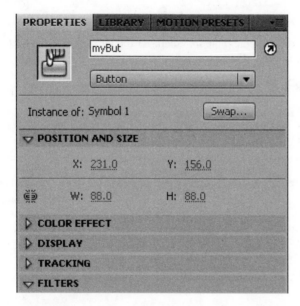

Figure 8-36. Assigning an instance name to your button

We're now going to create some ActionScript that will make the button functional.

5. Create a new layer on the timeline and call it Actions, as shown in Figure 8-37.

Figure 8-37. Creating an Actions layer on the timeline

6. Select Window ➤ Actions to open the Actions panel, and then click the first frame in the Actions layer on the timeline.

247

7. Enter the following code into the Actions panel, as shown in Figure 8-38:

```
myBut.addEventListener(MouseEvent.CLICK, myClickFunction);
```

Figure 8-38. Adding an event listener to your button

This code tells the button labeled myBut to wait and listen for a mouse click. If the button is clicked, then the function myClickFunction is called.

8. Enter the following code, as shown in Figure 8-39:

```
function myClickFunction(event:MouseEvent):void {
        trace("click");
}
```

This is a standard function definition. Whenever the mouse clicks the button, the function traces the word click to the Output window.

```
1  myBut.addEventListener(MouseEvent.CLICK, myClickFunction);
2
3  function myClickFunction(event:MouseEvent):void {
4      trace("click");
5  }
6
7
```

Figure 8-39. The word click is traced whenever the mouse clicks the button.

Take a minute to test your file by selecting Control ➤ Test Movie. You will see that whenever you click the button in the published SWF, the word click appears in the Output window, as shown in Figure 8-40. As you have seen throughout this chapter, using the trace command is invaluable when testing your ActionScript.

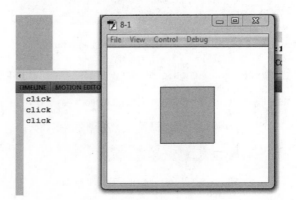

Figure 8-40. Tracing the click command

The next line of code will create a MouseEvent listener. This event listener is used to detect all mouse behaviors, as listed following:

- MouseEvent.CLICK detects when a button is being clicked.
- MouseEvent.MOUSE_OUT detects when the mouse has moved from hovering above the button to hovering off the button.
- MouseEvent.MOUSE_OVER detects when the mouse rolls over the button.

In the case of the following code, we are going to create a MouseEvent.MOUSE_OUT event listener.

9. Add the following code to your ActionScript, as shown in Figure 8-41:

```
myBut.addEventListener(MouseEvent.MOUSE_OUT, myClickOut);
```

```
1   myBut.addEventListener(MouseEvent.CLICK, myClickFunction);
2
3   function myClickFunction(event:MouseEvent):void {
4       trace("click");
5   }
6
7
8   myBut.addEventListener(MouseEvent.MOUSE_OUT, myClickOut);
9
10
11
12
```

Figure 8-41. Adding the MouseEvent listener to your ActionScript

Again, this code tells Flash that it needs to perform an action when the mouse rolls outside of the button's perimeter. The action is to perform the function myClickOut.

We're now going to see how the function myClickOut works by inserting a trace.

10. Enter the following code:

```
function myClickOut(event:MouseEvent):void {
        trace("Out");
}
```

The function myClickOut is called every time the mouse passes outside the button. Note that it is a void function, as it does not return a value. Now test the movie. Notice that when you click the button, the output reads click, and when you roll off the button, the output reads out.

This is a simplistic representation of how you can create interactions using MouseEvent listeners. We will use this again in the final exercise of this chapter, where we'll create a contact form to harness the power of buttons, dynamic text fields, ActionScript, and PHP code.

8

Text fields and ActionScript

Using ActionScript with dynamic text fields gives you the power to change text in your Flash CS4 movies on the fly. Dynamic text fields give you a way of displaying information and messages that can change, such as the time and date, navigation, scoring, measurements, and even greeting messages. Using a dynamic text field is very easy, as you saw in the countdown timer exercise previously in this chapter. You simply need to ensure that your text field is a dynamic text field and that you have assigned it an instance name.

You will now create a dynamic text field that uses the button from the last exercise to display information about the mouse. Continue along from the last exercise, or load up the exercise file 8-2.fla.

1. Using the Text tool **T** on the Tools panel, drag out a field, as shown in Figure 8-42.

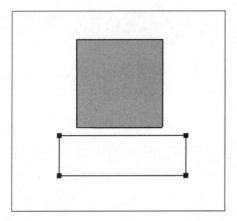

Figure 8-42. Placing a text field on the stage under the button

2. Assign the text field an instance name of myTextField in the Properties Inspector. Also ensure that the text field is set to Dynamic Text, as shown in Figure 8-43.

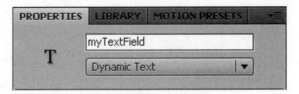

Figure 8-43. Assigning an instance name and defining the kind of text field in the Properties Inspector

3. Open the Actions panel, and add the following text field code under the first trace statement, as shown in Figure 8-44:

```
myTextField.text = "click";
```

```
1   myBut.addEventListener(MouseEvent.CLICK, myClickFunction);
2
3   function myClickFunction(event:MouseEvent):void {
4       trace("click");
5       myTextField.text = "click";
6   }
7
8
9   myBut.addEventListener(MouseEvent.MOUSE_OUT, myClickOut);
10
11  function myClickOut(event:MouseEvent):void {
12      trace("out");
13
14  }
```

Figure 8-44. Adding text field code to your ActionScript

4. Now add the following code under the second trace statement, as shown in Figure 8-45:

```
myTextField.text = "out";
```

```
1   myBut.addEventListener(MouseEvent.CLICK, myClickFunction);
2
3   function myClickFunction(event:MouseEvent):void {
4       trace("click");
5       myTextField.text = "click";
6   }
7
8
9   myBut.addEventListener(MouseEvent.MOUSE_OUT, myClickOut);
10
11  function myClickOut(event:MouseEvent):void {
12      trace("out");
13      myTextField.text = "out";
14  }
15
```

Figure 8-45. Inserting the output to appear on the stage

Let's test the movie now. Mouse over the button and you will see the output out appear in the dynamic text field on the stage. Click the button and you will see the output click appear in the text field.

These exercises might seem basic, but they are designed to give you an idea of the power of buttons and text fields. In the following exercise, the final exercise of this chapter, we are going to create a contact form, harnessing the power of PHP and Flash CS4.

Sending e-mail with fields and buttons

This next section is a concise guide to sending variables to a server-side script. Server-side scripting implements processes on a web server to create dynamic web pages. In this case, the user will be sending an e-mail address entered from a text field in a SWF document.

The information entered into the form will then be e-mailed to your e-mail address. This is typical of the way that contact forms function. It consists of a Flash SWF front end and a PHP script back end. The Flash side passes the e-mail address to the back end. The back end then takes the e-mail address and processes it through a PHP script, which composes the e-mail address as the content in an e-mail sent to you. You don't have to use PHP—you could use any server-side language, such as ASP or JSP. We have chosen to use PHP due to its popularity in the market and the fact that it is open source—it doesn't cost anything to use. The exercise requires an environment that uses PHP 4 or later to work correctly, so make sure that your hosting platform is running PHP.

Ensure that you have downloaded the exercise files from the friends of ED website to complete this exercise.

1. Begin the e-mail contact form by opening 802.fla. You will see a brown strip with some words, a light strip, and a Send button appear on the stage.

2. Create a new layer on top of these background elements and call it inputText.

3. With the inputText layer highlighted, select the Text tool and drag out a text field the length of the rounded rectangle adjacent to the words Enter Your Email, as shown in Figure 8-46.

Figure 8-46. Creating a text field on the stage

We're now going to ensure that the text that the user inputs into the text field will sit nicely upon the stage.

4. With the text field on the stage selected, give it an instance name of emailAddress in the Properties Inspector and ensure that it is assigned the type Input Text. Change the Character Family to Arial, assign it a size of 12 points, and make the font color a dark brown. Use the Eyedropper tool to match the text color to that of the dark brown in the background. See Figure 8-47 for a guide to the settings.

5. Save your document, as we will be using it in the next exercise.

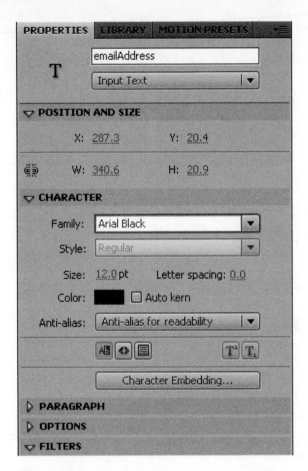

Figure 8-47. Assigning the font properties in the Properties Inspector

Now that we have set up the input field where the user will enter their e-mail address, we will enable the button to send the user-entered information to the PHP script on your server, which will send the information directly to your e-mail address.

6. Click the Send button on the stage (located next to the text field you have just created).

7. Give the Send button an instance name of sendButton.

The groundwork has now been done, and all that remains is to apply the ActionScript to the button.

8. Create a new layer and call it Actions.

9. Open the Actions panel by selecting Window ➤ Actions, and click the first frame of the Actions layer on the timeline.

10. You want to catch whenever a user clicks the Send button, so add an event listener to your button by entering the following code, as shown in Figure 8-48:

```
sendButton.addEventListener(MouseEvent.CLICK, sendEmailAddress);
```

```
1   sendButton.addEventListener(MouseEvent.CLICK, sendEmailAddress);
2
3
4
5
6
```

Figure 8-48. Adding an event listener to the ActionScript

This code attaches a mouse click event listener to the sendButton instance on the stage. When a click is performed, the sendEmailAddress function is called. Now you need to add the sendEmailAddress function.

11. Enter the following code to the Actions panel, as shown in Figure 8-49:

```
function sendEmailAddress(event:MouseEvent):void {
```

```
1   sendButton.addEventListener(MouseEvent.CLICK, sendEmailAddress);
2
3   function sendEmailAddress(event:MouseEvent):void {
4
5
6
```

Figure 8-49. Adding the sendEmailAddress function to your ActionScript

This line defines the function as a void MouseEvent function. All code inside this function is carried out whenever a user clicks the button.

12. The next line is the workhorse of the contact form. Enter the following, as shown in Figure 8-50:

```
sendToURL(new URLRequest
    ("http://www.myWebSite.com/email.PHP?email=" + emailAddress.text));
```

```
1   sendButton.addEventListener(MouseEvent.CLICK, sendEmailAddress);
2
3   function sendEmailAddress(event:MouseEvent):void {
4       sendToURL(new URLRequest("http://www.myWebSite.com/email.php?email=" + emailAddress.text));
5
6
```

Figure 8-50. Adding the URLRequest code to your ActionScript

> *This statement must be customized with your own URL. Here, we have used the very real-sounding www.myWebSite.com, but you will need to use your own for this exercise to work. If you are unsure about hosting, ask your Internet provider for more details about web hosting packages, and make sure they support PHP 4 or later.*

This statement utilizes the sendToURL command. This is the command you use to move data from ActionScript to your server. The data used in this example comes from a form where the user enters their e-mail address and clicks the Send button. You can also use this command to send data from any ActionScript variable, such as a high score in a game. The sendToURL command requires that you encode your variables with URL formatting. That means that you use the new URLRequest("") command to point to the server script file. In this case, the email.PHP script is sitting in the root of the myWebSite directory. Use the quotation mark to signify you are about to pass variables. In this case, the variable name is email, and you are making it equal to whatever has been entered in the input text field. If you wanted to pass the variable name instead of email, the line of code would read as follows:

```
sendToURL(new URLRequest
         ("http://www.myWebSite.com/email.PHP?name=" + name.text));
```

Obviously you would need to create another input text field to cater for the extra name variable. If you wanted to pass both variables, you would use the ampersand (&) to signify additional variables. As an illustration of this principle, to pass both the email and name variables, the preceding line would read

```
sendToURL(new URLRequest
                    ("http://www.myWebSite.com/email.PHP?name="
                     + name.text));
```

We are going to add a line of code that will clear the field once the information has been sent to the server.

13. Add the following code so that the text field becomes cleared after you have clicked the Send button, as shown in Figure 8-51:

```
emailAddress.text = "";
}
```

```
1  sendButton.addEventListener(MouseEvent.CLICK, sendEmailAddress);
2
3  function sendEmailAddress(event:MouseEvent):void {
4      sendToURL(new URLRequest("http://www.myWebSite.com/email.php?email=" + emailAddress.text));
5      emailAddress.text = "";
6  }
```

Figure 8-51. Adding the code that will clear the information from the input text once it has been submitted

14. Save the file as contact.fla and select Control ➤ Test Movie.

The form will appear, but if you were to enter your e-mail address and click the Send button, nothing would happen. There are two reasons for this, the first being that the sendToURL command is trying to contact an email.PHP script file that does not exist yet. Secondly, all the files need to be located on your server (usually a different computer from the one you are using). Once you are finished writing the PHP script, you should use an FTP client, such as Filezilla, to upload the SWF and PHP files to your server.

With the Flash front end complete, now we can jump into PHP mode! We will do this in the following exercise.

1. Open a simple text editor; on Windows you can use Notepad, and on the Mac you can use TextEdit.

2. Enter the following PHP script:

```
<?PHP
$address = $_REQUEST['email'];
mail("myEmailAddress@somewhere.com", $address ,$address);
?>
```

This PHP script uses the command $_REQUEST to fetch the variable email that is being passed from the Flash movie. The string email is then stored in the PHP variable $address. The mail command is then used to create and send an e-mail to myEmailAddress@somewhere.com. The e-mail address is used as the subject line and body copy of the e-mail that is delivered to your inbox.

As a note for future reference, the PHP mail command uses the following syntax:

```
Mail(Email address to be sent to,
Email subject headline, Email message copy, Headers);
```

In the preceding case, an e-mail is being sent to myEmailAddress@somewhere.com. Customize this e-mail address to suit where you would like the e-mails to be sent.

On receiving the e-mail, you will find that the e-mail subject headline will be the string that was entered into the Flash form. The same string will also occupy the content of the e-mail. Given multiple fields, the possibilities of the e-mail content are endless. To learn more about PHP, visit www.PHP.net/ or www.w3schools.com/.

We are now going to complete our PHP.

3. Save the file as email.PHP. Ensure that you actually type the .PHP suffix to ensure that the text editor saves the file as a PHP file, not as a text file. Notice that this is the same name used in the preceding ActionScript.

4. Upload the email.PHP and contact.swf files to your own web server. The preceding ActionScript code used www.myWebSite.com as the address of the web host directory, so you would use an FTP client to upload the two files to the root directory of www.myWebSite.com. If you wanted the contact form to appear on http://redtomatoes.com/webpage/contacts, you would have to upload the files to that location.

Now open your browser and point it to www.myWebSite.com/contact.swf. Enter an e-mail address in the text field and click Send. You may have to clear your cache or refresh your browser. Check your e-mail account. Within seconds, depending on the speed of your server, you will see an e-mail filled with all the details sent via your Flash form.

This has been a brief overview of combining Flash CS4 and PHP; however, there is much more that these tools working together can accomplish. If you are interested in finding out more about PHP, we recommend reading *PHP Object-Oriented Solutions*, by David Powers (friends of ED, 2008).

Summary

In this chapter you learned the basics of ActionScript 3.0, its intricacies and functions, and how it works. You built a contact form and a countdown timer in ActionScript 3.0, and you learned how to apply ActionScript 3.0 in various situations. ActionScript is a powerful but involved tool. It requires detailed attention to every character on every string to ensure that it works correctly.

The upcoming chapters will show you how potent ActionScript is. In Chapter 9 you will be using ActionScript to build a carousel gallery, and in Chapter 10 you will be using it to create a banner with a mute button.

8

CHAPTER 9
USING 3D SPACE IN FLASH CS4

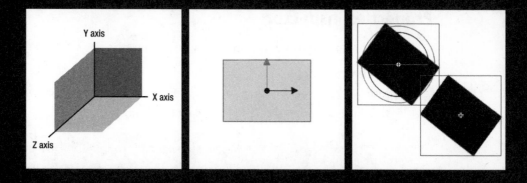

So far this entire book has been about using Flash CS4 to create traditional Flash movies. You are now going to learn about creating 3D animations using Flash CS4's 3D tools. Up until now, you have mostly moved objects across the x- and y-axes and along the timeline. Enter the z-axis. 3D graphics occur on the z-axis, which journeys deep into the display and projects out of the display.

In Flash CS4 there are two ways to access the z-axis. The first, and most intuitive, is to use the 3D tool on the toolbar. The 3D tool provides you with a way to manipulate 2D movie clips in a 3D space. This creates the illusion of a complex 3D engine. You can create something like a spinning image carousel using just the 3D tool, which is exactly what we'll do a little later in the chapter. The second way to do real 3D in Flash is to use a real 3D engine. A 3D engine makes use of ActionScript libraries that hide the advanced mathematical calculations involved in creating purely 3D scenes. Most of the movement and interaction is created programmatically. This means that you write ActionScript to set up complex scenes, and you import meshes, textures, rigs, and animations. It also means that you can control lighting and materials in real time. In the final section of this chapter, we will briefly look at what 3D engines offer your Flash CS4 animations.

Moving stuff in 3D space

Flash CS4 contains two new tools that allow you to manipulate objects in 3D space: the 3D Translation tool, which moves an object in 3D space, and the 3D Rotation tool, which rotates an object in 3D space. They're found on the Tools panel, as shown in Figure 9-1.

Figure 9-1. The 3D Translation tool enables you to move objects in 3D space.

> If you cannot see the 3D Translation tool, simply click and hold the 3D Rotation tool and select the 3D Translation tool from the menu that appears.

Manipulating an object in 3D space using the Properties Inspector

In the following exercise we will explore how to manipulate an object in 3D space.

1. Open a new document in Flash CS4.
2. Draw a black rectangle, sans stroke, on the stage (as shown in Figure 9-2).
3. Right-click on the rectangle and convert it to a movie clip symbol.

> To rotate your objects in 3D space you must first convert them to movie clip symbols.

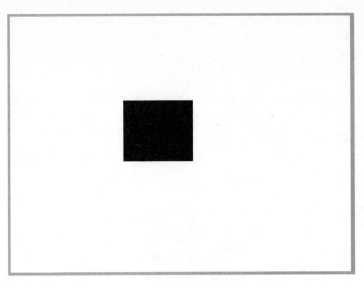

Figure 9-2. Drawing an object on the stage in preparation for moving it in 3D space

4. With the Selection tool, click on the rectangle on the stage. You can now move the black rectangle in 3D space. First we will move the rectangle along axes you're already familiar with: the x- and y-axis.

5. Change the x value in the Properties Inspector to 100. You will see the rectangle slide along the x-axis to the left. Experiment with different values along the x-axis.

6. Change the y value in the Properties Inspector to 100. You will see the rectangle slide upward along the y-axis. Experiment with different y-axis values.

Now let's manipulate the z-axis and start to move the object in 3D. To manipulate the z-axis in the Properties Inspector you will need to open the 3D Position and View section, as shown in Figure 9-3.

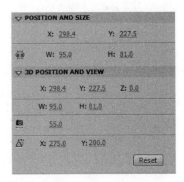

Figure 9-3. 3D Position and View is accessed by the drop-down in the Properties Inspector.

7. Change the z value in the Properties Inspector to 1000. What happens? A-ha! The rectangle moves away from you on the z-axis!

8. Change the z value in the Properties Inspector to 1. You will now see the rectangle move forward, toward you, on the z-axis.

We've now moved the objects along the three axes. Those familiar with Flash will be familiar with moving objects along the x-axis and y-axis, but the z-axis adds another element to your animation. Zero is the value at which items are placed on the stage by default. Assigning a negative value to an object will move the object closer to you. Assigning a positive value to the object will move it farther away from you. This is demonstrated in Figure 9-4.

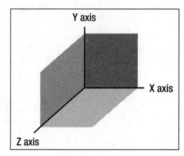

Figure 9-4. The z-axis moves objects in 3D space.

Moving objects in 3D space using the 3D Translation tool

The previous exercise demonstrated moving the object in 3D space using the Properties Inspector. I recommend manipulating objects this way because it allows you a finer control and the ability to easily position the object exactly where you want it to be. You can also move objects in 3D space using the 3D Translation tool. Here's how.

1. Open a new blank document in Flash CS4.

2. Draw another rectangle on the stage. Make this one a light color, like yellow, as shown in Figure 9-5.

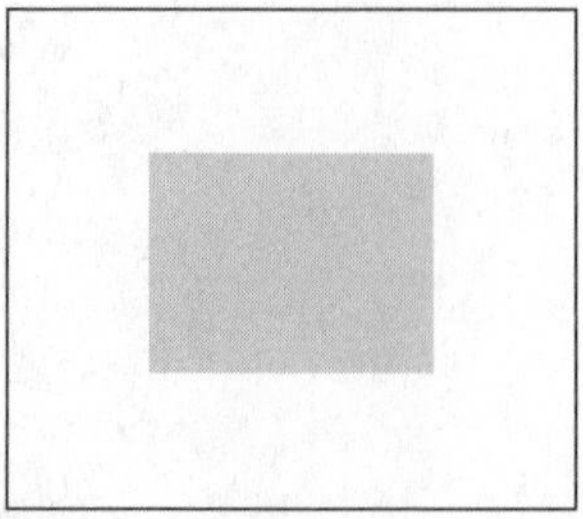

Figure 9-5. Draw a light-colored rectangle on the stage.

3. Convert the rectangle to a movie clip symbol by right-clicking it and selecting Convert to Symbol from the context menu.

4. Name your symbol and select Movie Clip from the Type drop-down.

5. Click on the 3D Translation tool in the Tools panel.

Remember, the 3D Translation tool exists in the same space as the 3D Rotation tool 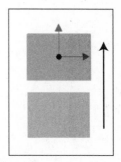.

When you click on the 3D Translation tool, the movie clip on the stage is overlaid by the 3D axis. The vertical axis is y, the horizontal is x, and the black dot in the middle of the movie clip is z, as shown in Figure 9-6.

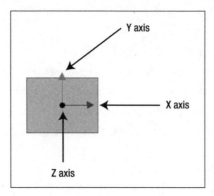

Figure 9-6. The 3D axis represented by the 3D Translation tool

We will now continue the exercise and see how you can move the object using these axes on the stage. First we will move along the x-axis.

6. With the 3D Translation tool, click on the x-axis and drag it to the right, as shown in Figure 9-7.

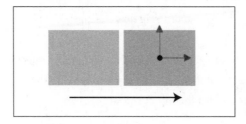

Figure 9-7. Moving the rectangle along the x-axis

You will notice that when you click on the x-axis on the object on the stage, the y-axis and x-axis are grayed out and you can move the object along only the chosen axis. Try it now on the y-axis.

7. With the 3D Translation tool still selected, click on the y-axis, and drag it up as shown in Figure 9-8.

Another thing to note is that as you move the movie clip on the stage, the coordinates are changed in the 3D Position and View section in the Properties Inspector just as if you had manually manipulated them as we did in the previous exercise. Moving along the x- and y-axis is pretty commonplace; we are used to moving objects in this 2D space. We'll now move the movie clip along the z-axis using the 3D overlay on the stage.

Figure 9-8. Moving the yellow rectangle along the y-axis

Moving the object along the z-axis using the 3D Translation tool

As we have discussed, the black dot in the middle of the object that appears when you click on the 3D Translation tool is the z-axis, and when you move objects along the z-axis you can make the object appear to move closer or farther away from the viewer. Previously we have used the 3D Position and View section in the Properties Inspector to move objects on the z-axis. We will now use the black dot to move the yellow rectangle along the z-axis.

1. Click on the movie clip on the stage to select it.
2. Click on the 3D Translation tool if it isn't already selected from the prior exercises.
3. Click on the black dot in the middle of the object on the stage.
4. Drag the mouse to the bottom on the stage.

What happens? The rectangle becomes larger, as if it has traveled toward you, as shown in Figure 9-9.

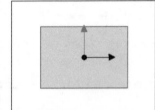

Figure 9-9. The object appears closer to you.

We'll continue the exercise to demonstrate how the z-axis can be used to make the objects move farther away from you.

5. Again click on the 3D Translation tool if it is no longer selected.
6. Click on the black dot in the middle of the object on the stage.
7. Drag the mouse toward the top of the stage.

The object will now appear to move away from you, as shown in Figure 9-10.

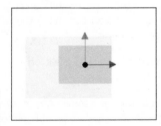

Figure 9-10. The object moves farther away.

Moving multiple objects in 3D space

We'll now investigate moving groups of objects in 3D space. With the preceding exercise completed, draw a second rectangle on the stage alongside the existing one, as shown in Figure 9-11.

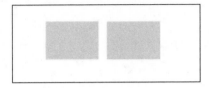

Figure 9-11. Drawing two rectangles on the stage to be manipulated in the 3D space

1. Convert the second rectangle into a movie clip symbol the same way as we did in the previous exercise.
2. With the Selection tool enabled, click first on one movie clip on the stage, and then on the other. They should both be selected.

As the first has already had the 3D Translation tool applied to it, we don't need to apply it again.

3. Experiment again with the x-, y-, and z-axes in the Properties Inspector.

You will see both the rectangles move in a group.

Rotating stuff in 3D space

Not only does Flash CS4 allow you to move objects within 3D space; it also allows you to rotate objects in 3D space using the 3D Rotation tool, as shown in Figure 9-12.

The following exercise will demonstrate how to rotate an object in Flash CS4.

1. Open a new document in Flash CS4.
2. Draw a black rectangle, sans stroke, on the stage.
3. Right-click the rectangle on the stage and select Convert to Symbol to convert the object to a movie clip.
4. Click on the 3D Rotation button on the Tools panel.

Figure 9-12. The 3D Rotation tool

What happens? Well, you will see a kind of crosshair appear on the movie clip on stage, as shown in Figure 9-13. Each line of the crosshair has a different color: the x-axis is red, the y-axis is green, the z-axis is blue, and the orange has free movement. To rotate the object in 3D space, simply experiment with manipulating it on the stage with your mouse.

To change where the rotation point is on the movie clip, simply click on it and drag it as shown in Figure 9-14.

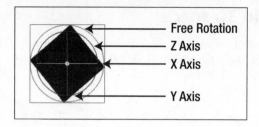

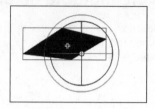

Figure 9-13. The 3D Rotation axis

Figure 9-14. Changing the position of the rotation point

Rotating groups of objects in 3D space

Rotating multiple objects in 3D space is similar to the way that we moved objects in 3D space in the previous exercise. Let's check it out now.

1. With the previous exercise open in Flash CS4, draw another rectangle on the stage, as shown in Figure 9-15.

2. Convert the new rectangle to a movie clip.

Figure 9-15. Drawing two movie clips on the stage

3. Select both the rectangles.

4. Manipulate the shapes by moving the x-, y-, and z-axes on the stage.

You will see both of the shapes rotate in 3D space, as shown in Figure 9-16.

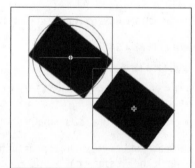

Figure 9-16. Two figures rotated in 3D space on the stage

Just as you can change the x-, y-, and z-axes using the Properties Inspector when you have the 3D Translation tool selected, you can adjust them when you have the 3D Rotation tool activated. We'll investigate this now.

Rotating an object in 3D space using the Properties Inspector

This feature is a particularly handy one, as it allows you to exert exact control over the rotation of your objects, to ensure a fine and precise animation. We'll see how easy this is.

1. Open a new document in Flash CS4.

2. Draw a light-colored rectangle on the stage.

3. Right-click and chose Convert to Symbol from the context menu. Choose Movie Clip from the Type drop-down list that appears in the Convert to Symbol dialog box.

4. Click on the 3D Rotation tool in the Tools panel to select it.

You will see the 3D Rotation tool overlay appear on the stage as before, but we are not going to be manipulating the movie clip that way this time.

5. Click on the Properties tab to reveal the Properties Inspector.

This time we are concentrating on the 3D Position and View section of the Properties Inspector, as shown in Figure 9-17.

6. Double-click on the X value and change it to –10.

As before, the movie clip on the stage will move along the x-axis. In this case, it will move to the left side of the stage. This is because negative values move the object left along the x-axis and positive values move it right. Play with different values to get a feel for the exact adjustment you can make.

We will now change the y-axis with the Properties Inspector.

7. Return the movie clip to the center of the stage.

8. Double-click on the Y value in the 3D Position and View section in the Properties Inspector and change it to –10.

You will notice that the movie clip moves to the top of the stage. On the y-axis, positive values will move your movie clip downward, while negative values on the y-axis will move your movie clip upward.

We will now change the z-axis with the Properties Inspector.

9. Double-click on the Z value in the 3D Position and View section in the Properties Inspector and change it to 400.

What happens? The movie clip moves away from you on the stage and appears smaller. We'll now make it move toward you.

10. Double-click on the Z value in the 3D Position and View section in the Properties Inspector and change it to –400.

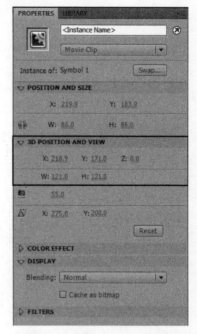

Figure 9-17. The 3D Position and View section of the Properties Inspector allows you exact control over your animations' 3D rotation.

9

The movie clip moves toward you on the stage and appears larger. On the z-axis, negative values will make your symbol move toward you, while positive values will make your symbol move away.

Creating a simple spinning logo

Now that you have learned the various ways to manipulate objects on the stage in 3D space, we will apply this to the gene-with-envy logo that you created in Chapter 4; however, be sure you have downloaded the exercise files for this chapter for best results.

1. Open the exercise file 9-01.fla.

The logo has been separated into two layers. Both the snail and the logo type have already been converted to movie clips. This is a crucial step. The 3D tool will work only on movie clips.

2. Right-click the 100th frame on the timeline and select Insert Frame on both layers, as in Figure 9-18.

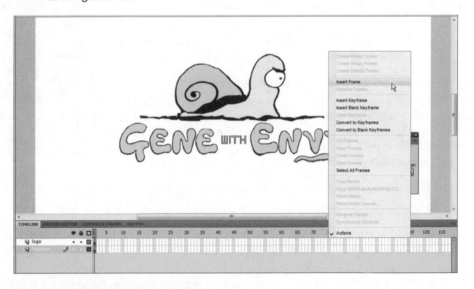

Figure 9-18. Insert 100 frames into both layers.

3. Right-click the timeline on the snail layer.

4. Create a motion tween by selecting Create Motion Tween from the context menu.

You already know that if you reposition the snail movie clip, you will create an ordinary two-dimensional transformation. This chapter is all about three dimensions, so read on to discover how you can tween in 3D.

5. Slide the playhead so that you are on the 100th frame.

6. Using the Selection tool (v), select the snail.

7. Choose the 3D Rotation tool from the toolbar.

After you select the 3D Rotation tool a crosshair guide will appear. As we saw before, the vertical red line represents the x-axis. The green horizontal line represents the y-axis. The blue circle represents the z-axis. The red circle that encloses the crosshair is the free-transform axis. If you click and drag on the red line, the x-axis, the snail will rotate horizontally. The same behavior translates to each of the other axes.

8. Starting from the left side of the crosshair, click and drag the green line from left to right.

The snail will rotate about the y-axis, with the head coming forward in a clockwise manner. Keep dragging until the snail has rotated 180° as in Figure 9-19.

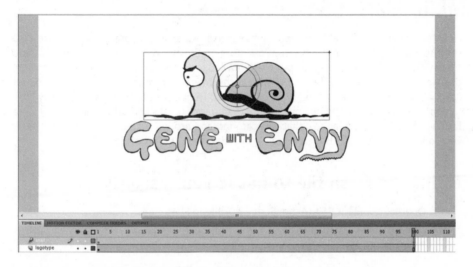

Figure 9-19. Rotating the snail 180°

As you click and drag, notice an opaque gray segment is drawn in relation to the rotation. A horizontally or vertically lined segment represents a multiple of 90°.

9. Open the Motion Editor as shown in Figure 9-20.

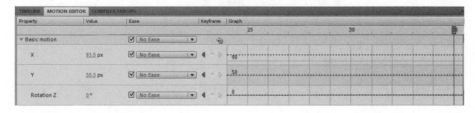

Figure 9-20. The Motion Editor

3D transforms can be tweaked in the same way as 2D transforms using the Motion Editor.

10. Find the Rotation Y entry and set it to 360°. The value should initially be 180° or close to it from our efforts with the 3D Rotation tool, so we'll double it here to make the snail spin around completely.

11. Test the movie by selecting Control ➤ Test Movie to publish the movie, and you will see the snail spin around and around. You could, of course, add more effects to the 3D animation here, such as having the logo zoom in as it spins, or rotating on more than one axis at a time. It goes without saying that you should show restraint on your final logo animation, though—less is almost certainly more here.

Creating a 3D carousel with ActionScript and XML in Flash CS4

Now that we are comfortable manipulating objects in 3D space, we are going to create a 3D carousel that will display products from our store. In Chapter 8 you learned about XML and ActionScript 3.0. We are going to put that knowledge to the test and create a 3D carousel that we are calling our "genosel," which will call the images into your Flash file via ActionScript 3.0 and XML. Our genosel, will be a virtual carousel. Think about the carousels you may have ridden on as a child. They were basically static statues of horses and other animals that were fastened to a large circular disc that spun around and around a central axis. This is exactly what our genosel will be, though with images rather than statues of horses!

Creating the Flash file to house your carousel

1. Open a new Flash CS4 (ActionScript 3.0) file in Flash CS4.

2. Open the Properties Inspector and set the stage dimensions to 600×300 in the Properties section, as shown in Figure 9-21.

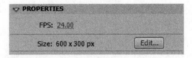

Figure 9-21. Setting the stage dimensions in the Properties section of the Properties Inspector

The file displays as a simple white stage with the dimensions 600×300. We're going to color this background to give the animation a little more depth and substance, and to suit the gene-with-envy website.

3. Click on the color tile (the default is white) in the Stage section of the Properties Inspector.

4. Type the following into the RGB values field, as shown in Figure 9-22:

#c8e500

5. Save your file as 9-02.fla.

The stage for your genosel is now set up. Next we will be creating the XML file that your ActionScript will use to call the images to the stage.

Creating the XML file

We are now going to create the XML file that will call the image into your Flash file. You are familiar with XML files from Chapter 8. This particular XML is going to specify how many images we are using in our 3D carousel, and the URL where the images are located. We have uploaded the images to one of our servers. If you were going to tailor this exercise to call your own set of images, you would simply need to replace the existing image URLs with your own.

1. Open your preferred ASCII text editor. I will be using Dreamweaver for this exercise.

2. Create the first node for the file by typing <genosel> into the second line, as shown in Figure 9-23.

```
1  <?xml version="1.0" encoding="utf-8"?>
2  <genosel>
```

Figure 9-23. Opening the XML structure

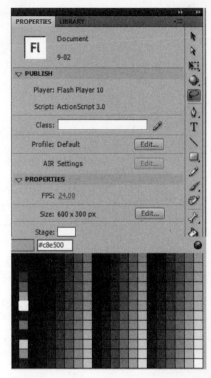

Figure 9-22. Choosing the stage color to suit your website

9

First we are going to specify the number of images that will be called into the Flash file.

3. Add the following code into your XML document under the existing code, as shown in Figure 9-24:

<number_of_images>5</number_of_images>

```
<?xml version="1.0" encoding="utf-8"?>
<genosel>
    <number_of_images>5</number_of_images>
```

Figure 9-24. Specifying the number of images in your animation

The next step specifies the URL of each of the images.

4. Add the following code to your XML document, as shown in Figure 9-25:

```
<images>

    <image>

<url>http://www.cheridankerr.com/gene/cabbage.png</url>
    </image>

    <image>

<url> http://www.cheridankerr.com/gene/tomtee.png</url>
    </image>

    <image>

<url>http://www.cheridankerr.com/gene/sqwidge.png</url>
    </image>

    <image>

<url>http://www.cheridankerr.com/gene/bug.png</url>
    </image>

    <image>

<url>http://www.cheridankerr.com/gene/blobby.png</url>
    </image>
<images>
```

```
1   <?xml version="1.0" encoding="utf-8"?>
2       <genosel>
3           <number_of_images>5</number_of_images>
4               <images>
5
6                   <image>
7                       <url>http://www.cheridankerr.com/gene/cabbage.png</url>
8                   </image>
9
10                  <image>
11                      <url> http://www.cheridankerr.com/gene/tomtee.png</url>
12                  </image>
13
14                  <image>
15                      <url>http://www.cheridankerr.com/gene/sqwidge.png</url>
16                  </image>
17
18                  <image>
19                      <url>http://www.cheridanerr.com/gene/bug.png</url>
20                  </image>
21
22                  <image>
23                      <url>http://www.cheridankerr.com/gene/blobby.png</url>
24                  </image>
25              </images>
```

Figure 9-25. Defining the image location and click-through URL in the XML file

5. Close the XML structure by adding `</genosel>` at the end of the code, as shown in Figure 9-26.

```
1   <?xml version="1.0" encoding="utf-8"?>
2       <genosel>
3           <number_of_images>5</number_of_images>
4               <images>
5
6                   <image>
7                       <url>http://www.cheridankerr.com/gene/cabbage.png</url>
8                   </image>
9
10                  <image>
11                      <url> http://www.cheridankerr.com/gene/tomtee.png</url>
12                  </image>
13
14                  <image>
15                      <url>http://www.cheridankerr.com/gene/sqwidge.png</url>
16                  </image>
17
18                  <image>
19                      <url>http://www.cheridanerr.com/gene/bug.png</url>
20                  </image>
21
22                  <image>
23                      <url>http://www.cheridankerr.com/gene/blobby.png</url>
24                  </image>
25              </images>
26      </genosel>
```

Figure 9-26. Your completed XML file

6. Save the file as genosel.xml.

> In the next section you will be calling the XML file from a server online, and we have already uploaded it to our website for you. However, if you were going to call the XML into your Flash file from your local computer, you'd be best off saving the XML file in the same directory where you are going to save your Flash file so you have to create only a relative link.

You have completed the XML document that will pull the information into your Flash CS4 file. The beauty of using XML is that it allows you to quickly change information within your Flash document without having to revise the animation or the actual Flash file structure. For example, you can easily change images by simply replacing their location URL in the XML file.

Next we will set up the variables that communicate with your created XML file.

Creating the variables to call the XML file in ActionScript 3.0

The following exercise is the first step in creating your 3D carousel. The first part of the exercise creates all of the variables that the Flash file requires to work the 3D carousel. We will then load the XML file that we created previously, which contains all of the image information that will be utilized in the 3D carousel.

The first thing we are going to do with ActionScript in this exercise is to define the size of the images that are being called into the Flash file. The dimensions are 150 pixels wide by 141 pixels high.

1. Open the previously saved 9-02.fla in Flash CS4.

2. Click on the first frame of layer 1.

3. Open the ActionScript window by pressing F9 on the keyboard or selecting Window ➤ Actions.

4. Add the following code to the first line of the ActionScript panel, as shown in Figure 9-27:

```
const IMAGE_WIDTH:uint = 150;
const IMAGE_HEIGHT:uint = 141;
```

```
1   const IMAGE_WIDTH:uint = 420;
2   const IMAGE_HEIGHT:uint = 396;
3
```

Figure 9-27. Specifying the height and width of your images in ActionScript 3.0

This code specifies the size of the image. In this case, each of our images totals 150 pixels wide by 141 pixels high. If you are customizing this animation to suit your own images, simply ensure that they are a uniform shape, and specify the different dimension in the code.

We are now going to set a focal point for the animation. The focal point determines the amount of perspective given to the viewer. It defines the distance between the viewer's perspective and that of the object upon the 3D z-axis. We do this by simply adding a line of code to the ActionScript.

5. Add the following code to the first free line in your ActionScript pane, as shown in Figure 9-28:

```
var focalLength:Number = 2000;
```

```
1   const IMAGE_WIDTH:uint = 150;
2   const IMAGE_HEIGHT:uint = 141;
3   var focalLength:Number = 2000;
```

Figure 9-28. Setting the focal point in ActionScript 3.0

> *When you have finished this tutorial, feel free to have a play with the focal point to find a setting that suits you. In this example, setting a focal point of 175 makes the animation come up close and personal, displaying only a couple of the images on the stage, while setting your focal point to 2000 displays the images at a nice proportion to the size of the stage.*

With the focal point set, it's time to determine the vanishing point. The vanishing point is the location where your carousel will disappear into the distance, and it positions your animation on the stage on the x- and y-axes.

6. Add the following code beneath the focal-point code you added in step 5, as shown in Figure 9-29:

```
var vanishingPointX:Number = stage.stageWidth / 2;
var vanishingPointY:Number = stage.stageHeight / 2;
```

```
1  const IMAGE_WIDTH:uint = 420;
2  const IMAGE_HEIGHT:uint = 396;
3  var focalLength:Number = 500;
4  var vanishingPointX:Number = stage.stageWidth / 2;
5  var vanishingPointY:Number = stage.stageHeight / 2;
```

Figure 9-29. Setting the x- and y-axis vanishing point in ActionScript 3

We are going to now use ActionScript to position the carousel on stage. In the next step, we are going to define the 3D Floor at 0, which is the absolute center of the vertical axis. Again, when you have completed this tutorial, feel free to play with the Floor settings to find a setting that suits you. As with positioning on the y-axis, negative values display the animation on an increased vertical scale, whereas positive values display the animation toward the bottom of the stage.

7. Add the following code to line 6 of your ActionScript, as shown in Figure 9-30:

```
var floor:Number = 0;
```

```
1  const IMAGE_WIDTH:uint = 150;
2  const IMAGE_HEIGHT:uint = 141;
3  var focalLength:Number = 2000;
4  var vanishingPointX:Number = stage.stageWidth / 2;
5  var vanishingPointY:Number = stage.stageHeight / 2;
6  var floor:Number = 0;
```

Figure 9-30. The Floor:Number value in ActionScript 3.0 dictates the vertical positioning of your carousel.

We are going to specify how fast the animation rotates. This is called angleSpeed. We'll set this now.

8. Insert the following code at line 7 of your ActionScript, as shown in Figure 9-31:

```
var angleSpeed:Number = 10;
```

```
1  const IMAGE_WIDTH:uint = 150;
2  const IMAGE_HEIGHT:uint = 141;
3  var focalLength:Number = 2000;
4  var vanishingPointX:Number = stage.stageWidth / 2;
5  var vanishingPointY:Number = stage.stageHeight / 2;
6  var floor:Number = 0;
7  var angleSpeed:Number = 10;
```

Figure 9-31. Determining the speed at which your carousel rotates

The next line will define the radius of the circle of rotation of the carousel. A positive value creates a larger radius, which increases the distance between the images in your animation.

9

9. Add the following line to line 8 of your ActionScript, as shown in Figure 9-32:

```
var radius:Number = 200;
```

```
1   const IMAGE_WIDTH:uint = 150;
2   const IMAGE_HEIGHT:uint = 141;
3   var focalLength:Number = 2000;
4   var vanishingPointX:Number = stage.stageWidth / 2;
5   var vanishingPointY:Number = stage.stageHeight / 2;
6   var floor:Number = 0;
7   var angleSpeed:Number = 10;
8   var radius:Number = 200;
```

Figure 9-32. Defining the radius in your carousel

10. Save your animation.

We have saved the animation, only so that if we accidentally close the file or make a mistake, we can bring it back to this point. We have now set up the basic information that will control your carousel, though if you test your movie you will not see anything other than the green stage.

The next part of the exercise will call on the XML file that will allow you to begin to see the animation on stage. The first step is to define the path of the XML file that you created earlier. For the purposes of this exercise, I have uploaded this file to my own server.

11. Add the following code to line 9 of your ActionScript file, as shown in Figure 9-33:

```
var xmlFilePath:String = "http://www.cheridankerr.com/gene/genosel.xml";
```

```
8   var radius:Number = 200;
9   var xmlFilePath:String = "http://www.cheridankerr.com/gene/genosel.xml";
```

Figure 9-33. Defining the path to the genosel.xml file in ActionScript 3.0

We will now define a variable in which the XML file is saved when it is loaded.

12. Add the following code to line 10 of your ActionScript file, as shown in Figure 9-34:

```
1    const IMAGE_WIDTH:uint = 150;
2    const IMAGE_HEIGHT:uint = 141;
3    var focalLength:Number = 2000;
4    var vanishingPointX:Number = stage.stageWidth / 2;
5    var vanishingPointY:Number = stage.stageHeight / 2;
6    var floor:Number = 0;
7    var angleSpeed:Number = 10;
8    var radius:Number = 200;
9    var xmlFilePath:String = "http://www.cheridankerr.com/gene/genosel.xml";
10   var xml:XML;
```

Figure 9-34. Defining the variable that calls the XML file

The next three lines will define the array that contains the imageHolders, the number of images that have been loaded into the Flash animation, and the total number of images that the genosel.xml file specifies.

13. Type the following code into your ActionScript panel at the first available free line, as shown in Figure 9-35:

```
var imageHolders:Array = new Array();
var numberOfLoadedImages:uint = 0;
var numberOfImages:uint = 0;
```

```
 9   var xmlFilePath:String = "http://www.cheridankerr.com/gene/genosel.xml";
10   var xml:XML;
11   var imageHolders:Array = new Array();
12   var numberOfLoadedImages:uint = 0;
13   var numberOfImages:uint = 0;
```

Figure 9-35. Defining the array containing the imageHolders, the images loaded, and the total images in your Flash animation

Next we're going to call the XML URL via the URLLoader. In previous versions of Flash (prior to ActionScript 3.0), there were a number of classes that loaded external content. In ActionScript 3.0, this has evolved to the URLLoader class, which is simply a method to load content from an external XML file. Events triggered from the URLLoader indicate when the loading of the external content is complete. The following step will achieve that.

14. Add the following four lines to your ActionScript, as shown in Figure 9-36:

```
var loader = new URLLoader();
loader.load(new URLRequest(xmlFilePath));
loader.addEventListener(Event.COMPLETE, xmlLoaded);
function xmlLoaded(e:Event):void {
```

```
10   var xml:XML;
11   var imageHolders:Array = new Array();
12   var numberOfLoadedImages:uint = 0;
13   var numberOfImages:uint = 0;
14   var loader = new URLLoader();
15   loader.load(new URLRequest(xmlFilePath));
16   loader.addEventListener(Event.COMPLETE, xmlLoaded);
17   function xmlLoaded(e:Event):void {
```

Figure 9-36. Calling the XML file via the URLLoader

The final line of the previous code is a function that is called after the XML file has been loaded.

We're now going to use the function we built to make a new XML object, and create a function that loads the images from the XML file.

15. Add the following code to the tail end of your ActionScript pane:

```
            xml = new XML(loader.data);
            xml.ignoreWhitespace = true;
            loadImages();
}
```

Remember to save your work regularly!

9

The following code will create holders for the images specified in your 3D carousel via the XML file, and will pull the specified number of images defined in your XML file and loop through each of them.

16. Add the following code to lines 22, 23, and 24 of your ActionScript:

```
function loadImages():void {
            numberOfImages = xml.number_of_images;
        for each (var image:XML in xml.images.image) {
```

Your ActionScript panel should now resemble Figure 9-37.

```
1   const IMAGE_WIDTH:uint = 150;
2   const IMAGE_HEIGHT:uint = 141;
3   var focalLength:Number = 2000;
4   var vanishingPointX:Number = stage.stageWidth / 2;
5   var vanishingPointY:Number = stage.stageHeight / 2;
6   var floor:Number = 0;
7   var angleSpeed:Number = 10;
8   var radius:Number = 200;
9   var xmlFilePath:String = "http://www.cheridankerr.com/gene/genosel.xml";
10  var xml:XML;
11  var imageHolders:Array = new Array();
12  var numberOfLoadedImages:uint = 0;
13  var numberOfImages:uint = 0;
14  var loader = new URLLoader();
15  loader.load(new URLRequest(xmlFilePath));
16  loader.addEventListener(Event.COMPLETE, xmlLoaded);
17  function xmlLoaded(e:Event):void {
18      xml = new XML(loader.data);
19      xml.ignoreWhitespace = true;
20      loadImages();
21  }
22  function loadImages():void {
23      numberOfImages = xml.number_of_images;
24      for each (var image:XML in xml.images.image) {
```

Figure 9-37. Your ActionScript so far

The next three lines of code are going to create imageHolders, which are movie clips that appear on your stage to hold the images, and a new image loader that exists to display the external images pointed to from the genosel.xml file. The third line then combines the image loader with the imageHolder.

17. Add the following code to lines 25-27 of your ActionScript:

```
var imageHolder:MovieClip = new MovieClip();
var imageLoader = new Loader();
imageHolder.addChild(imageLoader);
```

The following line of code will ensure that any errant mouse clicks do not affect the image behaviors:

18. Enter the following code on line 28 of your ActionScript, as shown in Figure 9-38:

```
imageHolder.mouseChildren = false;
```

```
22  function loadImages():void {
23      numberOfImages = xml.number_of_images;
24      for each (var image:XML in xml.images.image) {
25      var imageHolder:MovieClip = new MovieClip();
26      var imageLoader = new Loader();
27          imageHolder.addChild(imageLoader);
28          imageHolder.mouseChildren = false;
```

Figure 9-38. Setting mouseChildren to false ensures protection against errant mouse clicks.

The next step involves ensuring the registration point of the imageHolder is centered, by positioning the image loader along the x-and the y-axes. The registration point is the point to which Flash attaches the symbol when it's in motion. In Chapter 7 we changed the registration point of the multiarmed monster so that when its arms moved around they stayed attached to the body. The following code will ensure that the images in your carousel stay in position when the carousel moves them around.

19. Add the following two lines to the end of your current ActionScript code:

```
imageLoader.x = - (IMAGE_WIDTH / 2);
imageLoader.y = - (IMAGE_HEIGHT / 2);
```

The following five lines will ensure that the imageHolder has been added to the imageHolder array and that the images load correctly.

20. Add the following five lines under the previous code entered, as shown in Figure 9-39:

```
imageHolders.push(imageHolder);
imageLoader.load(new URLRequest(image.url));

imageLoader.contentLoaderInfo.addEventListener(Event.COMPLETE,
imageLoaded);
        }
}
```

```
22  function loadImages():void {
23      numberOfImages = xml.number_of_images;
24      for each (var image:XML in xml.images.image) {
25      var imageHolder:MovieClip = new MovieClip();
26      var imageLoader = new Loader();
27          imageHolder.addChild(imageLoader);
28          imageHolder.mouseChildren = false;
29          imageLoader.x = - (IMAGE_WIDTH / 2);
30          imageLoader.y = - (IMAGE_HEIGHT / 2);
31          imageHolders.push(imageHolder);
32          imageLoader.load(new URLRequest(image.url));
33          imageLoader.contentLoaderInfo.addEventListener(Event.COMPLETE, imageLoaded);
34      }
35  }
```

Figure 9-39. Ensuring the images load correctly into the carousel

The final three lines that need to be added for this section of the exercise create a function that is called when an image is loaded and update the number of images defined by the XML file, which will then flag when the last image has been uploaded and set up the genosel.

21. Add the following code to the ActionScript panel, as shown in Figure 9-40:

```
function imageLoaded(e:Event):void {
                             numberOfLoadedImages++;
        if (numberOfLoadedImages == numberOfImages) {
```

```
1    const IMAGE_WIDTH:uint = 150;
2    const IMAGE_HEIGHT:uint = 141;
3    var focalLength:Number = 2000;
4    var vanishingPointX:Number = stage.stageWidth / 2;
5    var vanishingPointY:Number = stage.stageHeight / 2;
6    var floor:Number = 0;
7    var angleSpeed:Number = 10;
8    var radius:Number = 200;
9    var xmlFilePath:String = "http://www.cheridankerr.com/gene/genosel.xml";
10   var xml:XML;
11   var imageHolders:Array = new Array();
12   var numberOfLoadedImages:uint = 0;
13   var numberOfImages:uint = 0;
14   var loader = new URLLoader();
15   loader.load(new URLRequest(xmlFilePath));
16   loader.addEventListener(Event.COMPLETE, xmlLoaded);
17   function xmlLoaded(e:Event):void {
18       xml = new XML(loader.data);
19       xml.ignoreWhitespace = true;
20       loadImages();
21   }
22   function loadImages():void {
23       numberOfImages = xml.number_of_images;
24       for each (var image:XML in xml.images.image) {
25       var imageHolder:MovieClip = new MovieClip();
26       var imageLoader = new Loader();
27           imageHolder.addChild(imageLoader);
28           imageHolder.mouseChildren = false;
29           imageLoader.x = - (IMAGE_WIDTH / 2);
30           imageLoader.y = - (IMAGE_HEIGHT / 2);
31           imageHolders.push(imageHolder);
32           imageLoader.load(new URLRequest(image.url));
33           imageLoader.contentLoaderInfo.addEventListener(Event.COMPLETE, imageLoaded);
34       }
35   }
36   function imageLoaded(e:Event):void {
37           numberOfLoadedImages++;
38       if (numberOfLoadedImages == numberOfImages) {
39
```

Figure 9-40. The final code for this exercise

22. Save your Flash file.

We have accomplished what we set out to do—to create the variables that enable the Flash file to call the information in the XML file. Though we haven't finished creating the 3D carousel yet, we are going to finish this exercise here and continue with this saved file in the next exercise. If you tried to test your movie now, it would throw an output error, and naught would display on the screen. In the next exercise we will remedy that with the creation of the genosel.

Displaying the information on stage

This second part of the genosel-creation process continues the build of the carousel component of the genosel.

1. Add the following code to the end of your saved Flash document from the previous exercise, as shown in Figure 9-41:

```
initializeCarousel();
        }
}
```

```
32          imageLoader.load(new URLRequest(image.url));
33          imageLoader.contentLoaderInfo.addEventListener(Event.COMPLETE, imageLoaded);
34      }
35  }
36  function imageLoaded(e:Event):void {
37          numberOfLoadedImages++;
38      if (numberOfLoadedImages == numberOfImages) {
39  initializeCarousel();
40      }
41  }
```

Figure 9-41. Setting up the genosel

The next step in this exercise is to create the function that will be used when all of the images have loaded into the genosel.

2. Add the following line of code to line 42 of the ActionScript panel, as shown in Figure 9-42:

```
function initializeCarousel():void {
```

```
36  function imageLoaded(e:Event):void {
37          numberOfLoadedImages++;
38      if (numberOfLoadedImages == numberOfImages) {
39  initializeCarousel();
40      }
41  }
42  function initializeCarousel():void {
```

Figure 9-42. Creating the InitializeCarousel function

The next lines of code that you add will determine the angle of the distance between each of the images in radians (the standard unit of a plane angular measure). A radian is the standard international unit of plane angle.

3. The following code is tacked onto the first available line below the rest of the code you have already entered to determine the distance between the images in the carousel:

```
var angleDifference:Number = Math.PI * (360 / numberOfImages) / 180;
```

To assign the imageHolder that we created in the previous exercise to a local variable, we must ensure that we space the images evenly and that we loop through them all.

4. The following code is to be inserted below the code from the prior exercise, as shown in Figure 9-43:

```
for (var i:uint = 0; i < imageHolders.length; i++) {
var imageHolder:MovieClip = (MovieClip)(imageHolders[i]);
var startingAngle:Number = angleDifference * i;
```

```
39   initializeCarousel();
40      }
41  }
42  function initializeCarousel():void {
43      var angleDifference:Number = Math.PI * (360 / numberOfImages) / 180;
44      for (var i:uint = 0; i < imageHolders.length; i++) {
45      var imageHolder:MovieClip = (MovieClip)(imageHolders[i]);
46      var startingAngle:Number = angleDifference * i;
```

Figure 9-43. Assigning imageHolders to the local variable, looping through them all, and spacing them evenly via ActionScript 3.0

5. Add the following code to lines 47 through 50 in your ActionScript panel to ensure that the imageHolders are positioned correctly on stage:

```
imageHolder.xpos3D = radius * Math.cos(startingAngle);
imageHolder.zpos3D = radius * Math.sin(startingAngle);
imageHolder.ypos3D = floor;
imageHolder.currentAngle = startingAngle;
```

The next line of code that we are going to enter into the ActionScript panel will calculate the ratio of scale for the imageHolder; that is, the farther away the image appears, the smaller the scale is going to be. Likewise, as the image appears closer to you, the scale becomes larger.

6. Add the following code below the rest of the code in your ActionScript panel:

```
var scaleRatio = focalLength/(focalLength + imageHolder.zpos3D)
```

The following code then uses the scale ratio to scale the imageHolder.

7. Immediately below the code in the preceding step, add the following, as shown in Figure 9-44:

```
imageHolder.scaleX = imageHolder.scaleY = scaleRatio;
```

```
42  function initializeCarousel():void {
43      var angleDifference:Number = Math.PI * (360 / numberOfImages) / 180;
44      for (var i:uint = 0; i < imageHolders.length; i++) {
45      var imageHolder:MovieClip = (MovieClip)(imageHolders[i]);
46      var startingAngle:Number = angleDifference * i;
47          imageHolder.xpos3D = radius * Math.cos(startingAngle);
48          imageHolder.zpos3D = radius * Math.sin(startingAngle);
49          imageHolder.ypos3D = floor;
50          imageHolder.currentAngle = startingAngle;
51      var scaleRatio = focalLength/(focalLength + imageHolder.zpos3D);
```

Figure 9-44. Calculating the scaleRatio on the x- and y-axes in your genosel

The final four lines of code for this exercise will add the imageHolder to the stage, and position it on 2D coordinates.

```
imageHolder.x = vanishingPointX + imageHolder.xpos3D * scaleRatio;
        imageHolder.y = vanishingPointY + imageHolder.ypos3D *
scaleRatio;
            addChild(imageHolder);
}
```

```
42  function initializeCarousel():void {
43      var angleDifference:Number = Math.PI * (360 / numberOfImages) / 180;
44      for (var i:uint = 0; i < imageHolders.length; i++) {
45      var imageHolder:MovieClip = (MovieClip)(imageHolders[i]);
46      var startingAngle:Number = angleDifference * i;
47          imageHolder.xpos3D = radius * Math.cos(startingAngle);
48          imageHolder.zpos3D = radius * Math.sin(startingAngle);
49          imageHolder.ypos3D = floor;
50          imageHolder.currentAngle = startingAngle;
51      var scaleRatio = focalLength/(focalLength + imageHolder.zpos3D);
52          imageHolder.scaleX = imageHolder.scaleY = scaleRatio;
53          imageHolder.x = vanishingPointX + imageHolder.xpos3D * scaleRatio;
54          imageHolder.y = vanishingPointY + imageHolder.ypos3D * scaleRatio;
55          addChild(imageHolder);
56      }
```

Figure 9-45. The entire exercise code in the ActionScript panel

8. Save your Flash CS4 document.

The entire code for this exercise is available to download from the Downloads section of the friends of ED website, http://friendsofed.com/.

We're at a junction where we could theoretically see the elements appear on stage, as shown in Figure 9-46, by adding a second } to the bottom of the code to close it. Should you choose to do this, you will need to remember to delete the bracket prior to continuing the next exercise.

Figure 9-46. The static carousel

The final exercise to complete your 3D genosel will show you how to bring your animation to life by rotating it.

Rotating your carousel

The first exercise in this section set up our XML file, which specified how many images we were going to use in our genosel and the URLs where they were located. The second exercise defined variables in ActionScript 3.0 to call the information in the XML file, and the third exercise enabled you to display the information on the stage. This final exercise is going to animate the genosel!

9

The first thing we are going to do is add an ENTER_FRAME for the rotation. The ENTER_FRAME is a class that enables the creation of animations. Let's add this now, and we can begin to build the animation!

> Remember: if you added the } at the end of the last exercise to view the static movie, you must remove it before commencing this exercise!

1. Add the following code to the first free line under the code from the previous exercise, as shown in Figure 9-47:

```
        addEventListener(Event.ENTER_FRAME, rotateCarousel);
}
function rotateCarousel(e:Event):void {
```

```
50      imageHolder.currentAngle = startingAngle;
51   var scaleRatio = focalLength/(focalLength + imageHolder.zpos3D);
52      imageHolder.scaleX = imageHolder.scaleY = scaleRatio;
53      imageHolder.x = vanishingPointX + imageHolder.xpos3D * scaleRatio;
54      imageHolder.y = vanishingPointY + imageHolder.ypos3D * scaleRatio;
55   addChild(imageHolder);
56   }
57   addEventListener(Event.ENTER_FRAME, rotateCarousel);
58 }
59 function rotateCarousel(e:Event):void {
```

Figure 9-47. Adding the ENTER_FRAME class to your ActionScript 3.0

The next line of code we add is going to enable the user to adjust the speed of the carousel mousing over the images as the carousel turns. The second line will ensure that this is looped throughout the images.

2. Add the following code to lines 60 and 61 of your ActionScript pane, directly under the preceding code:

```
angleSpeed = (mouseX - vanishingPointX) / 5000;
```

Once again we are going to assign the imageHolder to a local variable and update its angle as the genosel rotates.

3. Add the following code to the ActionScript panel, as shown in Figure 9-48:

```
for (var i:uint = 0; i < imageHolders.length; i++) {
var imageHolder:MovieClip = (MovieClip)(imageHolders[i]);
imageHolder.currentAngle += angleSpeed;
```

```
57      addEventListener(Event.ENTER_FRAME, rotateCarousel);
58 }
59 function rotateCarousel(e:Event):void {
60      angleSpeed = (mouseX - vanishingPointX) / 5000;
61      for (var i:uint = 0; i < imageHolders.length; i++) {
62      imageHolder.currentAngle += angleSpeed;
```

Figure 9-48. The code for this exercise, up to step 3

4. The following code will set a new position for the imageHolder as the genosel rotates:

```
imageHolder.xpos3D=radius*Math.cos(imageHolder.currentAngle);
imageHolder.zpos3D=radius*Math.sin(imageHolder.currentAngle);
```

5. Add the following code to calculate the ratio of scaling required as the carousel moves along the 3D axis. We'll use this information to scale the imageHolder and then to refresh the imageHolder's coordinates as it moves around the carousel:

```
var scaleRatio = focalLength/(focalLength + imageHolder.zpos3D);
            imageHolder.scaleX=imageHolder.scaleY=scaleRatio;
        imageHolder.x=vanishingPointX+imageHolder.xpos3D*scaleRatio;
        imageHolder.y=vanishingPointY+imageHolder.ypos3D*scaleRatio;
}
```

6. The following lines of code will call the function that sorts the images in the genosel and ensures they overlap each other correctly, as shown in Figure 9-49:

```
sortZ();
}
function sortZ():void {
```

Your ActionScript panel should be displaying as shown in Figure 9-49.

```
57      addEventListener(Event.ENTER_FRAME, rotateCarousel);
58  }
59  function rotateCarousel(e:Event):void {
60      angleSpeed = (mouseX - vanishingPointX) / 5000;
61      for (var i:uint = 0; i < imageHolders.length; i++) {
62      imageHolder.currentAngle += angleSpeed;
63      imageHolder.xpos3D=radius*Math.cos(imageHolder.currentAngle);
64      imageHolder.zpos3D=radius*Math.sin(imageHolder.currentAngle);
65      var scaleRatio = focalLength/(focalLength + imageHolder.zpos3D);
66      imageHolder.scaleX=imageHolder.scaleY=scaleRatio;
67      imageHolder.x=vanishingPointX+imageHolder.xpos3D*scaleRatio;
68      imageHolder.y=vanishingPointY+imageHolder.ypos3D*scaleRatio;
69      }
70      sortZ();
71  }
72  function sortZ():void {
```

Figure 9-49. Ensuring your images overlap each other correctly in your animation

7. The final lines of code ensure that the image that has the highest Z position is displayed first in the array and defines a new set of child indexes for the images that are called from the XML file.

```
imageHolders.sortOn("zpos3D", Array.NUMERIC | Array.DESCENDING);
        for (var i:uint = 0; i < imageHolders.length; i++) {
                setChildIndex(imageHolders[i], i);
        }
}
```

8. Save your movie.

It is now time to test your genosel by selecting Control ➤ Test Movie.

What do you see? Familiar creatures from previous chapters in this book rotate serenely around a carousel. Where, though, would you use an application like this?

When you are considering planning your website or animation, at all times you must consider usability. If your website is commercial, your goal is probably to drive your customer to buy your product, either online or in a store. If your carousel moves too quickly or is confusing for the user to get all of the information that you wish to give them, you may want to reconsider using it, or adjust the settings to slow it down to a usable speed. See Chapter 11 for more usability hints.

Flash CS4 and 3D engines

A 3D engine provides an easy and efficient way to create 3D interactivity with real-time animation and lighting, material changes, and rendering. Traditionally 3D was faked in Flash by either prerendering from dedicated 3D-modeling software or by using clever mathematical algorithms. 3D engines let you use your imagination without having to worry about how things work. Typically, 3D engines are delivered as part of a downloadable library—a collection of ActionScript functions and routines for creating 3D in Flash. Most of the common 3D engines are hosted at code.google.com and are downloaded using a version-control system, such as the Subversion (SVN) tool available from http://subversion.tigris.org. Once the libraries are downloaded to your system you can either place the library folders into the same project directory that you are working on, or you can place the library folders on a given local spot on your computer. You then use the Preferences panel in Flash to point to the specific class-path location. For full instructions on downloading and setting up 3D engines and SVN, for both Windows and OSX, please refer to Appendix A.

As an alternative you can download the class libraries to the same directory as your project. The advantage of using the libraries in this way is that you will not need to set up an external path library. The disadvantage is that for every project you will need to copy the same folders to every 3D project you create. Also, 3D engines do get updated regularly, and it is much easier to update one folder rather than a plethora scattered through your work directories.

Papervison3D, Sandy 3D, and Away3D

There are a heap of 3D engines out there, some free to use, and some that you must buy. Papervision3D is without a doubt the best known—and best of all, it's free. The other two engines worth a mention are Sandy 3D and Away3D. All engines have advantages and disadvantages. In this book will discuss Away3D because of its ease of use, great interactive features, and friendly community. If you venture to http://away3d.com/ you will see some examples built using the engine that you can interact with to get an idea of the engine's power. Away3D also has a welcoming user group at http://groups.google.com/group/away3d-dev. Go there to find an answer to a question, to get feedback, or to speak with like minds.

Summary

In our largest coding exercise so far, we have created carousel in ActionScript 3 and Flash CS4. You have learned about external 3D engines such as Papervision3D, Sandy 3D, and Away3D. Using 3D graphics is a wonderful way to bring your Flash CS4 animations to life.

In the next chapter we add sound to Flash animations and you'll learn about ways to use video.

9

CHAPTER 10

SEEING AND HEARING ARE
BELIEVING!

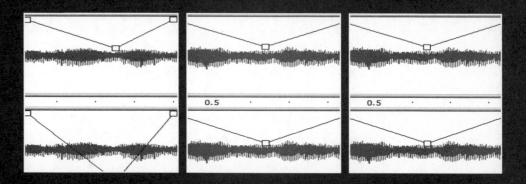

Flash CS4 allows Flash designers to build animations that as little as ten years ago could only be dreamed about. Sound and video are no longer just the realm of film and music makers. Flash CS4 allows you to create compelling and interactive documents using both sound and video imported right onto the stage.

Until recent years, video and sound in Flash CS4 animations has been looked upon with trepidation because the speed of Internet was slower and it would take a long time to download a video. Now fast Internet is the order of the day, and you can use video and sound knowing that they will be delivered to the user in the best possible format.

Ad-serving technologies such as Eyeblaster offer developers rich media advertising banner formats that are ready to have video and sound inserted into them. Yet just because you can use it doesn't necessarily mean that you always should. Sound and video should be used to enhance your movie, not to dominate your Flash CS4 application.

Over the course of this chapter, you will learn how to apply sound to an animation you previously created, and to create videos in Flash CS4.

Sweet, sweet sounds in Flash

Flash CS4 allows you to incorporate sounds in many ways in your Flash movie clips and animations. You can add sounds to your animation that will play repeatedly and continuously, separate from your timeline, or you can harness the timeline to synchronize animation and sound to create some really cool effects. You can also control sounds via ActionScript. Flash CS4 might offer great 3D stuff, but sound and video take your Flash applications to a whole new level, which enables you as a commercial web developer/designer to give your clients the vehicle with which to sell their product.

There are two ways that you can control sound in Flash CS4. One is inserting it into a timeline by importing it directly to the stage or from the library. The other way is by implementing a Sound object in ActionScript. For fine control of your animations and sounds, it is preferable to use the Sound object, as timeline sounds are largely dependent upon the speed of the user's computer. This makes syncing animation and sounds a largely hit-or-miss effort for timeline animations. Luckily, the Sound object will save the day. We will examine the Sound object later on in this chapter when we apply a sound to a banner.

You can use Flash CS4 in a variety of ways to manipulate sounds:

- Adding sound to buttons
- Fading sound in and out to enhance your Flash CS4 movie clips
- Streaming sound to an animation

Flash CS4 allows you to work with two kinds of sounds: event sounds and streaming sounds, which are sounds that need to be downloaded completely before they play, and streaming sounds are sounds that play as soon the first couple of frames have downloaded. Streaming sounds are synchronized on a timeline. Table 10-1 displays the sound formats that you can import into Flash CS4 if you have QuickTime 4 or later installed on your computer.

> The latest version of QuickTime can be downloaded for free from www.apple.com/downloads.

Table 10-1. Supported sounds in Flash CS4

Sound	Descriptor
AIFF	Macintosh native sound format
ASND	Adobe Soundbooth native sound format
WAV	Waveform audio format (Windows and Mac OS compatible)
MP3	MPEG-1, Audio Layer 3 cross-platform (Windows and Mac OS) sound file
Sound Designer II	Mac-only sound
Audio-only QuickTime movies	Windows and Mac compatible
Sun AU	Cross-platform (Windows and Mac) sound
System 7	Cross-platform (Windows and Mac) sound

Importing sounds

Importing sounds into Flash CS4 is as simple as importing images. The following exercise will show you how to import the sound of a wasp. Be sure to have downloaded the source files for this chapter from the friends of ED website (www.friendsofed.com).

1. Open a new document in Flash CS4.

2. Select File ➤ Import ➤ Import to Library, as shown in Figure 10-1.

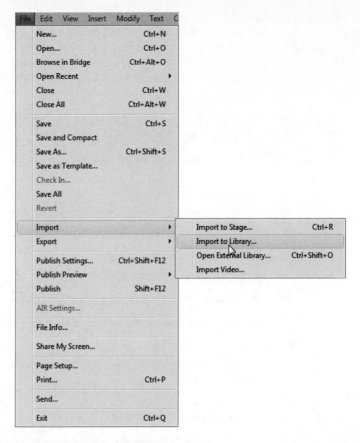

Figure 10-1. Importing a sound to the library

3. Navigate to where the wasp.wav file is saved on your system, in the Import dialog box, and ensure that the selected file type to view is WAV Sound (*wav).

4. Select wasp.wav and click Open to import the sound into the Library, as shown in Figure 10-2.

Figure 10-2. The file wasp.wav imported into the Library

As you can see, sounds are saved into the Flash CS4 document's Library along with any images, movie clips, and symbols that make up the Flash CS4 animation. Just as you can use an image multiple ways in an animation with just one copy in the Library, you can use one sound in the Library multiple ways.

> *You can also preview the sound in the Sound Library by clicking the play controls at the top right of the preview panel.*

Let's hear how the sound file that we have just imported plays:

1. Double-click the `wasp.wav` file in the Library. The Sound Properties dialog box will appear, as shown in Figure 10-3.

Figure 10-3. The Sound Properties dialog box displaying the wasp.wav file

> *You need to click the speaker icon rather than the file name in the Library to get the* Sound Properties *dialog box to display. Clicking the file name merely allows you to rename the file in the Library.*

2. Click the Test button in the Sound Properties dialog box. You will hear the wasp buzzing for about 15 seconds.

3. Save this Flash CS4 document as `wasp.fla`, as we will be using it in the next exercise.

Though it hasn't been seen since Flash 8, Flash CS4 also contains a comprehensive Sound Library. To access the Sound Library, as shown in Figure 10-4, select Window ➤ Common Libraries ➤ Sounds.

The Sound Library is completely royalty free and may be used on commercial and personal websites. It contains a variety of sounds to help bring your Flash CS4 movies to life, such as ambient background noises, animal noises, explosions, screams, and general household sounds.

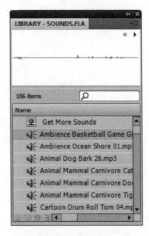

Figure 10-4. The Sound Library installed with Flash CS4

Exporting sounds

Sound and video files can be large and slow to download, so Flash can compress them so that they're smaller and quicker. Flash CS4 offers you the ability to select compression options for individual event and stream sounds, and also for videos, which we will be using later on in this chapter. For now, let's check out how to export sounds and use the Sound section of the Properties Inspector.

When you need to be careful about file size, it's a good idea to compress sounds, though the quality of the sound deteriorates the more you compress it. As you will discover in Chapter 11, there are international standards for file size in online advertising collateral. Likewise, when visiting your website, users can be fickle. If you keep them waiting to see your content, there is no guarantee that they will stick around to see your offering. Therefore, as a Flash developer, when it comes to sounds and video, you are constantly walking a fine line between optimal performance and preserving the integrity of your files.

Sound file compression in Flash CS4

In the Sound Properties dialog box, you can choose from different types of compression, as shown in Figure 10-5. We'll momentarily deviate from our exercise to investigate what each of these are.

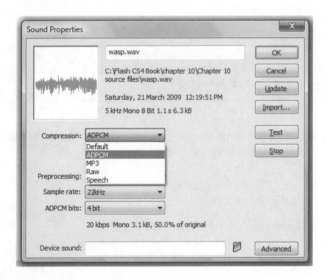

Figure 10-5. Types of sound compression available in Flash CS4

ADPCM compression

ADPCM (Adaptive Differential Pulse Code Modulation) compression enables you to compress 8- and 16-bit sound data. This is the best kind of compression to use when you have very short and light sound files, such as a button click or page transition click, as ADPCM compression does not compress the sound file very much. As shown in Figure 10-6, when you select ADPCM, a number of options become available for exporting the file.

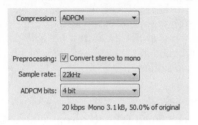

Figure 10-6. The ADPCM compression options

Preprocessing enables you to convert stereo sound to monaural (better known as mono) sound, which is a single-channel sound that can be channeled to two or more speakers.

Changing the sample rate enables you to control the file size and the sound quality (defined in kilohertz [kHz]). Generally, the lower the sample rate, the smaller the file size, but this decrease in file size is often at the expense of sound quality. As a Flash developer, you are constantly walking the line between high-quality sounds, videos, and graphics, and acceptable files size for users. You cannot increase the kHz of a sound file beyond that of the original imported file—that means that you cannot improve the sound quality of the original file.

Changing the ADPCM Bits setting enables you to manipulate the bit rate of the sound compression. The lower the bit rate, the lower the sound quality; and the higher the bit rate, the better. If file size is not an issue, choose the higher-quality sound. If you have file weight restrictions, you will be required to compromise on sound quality.

MP3 compression

MP3 compression allows you to export sound files employing MP3 compression. This is the option to use when you are exporting longer-playing sounds, such as movie clip sound-tracks and songs. Again, the MP3 compression option, as shown in Figure 10-7, offers a number of different choices when exporting your movie.

Figure 10-7. The MP3 compression options

The Preprocessing option is exactly as per other compressions—that is, it enables you to change stereo sound to mono. The difference with MP3 compression is that you are only able to make this conversion if the file that you are converting has a bit rate of 20kbps (kilobits per second) or higher.

10

Once again, changing the bit rate determines the exported sound file's bits per second, at a range between 8 and 160kbps. If you are exporting music soundtracks, for best sound results, ensure that the bit rate is set to 16kbps or higher.

The options in the Quality drop-down box in the MP3 compression option are as follows: Fast, which offers most compression for the fastest possible download per bit rate; Best, which offers the best quality sound at the expense of download times; and Medium, which is a midpoint between the two settings.

Raw compression

Raw compression exports your sound with no sound compression—that is, it does not change the file size, regardless of the kHz quality. As shown in Figure 10-8, you are able to use the Preprocessing option to convert stereo sound files to mono, and to change the sample rate.

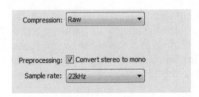

Figure 10-8. Raw compression preserves the original file size.

Raw compression exports the sound file without applying any compression to it at all.

Speech compression

Speech compression exports sounds using a compression that is especially created for human speech. As shown in Figure 10-9, it does not offer preprocessing conversion from mono to stereo sound, and the sample rate gives you control over file size and sound quality. While 5kHz is acceptable for speech, a sample rate of 11kHz or over is recommended. 44kHz is standard audio CD quality but a longer download time.

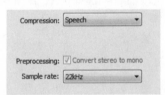

Figure 10-9. Speech compression options

Compressing a sound file

You will learn about the importance of optimizing your Flash CS4 movies in Chapter 11, but for now, let's learn how to compress a sound file.

1. Open the file wasp.fla that you created in the previous exercise in Flash CS4.

2. Double-click the speaker icon next to wasp.wav in the Library. The Sound Properties dialog box will appear, as shown in Figure 10-10.

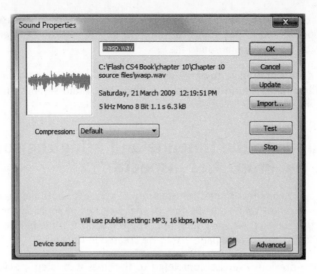

Figure 10-10. The Sound Properties dialog box

Notice that the details for the original file appear as shown in Figure 10-11. The unedited wasp.wav file is 6.3KB. In the next step, we'll see what happens when we change the compression rate.

5 kHz Mono 8 Bit 1.1 s 6.3 kB

Figure 10-11. The original file is 6.3KB.

3. Select MP3 from the Compression drop-down list.

Notice how the file size has changed from 6.3KB to 2.3KB—approximately 60 percent smaller. These conversions will prove invaluable in creating complicated Flash CS4 animations of small file size.

We're now going to test the sound.

4. Click Test to hear the sound.

You will hear the angry sound of a wasp! You can continue to play with the settings until you are happy with the sound.

5. Click OK to accept the sound.

Simple compression is not the only way that you can optimize sound files in your Flash CS4 animations. There are many ways that you can be clever with sound to prevent your files becoming too large, while still preserving their sound integrity. For example, you can set short sounds and music riffs to loop to provide background music for your animation. This will ensure that you have music throughout the animation, but will enable you to minimize the added weight to your file size from sound, as you are employing one small sound over and over again. It's important to note that you shouldn't ever loop streaming sound.

Similarly, if you have only certain points where different sounds need to be heard, set them to play from separate small sound files at the appropriate spot, instead of including a large sound file that has moments of silence, which would add weight to your Flash file.

10

Get more out of the same sounds by applying different effects for sounds (such as volume envelopes, looping, and in/out points) at different keyframes. You can get a number of sound effects by using only one sound file.

We will now demonstrate how to apply sounds to the timeline using an animation used previously in this book, and in the process explore the sound settings in the Properties Inspector.

Adding sounds to the timeline and using the sound settings in the Properties Inspector

We've seen how to compress sounds for optimum playback for both file loading times and sound quality, and now we'll start the first of the exercises in applying the sound to the timeline. For this exercise, we will continue to use the wasp.wav file before we move into completing another step on the banner that we created in Chapter 6.

1. With the previous exercise completed to the final step (step 4), click frame 1 of Layer 1.

2. Drag the wasp.wav file onto the stage.

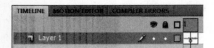

Figure 10-12. The sound populates frame 1 of the movie.

Notice that while you can't see anything on the stage, there is a small wavy line in the first frame of the timeline, as shown in Figure 10-12.

Now that you have placed a sound on the timeline, you can take advantage of the preset sound effects that come with Flash CS4.

3. Click frame 1 of Layer 1 to select it. The Properties Inspector will appear, as shown in Figure 10-13. It is here that you can apply different settings that will affect your sound.

Figure 10-13. The Sound section of the Properties Inspector

4. Choose an effect from the Effect drop-down menu, as shown in Figure 10-14.

Table 10-2 details what happens with each effect.

Table 10-2. Default sound effects in the Effect drop-down

Effect	Details
Left channel	The sound is played through the left speaker only.
Right channel	The sound is played through the right speaker only.
Fade to right	The sound plays normally but fades out to the right speaker.
Fade to left	The sound plays normally but fades out to the left speaker.
Fade in	The sound fades in from silence.
Fade out	The sound fades out from silence.
Custom	The Custom setting brings up the sound envelope, as shown in Figure 10-15, which allows you to customize the fading in and out of your sound.

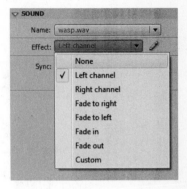

Figure 10-14. The preset sound effects in the Effects drop-down

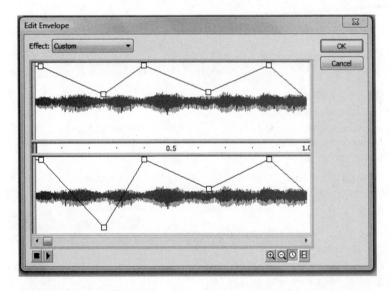

Figure 10-15. The Edit Envelope dialolg allows you to customize your sound on the stage.

299

The Stream option of the Sync drop-down box tells Flash CS4 to begin playing the sound before it is completely loaded into memory. The downside to it is that every time the sound is replayed, it needs to be reloaded. Setting Sync to stream also tells flash to line the sound up with the timeline—if you add frames to the layer with a streaming synced sound and scrub the playhead back and forth, you will hear a preview of the sound event at that frame.

Applying sounds to a button using ActionScript 3.0

Now that you've seen how to import a sound into the Library, we're going to revisit a familiar Flash CS4 movie. In Chapter 6, you learned how to animate a banner on motion paths. We're now going to give it some sound. Ensure that you have either completed the final exercise in Chapter 6, or that you have downloaded the source files for this chapter from the friends of ED website. When you have downloaded the file, take a moment to listen to it. You will find that we have built onto the original insect buzzing sound, adding some background noise and a sudden crunch—as if our fly is being consumed by a monster! If you have not completed the Chapter 6 exercise, you can download it from the Chapter 10 files for this book from the friends of ED website, along with the sound source file.

1. Open the final exercise from Chapter 6 or the downloaded source file from this chapter in Flash CS4. Your stage will display as shown in Figure 10-16.

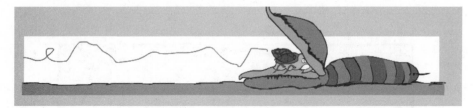

Figure 10-16. The open file

2. Save the sound file and the Flash source file in the same directory. Do not change their names; this is important to ensure that the ActionScript that we are about to code can reference the sound file and therefore works.

The first thing we are going to do is to create a button that will enable people to click to hear and mute sound after we have applied ActionScript to it.

3. Import the bee.mp3 file into the animation by selecting File ➤ Import to Library.

4. Create a new layer at the very top of the timeline, above all of the other layers.

5. Call it sound, as shown in Figure 10-17.

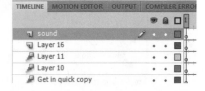

Figure 10-17. Creating the sound layer in Flash CS4

The next thing we need to do is create a button to which to attach the sound. We will do this on the sound layer of the timeline.

6. Select Insert ➤ New Symbol.

7. Give it the name of sound_btn and the type of Button, as shown in Figure 10-18.

Figure 10-18. Naming your button symbol

8. The button should open immediately on the stage, ready for you to edit. If it doesn't, double-click the sound_btn button in the Library.

The button symbol will open for editing. We're going to create a button that users click to hear or mute the sound. Ensuring that sound is user initiated is very important when creating banner ads for a client who is planning to distribute the ads through common publishers, as there are guidelines that must be adhered to for those ads to be published. See more about international publishing standards in Chapter 11.

9. Draw a small black rectangle on the stage within the sound_btn symbol.

10. Insert the text shown in Figure 10-19 in white on top of the black rectangle.

> Remember that the button needs to fit on the banner, so don't make it too big.

Figure 10-19.
Creating a button to
attach your sound to

11. Click Scene 1 at the top-left corner of the stage to exit the button editing screen.

12. Drag the sound_btn symbol from the Library to the right side of the stage, as shown in Figure 10-20.

13. In the Properties Inspector, give the button an instance name of sound_btn.

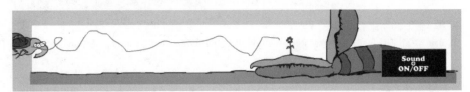

Figure 10-20. Placing the sound button on the stage

We have now prepared the movie, and it's time to move on to the ActionScript side of adding the sound.

14. With the first frame of the sound layer on the timeline, open the Actions panel by selecting Window ➤ Actions.

The first step in adding sound to your animation is to create a Sound object. This is a three-step process. First of all, we will declare a new sound and call it bee. This sound is named as it is because we are referencing the bee.mp3 file that is saved in the same directory as your Flash CS4 document. As discussed previously, the Sound object in ActionScript is the ideal way to finely control sounds in your animation, as it keeps the size of the animation smaller and enables you to specify exactly where you want sounds to occur, regardless of the size of the animation or the ability of the user's computer to display large-scale animations smoothly.

The second step is to tell Flash that bee is a new Sound object, and then you tell Flash exactly where the sound is located. This needn't always be a relative path; you could point it at an absolute URL such as www.friendsofed.com/sounds/bee.mp3 if you so wished.

All three steps are contained in one line of code!

15. Type the following code into line 1 of the Actions panel, as shown in Figure 10-21:

```
var bee:Sound  =  new Sound  (new URLRequest("bee.mp3"));
```

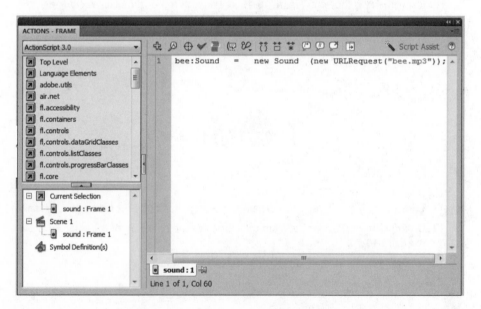

Figure 10-21. The first step in creating a Sound object is to declare the sound in ActionScript.

Now we'll create a SoundTransform object. SoundTransform objects control volume and stereo panning—that is, which stereo channel the sounds are directed to come out of. In this situation, we are allowing the users to decide if they want to hear the sound or not at the click of a button.

16. Add the following code at line 2 of the Actions panel, as shown in Figure 10-22:

```
var vol:SoundTransform = new SoundTransform(1,0);
```

Figure 10-22. Adding the SoundTransform object

Once again, a single line of code encompasses multiple steps. The first is setting the SoundTransform volume. Volume (in this case the number 1 in the code) is always represented by a value between 0 and 1.

The second step is to give the code a value for left and right stereo panning. Stereo panning in code is represented with values between −1 and 1, with −1 being the extreme left, 1 being the extreme right, and 0 being directly in the middle of left and right stereo—in which the sound is basically transmitted through two or more designated channels, creating a fuller sound experience.

The SoundChannel object controls the sound in your Flash CS4 movie. Every sound in your Flash CS4 ActionScript 3.0 document is assigned to a SoundChannel object, which acts like a speaker system for your sound file. Your Flash CS4 application can have many SoundChannels that can be mixed together to produce different kinds of sound effects, thus making it easier for the Flash designer to produce unique and compelling animations. So now we'll give our animation a SoundChannel object.

17. Add the following code to line 3 of the ActionScript, as shown in Figure 10-23:

```
var soundEffects:SoundChannel=bee.play(0,1,vol);
```

This new line of code gives the SoundChannel object the name soundEffects.

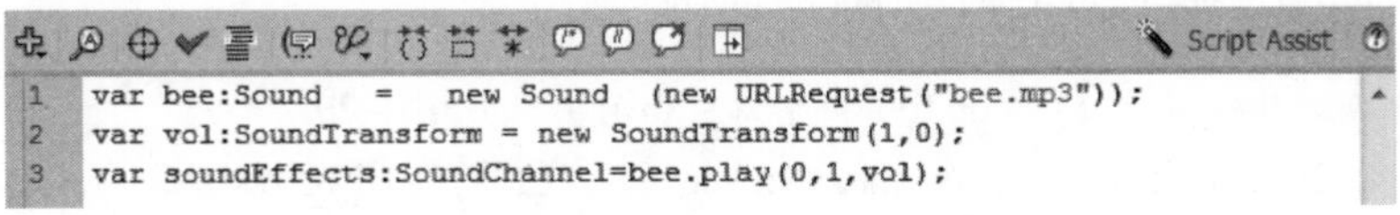

Figure 10-23. Naming the SoundChannel object

The code in step 17 tells the Flash file where to start playing the bee.mp3 file. The first number, 0, tells the file to start playing from 0 seconds, or the absolute start. The second number, 1, tells the file to play the sound once only. The reference to vol is referring to the SoundTransform you created in step 16, which contains the values for the volume and stereo panning.

If we pause for a moment here and test the movie by selecting Control ➤ Test Movie, we can see the wonderful effects that sound has upon an animation. Your bug now buzzes! Birds sing in the background and the caterpillar-like creature closes its mouth with a resounding lip smack. Now that we have the sound playing, we are going to give the user

10

the ability to control whether they want to hear it by toggling the button that we placed on the banner.

18. Add the following code to line 4 of the ActionScript, as shown in Figure 10-24.

```
var soundPlaying: Boolean = true;
```

This line creates a variable that enables the user to toggle the sound using the button that you inserted into the banner at the beginning of this exercise. With this line, we are setting a flag that is telling the banner that the sound is playing. Therefore, when the user clicks the button, the flag will be changed to tell the banner to stop playing the sound.

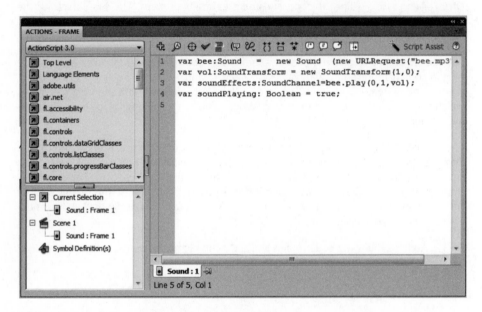

Figure 10-24. Beginning to create the button functionality

19. Add the following code to line 5, as shown in Figure 10-25:

```
sound_btn.addEventListener(MouseEvent.CLICK, toggleSound);
```

This code adds an event listener to the sound_btn button—this is a mouse click event that calls the toggleSound function whenever the button is clicked. Let's write that toggleSound function now.

Event listeners allow an object called the Listener object to receive events relayed from another object. In this example, we are registering the sound_btn object to toggle the sound when the mouse is clicked on the button.

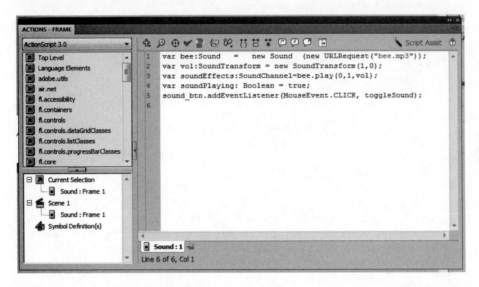

Figure 10-25. Adding the event listener

20. Add the following code from line 6 in the Actions panel, as shown in Figure 10-26:

```
function toggleSound(event:Event):void{

    if(soundPlaying==true){
        vol.volume=0;
        soundEffects.soundTransform = vol;
        soundPlaying=false;
    }else{
        vol.volume=1;
        soundEffects.soundTransform = vol;
        soundPlaying=true;
    }
}
```

This code is the function toggleSound, and it is basically telling Flash to turn the sound off if there is a sound playing and the button is clicked. If there is no sound playing and the user clicks the button, it means they want to hear it, so turn the sound on.

10

```
 3   var soundEffects:SoundChannel=bee.play(0,1,vol);
 4   command is bee.play(0,1,vol)
 5   var soundPlaying: Boolean = true;
 6   sound_btn.addEventListener(MouseEvent.CLICK, toggleSound);
 7   function toggleSound(event:Event):void{
 8
 9        if(soundPlaying==true){
10             vol.volume=0;
11             soundEffects.soundTransform = vol;
12             soundPlaying=false;
13        }else{
14             vol.volume=1;
15             soundEffects.soundTransform = vol;
16             soundPlaying=true;
17        }
18   }
```

Figure 10-26. Adding the toggleSound functionality

Let's examine what this code means. The line if(soundPlaying==true){ asks the Flash file if the sound is playing. If the answer is yes, when the button is clicked, the Flash file decreases the volume—denoted in the code volume=0. We then link the change of the volume back to the sound channel we previously defined. This is done using the following code: sound-Effects.soundTransform = vol.

Next, you need to tell the Flash file that the sound has decreased. This is done by setting the soundPlaying boolean to false.

```
vol.volume=0;
soundEffects.soundTransform = vol;
soundPlaying=false;
```

Following this code comes the else condition.

```
}else{
vol.volume=1;
soundEffects.soundTransform = vol;
soundPlaying=true;
```

The else condition gets executed only if the prior if statement returns false (i.e., the sound isn't playing)—that is, if a user clicks the button while the sound is muted. In this case, the code vol.volume=1 sets the volume to 100 percent output (the loudest output).

As per the previous volume transition, this change needs to be linked back to soundEffects, the SoundChannel object. And to finish it off, we need to tell Flash that the sound is playing! We do this by the code soundPlaying=true;.

Figure 10-27 demonstrates the way that the code should look in your Actions panel.

```
1    var bee:Sound = new Sound(new URLRequest("bee.mp3"));
2    var vol:SoundTransform = new SoundTransform(1,0);
3    var soundEffects:SoundChannel=bee.play(0,1,vol);
4    var soundVolume:SoundTransform=new SoundTransform();
5    var soundPlaying: Boolean = true;
6    sound_btn.addEventListener(MouseEvent.CLICK, toggleSound);
7    function toggleSound(event:Event):void{
8        if(soundPlaying==true){
9            vol.volume=0;
10           soundEffects.soundTransform = vol;
11           soundPlaying=false;
12       }else{
13           vol.volume=1;
14           soundEffects.soundTransform = vol;
15           soundPlaying=true;
16       }
17
18
19   }
20
```

Figure 10-27. The final code inserted into your movie

So let's test our banner! You should see the bee flying along *and* hear it buzzing! Let's click the Sound ON/OFF button. The sound should stop, which is very important when you are preparing any Flash animation. It is poor practice not to allow the user to disable sound, and publishers will not let your clients display banner advertising on their sites unless there is a clear and easily recognizable mute function. Likewise with sites, you should clearly label how the user can turn sound on and off. Sites with overpowering noises are likely to be visited only once by users, regardless of the functions that are offered.

This is simply an example of what you can do with volume control, and it doesn't necessarily need to be tied to a button. For instance, you could use the same volume control but add it to a volume slider, which would give the user even more control over the volume of the noise. Another idea could be to have the sound panning from left to right as the bee flies across it, which would be a great addition to a website or a static web banner.

Now that you have experimented with sound, let's see what lies in store in the wonderful world of video!

10

Moving pictures are worth a million words!

The video revolution is happening all around us. No longer is video the sole domain of social networking sites such as MySpace and YouTube—you can find video on many sites and advertising banners throughout the Internet. This section will demonstrate how Flash CS4 allows you to import and manipulate videos.

To import video into Flash CS4, you must use either FLV (Flash Video), which is the file format used to play video using Adobe Flash Player (and can also be embedded within SWF files), or H.264-encoded video. H.264-encoded video is an industry standard for video that allows users to stream high-quality video at a low data transfer rate.

You can convert Flash-incompatible videos using Adobe Media Encoder, shown in Figure 10-28, which is a stand-alone program used by the Adobe CS4 creative suite to output media to required media formats. To use Adobe Media Encoder, simply open the program, which is included in the Adobe CS4 bundle (and downloadable from www.adobe.com), add the file, and choose from the Format column drop-down list which format you would like to convert your media to. When you have chosen this, click the Queue button, and your video will be converted.

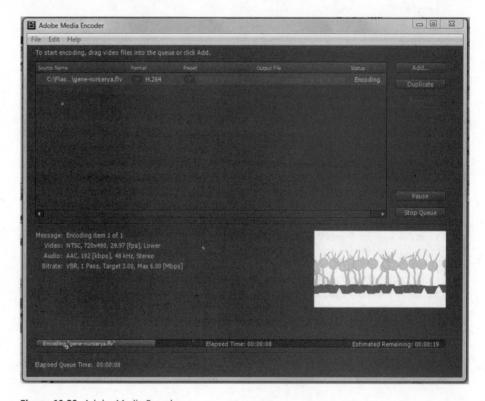

Figure 10-28. Adobe Media Encoder

There are a number of limitations when it comes to which version of Flash Player you can use. Table 10-3 describes them.

Table 10-3. Preferred video codecs for Flash and Flash Player versions

Video Codec	Published-to-SWF version	Flash Player Version
FLV	All	All
H.264/F4V	Version 9.2 or later	Version 9.2 or later
On2 VP6	Versions 6, 7, and 8	Version 8 and later
Sorenson Spark	Version 6 only	Versions 6, 7, and 8 only
Sorenson Spark	Version 7 only	Versions 7, 8, 9, and 10

The next section will jump straight into importing a video into Flash CS4.

Importing videos into Flash CS4

In the following exercise, we are going to import a video into Flash CS4! To complete this exercise, ensure that you have downloaded the source files for this chapter from www. friendsofed.com. We have already converted the movie to the preferred FLV format in Adobe Media Encoder for you. This is the first of three exercises that will step you through not only importing a video, but using the Flash CS4 controls for playing the video, and creating a Flash CS4 document that includes a separate sound.

1. Open a new document in Flash CS4.

We want the video to fill the entire Flash movie, and it is 600×338 pixels; so, if we create the Flash document the same size, the movie will not be cropped, and it won't have any bare borders around it.

2. Give the document the dimensions 600×338.

3. Save the document as gene-babies.fla in the same directory that you saved the gene-nursery.flv file that you downloaded.

We'll now import the gene-nursery.fla file. If you preview this movie in Flash Player, you'll find that it's an animation of a number of critters.

4. Select File ➤ Import ➤ Import Video to import the movie. The Import Video wizard will appear, as shown in Figure 10-29.

10

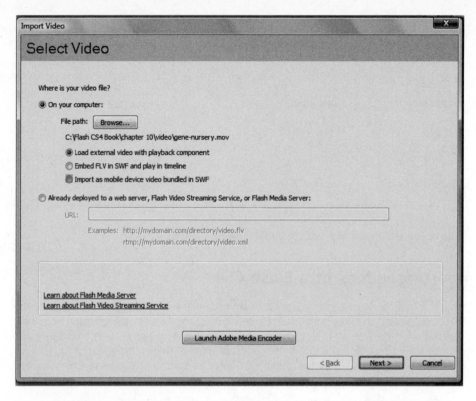

Figure 10-29. The Import Video wizard enables you to import movies into your Flash documents.

> *The* Import Video *wizard checks that the video that you are about to import is compatible with Flash CS4 and alerts you if it is not. Remember, you can convert videos that are Flash CS4 incompatible with Adobe Media Encoder.*

5. Navigate to where you have saved gene-nursery.flv and click Next. Information about the movie that you have selected will appear under the Browse button, as shown in Figure 10-30.

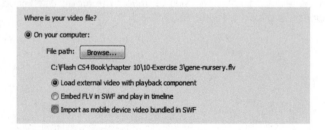

Figure 10-30. The gene-nursery.flv information in the Import Video dialog box

You are offered three options for importing your movie: Load external video with playback component, Embed FLV in SWF and play in timeline, **and** Import as mobile device video bundled in SWF.

Load external video with playback component **allows you to import the video, and automatically creates a playback component, which is a set of controls that allows users to control the video by starting, stopping, or scrubbing the controls forward and backward. This is the option we are going to use in this exercise.**

Embed FLV in SWF and play in timeline **places the movie that you have imported into the Flash document onto the timeline, where you can scrub the playhead backward and forward across individual frames to see the movie play frame by frame. This is best used for short videos with no audio track, as embedded video often causes synchronization issues with audio tracks. To choose this option, simply select the corresponding radio button.**

Import as mobile device video bundled in SWF **bundles a video into a Flash Lite document for mobile distribution.**

6. Select Load external video with playback component **and click** Next. As you have chosen to assign a playback component to the Library, the Skinning screen in the Import Video wizard will appear, as shown in Figure 10-31.

Figure 10-31. The Skinning screen

The Skinning *screen allows you to choose from a range of different playback components, and to specify where you want the playback controls to appear and what you want them to look like. Select a few different types to find one that you like.*

You also have the ability to link to your own custom playback controls. To do this, select Custom *from the* Skin *drop-down box and enter the URL for your custom skin into the* URL *field, ensuring it is relative to where you have saved your FLA file.*

If you wish to not have any play controls, simply select None *from the* Skin *drop-down box*

7. Select SkinOverPlaySeekMute.swf and click Next. The Finish Video Import screen will appear, as shown in Figure 10-32.

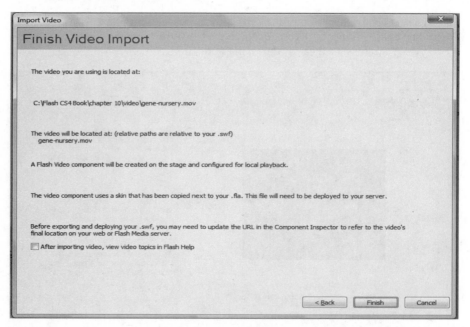

Figure 10-32. The Finish Video Import screen

8. Click Finish. A progress bar will keep you updated as to the import progress, as shown in Figure 10-33.

Figure 10-33. The Getting metadata progress bar

312

9. Save your movie as `gene-babies.fla`.

Your video has now been imported into Flash CS4! Your movie should appear in the Library, as shown in Figure 10-34. The next exercise will show you how to place your video into the document.

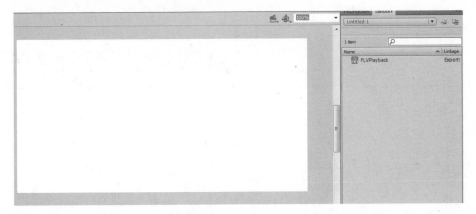

Figure 10-34. Your gene-babies.fla movie with the gene-nursery.flv file imported into the Library

Importing a movie from the Library to the stage

Now that we have accomplished the task of importing an FLV movie into the Library of a Flash CS4 document, we're going to import that movie onto the stage. Remember how we set the stage dimensions to fit the movie? This is where you will see that pay off, and you'll see the movie on the stage.

1. Ensure that the `gene-babies.fla` document is open in Flash CS4.

2. Drag the `gene-nursery.flv` movie from the Library and position it on the stage as shown in Figure 10-35.

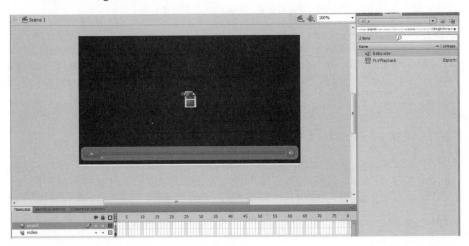

Figure 10-35. The gene-nursery.flv file on the stage

> You can position the movie with x and y values in the Properties Inspector.

3. Save your movie.

4. Select Control ➤ Test Movie to test your movie in Flash Player. The video will appear on the screen, as per Figure 10-36.

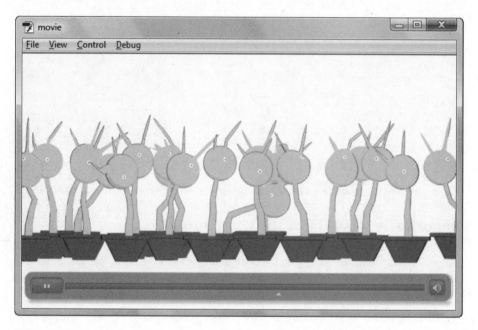

Figure 10-36. Your movie playing in Flash Player

Test your movie. You will see that it plays through and loops by default.

Let's first take a moment to consider what would have happened if we had chosen the second import option, Embed FLV in SWF and play in timeline. For a movie the size that we are currently importing, there would have been little difference. If you were importing a larger video, however—for example, a music video clip—you could not be guaranteed that the movie would play as smoothly as it should.

How to embed an FLV in a SWF file

The previous exercise showed us how to import an FLV file into a Flash CS4 document. The next exercise will demonstrate how to embed an FLV into a SWF file. To complete this exercise, be sure to have saved the gene-nursery.flv and the babies.wav files into a local directory. The FLV file provides your video content and the WAV file provides your audio content. Remember to download these files from the friends of ED website.

1. Open a new document in Flash CS4.

2. Give it the dimensions 600×338 so that it fills the entire Flash movie exactly.

3. Save the movie as video.fla in the same folder that you have the source files for this exercise.

We're now going to import the FLV into the document. We've been here before, in the last exercise, but this is where the similarities end!

4. Select File ➤ Import Video.

5. Browse to where the gene-nursery.flv file is saved.

6. Ensure the Embed FLV in SWF and play in timeline **radio button** is selected, as shown in Figure 10-37.

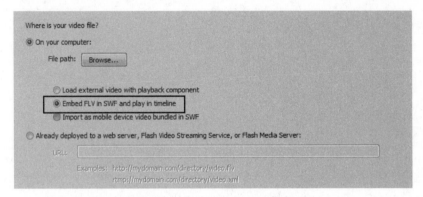

Figure 10-37. Selecting the Embed FLV in SWF and play in timeline option

7. Click Next, and you'll be taken to a new screen for the Import Video **Import wizard**: the Embedding **screen** (shown in Figure 10-38), which allows you to choose how to embed the video.

8. Ensure that the Embedded video **option** in the Symbol type **drop-down list is displayed, and that the** Place instance on stage **and** Expand timeline if needed **check boxes are checked (also as shown in Figure 10-38).**

We have chosen to select the Embedded video **option from the** Symbol type **drop-down because it is the most appropriate method of importing a video clip into Flash for linear playback.**

Other options in this drop-down include Movie clip, **which will enable you to place your video inside a movie clip (this is appropriate when you need to exert fine control over your movie); and** Graphic, **which does not allow you to interact with the video using ActionScript.**

> *Flash imports videos to the stage by default, which is fine if your video presentation is simple and contains little interaction.*

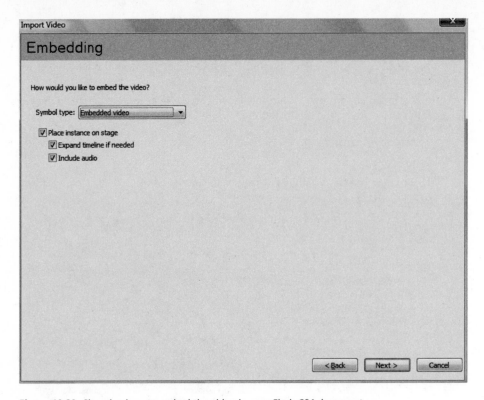

Figure 10-38. Choosing how to embed the video in your Flash CS4 document

9. Click Next, and the Finish Video Import screen will be displayed, confirming the options that you chose in the previous screen.

10. Click Finish.

The movie will display on the stage, as shown in Figure 10-39. Also note that the animation ends on frame 600 of the timeline. Take a moment to scrub the playhead back and forth along the timeline to see the baby genes move.

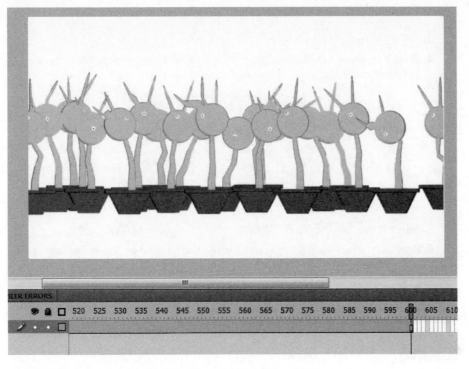

Figure 10-39. The embedded movie on the stage is 600 frames long.

Adding sounds to your video

Videos without audio can be a poor second cousin to videos with sound, which can inform users exactly what you are trying to relay to them and give your videos a different dimension. Let's look at this now, starting from the last step in the previous exercise.

1. Rename Layer 1 on the timeline to Video.

2. Insert a new layer above the Video layer and call it Sound, as shown in Figure 10-40.

Figure 10-40. Adding the Sound layer to the timeline

We'll now import the sound to the Library. We've done this before, remember? It's easy!

3. Select File ➤ Import to Library.

4. Browse to where the downloaded file baby.wav is saved, and click OK. You will see baby.wav in the Library, as shown in Figure 10-41.

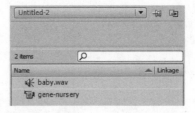

Figure 10-41. The Library displaying sound and video

5. Select frame 1 of the Sound layer.

6. Drag baby.wav onto the stage. You will see the timeline on the Sound layer populate, as shown in Figure 10-42.

Figure 10-42. baby.wav on the timeline of the Flash movie

If you scrub along the timeline, you will see that the Sound layer ends well before the Video layer. Flash CS4 provides an easy fix for this!

7. With the first frame on the Sound layer still selected, click the Properties tab.

8. Click the Repeat drop-down box and select Loop, as shown in Figure 10-43.

Figure 10-43. Looping the sound in the Properties Inspector

9. Save your movie.

Test your movie. What happens? Your cute little gene babies should be brought to life with a series of realistic giggles.

Using an external video file in your Flash CS4 animation

The following short exercise ends this section of video tutorials, and will show you how to connect to a video on the World Wide Web.

1. Open a new document in Flash CS4.
2. Give it the dimensions 600×338, as you'll be connecting to the same movie file as previously, with the same dimensions.
3. Save the movie as an FLA file.

We're now going to connect to a remotely hosted video.

4. Select File ➤ Import Video.
5. At the first screen of the Video Import wizard, choose Already deployed to a web server, Flash Video Streaming Service, or Flash Media Server.
6. Type the following URL into the URL field, as shown in Figure 10-44:

   `http://www.cheridankerr.com/gene-nursery.flv`

Figure 10-44. Entering the URL of the FLV file

7. Click Next.
8. As you did in the first video exercise, choose a skin, and click Next.
9. At the final screen, click Finish. You will see the FLV appear on the stage, as shown in Figure 10-45. You have now embedded a remote FLV file into a Flash CS4 document!

Test the movie by selecting Control ➤ Test Movie. What happens? It plays as before, but it's calling a movie from a remote server to your desktop, provided of course you are currently connected to the Internet. Play with the controls and see your movie move backward and forward. The downside to streaming video is that every time the animation is replayed or the page reloaded, it must load again.

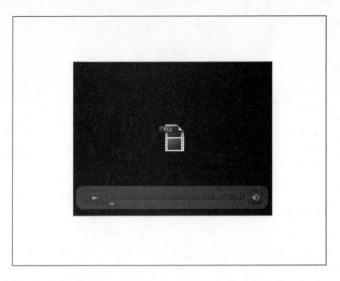

Figure 10-45. The remote FLV embedded in the Flash CS4 document

Summary

This chapter has shown some compelling ways to add sound and vision to your movies using Flash CS4. Sound can be applied many ways to your Flash CS4 movies, including dragging directly onto the timeline and using ActionScript to create an interactive experience.

Videos too add another dimension to your site, and Flash CS4 can have you up and running with video on your website in a matter of moments. In Chapter 12, you will learn how to import the video component of this chapter into a larger Flash website.

In the meantime, Chapter 11 gives you the ability to make your Flash animations available to an even wider group. In it, you'll learn about accessibility and the international publisher standards.

CHAPTER 11

UTILIZING BEST PRACTICES TO GET THE MOST OUT OF YOUR FLASH CS4 MOVIES

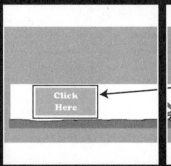

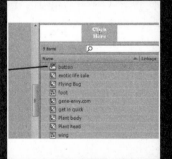

When Stan Lee, one of the founding fathers of the superhero comics that have kept generations in thrall, wrote the immortal words, "With great power there must also come great responsibility," he was referring to the power of fictional individuals such as Superman and Spider-Man. However, the idea is important to keep in mind as you are designing your Flash CS4 masterpieces. By ensuring that your Flash CS4 web animations are accessible to a wide range of people, you are helping them to succeed.

During the course of this book you have learned how to build amazing Flash CS4 animations and applications. You have learned how to make the characters in your animations move along prescribed guidelines and move in carousels, you've given them the power of sound, and you've used them in movies. With all you've learned, you now have absolute power with Flash. This chapter is designed to teach you how to wield that power wisely.

Part of that is following the guidelines of the World Wide Web Consortium (W3C), an internationally recognized body dedicated to enforcing and creating standards for the World Wide Web. You'll need to adhere to those standards to get the best possible result from the hard work you put into your Flash CS4 gems.

When the W3C was established in 1994, the Web was a blossoming technology without protocols or standards to guide developers and designers. The W3C's guidelines and best practices helped standardize user experience across the Web while allowing new technologies to be used to their full potential. Over time, these standards have evolved to include new developments. Although more than 90 percent of active Internet users in the US have broadband Internet (according to www.websiteoptimization.com), we still need to cater to the lowest common denominator—that is, the people with dial-up Internet speeds. After all, from a commercial perspective, their dollar is worth the same as a dollar from a customer with faster Internet speed. And at the end of the day, for Flash designers and developers, that's what building Flash CS4 applications is all about—getting the clients to your website to find the information that will drive them to purchase your client's product.

But best practice is not simply about your user's Internet-connection speed. It's about ensuring the widest possible range of your target demographic can access and interpret your website—that means everything from ensuring that you are creating Flash applications that can be read by the Adobe Flash Player with the most market penetration to ensuring that people with disabilities can read and interpret your site.

It is also important, having invested precious time and resources into building comprehensive Flash applications, that you can gauge the results of your efforts. For advertising, that is generally done in conjunction with publishers such as Yahoo! or MSN who generate reports from your ad campaign when it runs on their network, where you can see the number of people who have clicked on your ad to visit your site, see which areas of your site are most popular, and allow you to plan upgrades and redesigns to take advantage of this.

This chapter is about enabling you to take the guesswork out of your campaigns—to analyze results and change campaigns accordingly.

Accessibility is responsibility

When you create an *accessible* application or website, you are enabling people of all abilities and disabilities to use it. You must consider many factors when you are making your site accessible, including visual, mobility, cognitive, and auditory considerations, and seizures caused by strobing and similar effects.

Adobe Flash Player 10 is the first rich media player that allows people with disabilities to access all the content within your Flash application. It contains integrated supported for the widely used Microsoft Active Accessibility—an application programming interface that allows users of assistive technology products such as screen readers, touch-screen keyboards designed for people with limited physical abilities, and narrative software for users with limited hearing—and ensures that the content within Flash applications is immediately accessible with widely used screen readers (such as JAWS from Freedom Scientific and Window-Eyes from GW Micro). Creating Flash documents that are accessible, and support the user of assistive technologies ensures that your Flash applications can be seen by a wider audience. This coupled with Flash CS4's ability to create completely accessible rich-media applications enables you to develop Flash applications that are accessible to the vast majority of users. In the next section you will learn how to utilize accessibility options in Flash CS4.

> Currently, accessibility guidelines fall into four categories:
>
> **Auditory disabilities**: People who have disabled hearing may need subtitling software.
>
> **Cognitive disabilities**: People with learning disabilities and disabilities related to problem-solving and logic skills. These people may find the Web a better experience using assistive technology such as voice recognition and word-prediction software.
>
> **Motor disabilities**: People who have difficulty using the hands due to tremors, or loss of muscle control may use special touch screens.
>
> **Visual impairment**: People with color-blindness or limited vision. These people may use screen readers, screen magnification, and audio assistants.
>
> To make your site completely accessible, you need to ensure that people with these disabilities can use assistive technologies to view your Flash CS4 application.

Accessibility is more and more a prime consideration when developing Flash CS4 applications. This doesn't mean that you have to develop two stand-alone applications to ensure complete access; it means only that you have to plan your project wisely.

Ensuring your banners comply with publishers' standards

By now we are very much used to publishing files in Flash CS4. At the time of writing this book, the industry standard for Flash banner advertisements is mostly Flash 8 or Flash 9, with ActionScript 2.0 only. In the future it will be Flash 9 with ActionScript 3.0, and then

Flash 10. The current standard is because of the lowest-common-denominator rule mentioned in this chapter's introduction. Many publishers—companies such as MSN and Yahoo!—simply have not had the resources available to assist and debug files with ActionScript 3.0. Additionally, Flash 9 introduced some graphical filters that use a lot of CPU resources, and some users' computers can't yet handle that.

Pages that are set for advertising, such as those you will find on Yahoo! or MSN, have up to four banner ads apiece. The W3C and publishers must ensure that the ads shown on a page are light enough for the average user's computer to be able to display them correctly. Therefore, if you are creating advertising to be consumed on a popular site, be sure to check that site's specifications.

The following URLs are for three major international publishers' advertising specifications:

- **Yahoo!**: http://solutions.yahoo.com
- **MSN**: http://advertising.microsoft.com/creative-specs
- **AOL**: www.platform-a.com/ad-specs/rich-media/standard-rich-media-/-technical-guidelines/technical-guidelines/flash-coding-gui

This chapter's first exercise shows you how to publish your files in specific Flash Player versions. We will publish a banner that you completed in Chapter 6 in Flash Player 8 format, which means you would be able to send it to a publisher such as Yahoo! to be displayed on their site. If you have not completed the banner exercise in Chapter 6, you can download the completed FLA file from the Downloads section for this book on the friends of ED website, http://friendsofed.com.

1. Open the 728×90-pixel banner ad that you created in Chapter 6, or download 11-01.fla.
2. Locate the Properties panel.
3. Expand the Publish section by clicking the down arrow, as shown in Figure 11-1.

Figure 11-1. The Publish section of the Properties panel allows you to change the Publish options.

4. Click on the Edit button that corresponds to the Profile: Default **field. The** Publish Settings **dialog box will appear as shown in Figure 11-2.**

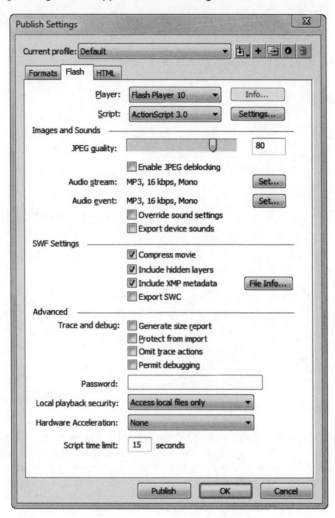

Figure 11-2. The Publish Settings dialog box allows you to specify the Flash Player version in which to publish.

5. Select Flash Player 9 from the Player **drop-down list.**

6. Select ActionScript 2.0 from the Script **drop-down list.**

7. Click OK to close the Publish Settings **dialog box.**

8. Save your FLA file.

9. Select Export ➤ Export Movie, as shown in Figure 11-3.

11

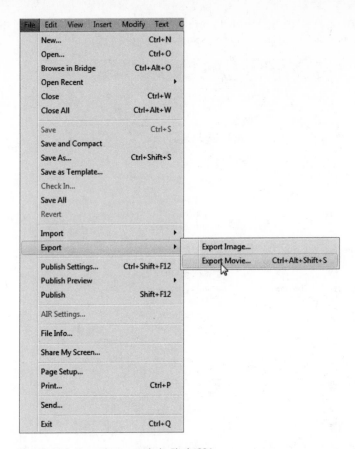

Figure 11-3. Exporting a movie in Flash CS4

Your banner ad is now ready to submit to publishers for display on their sites—but they will not accept your SWF file alone. Remember the lowest-common-denominator rule? It applies here, only this time you need to ensure that people who do not run Flash Player can see your ad. The next section will show you how to create a static backup GIF from Flash CS4.

Creating your backup GIF

Backup GIFs are served as alternatives to Flash files for people who cannot view Flash documents. This ensures that the largest group of people possible can see your ads.

Flash CS4 includes a handy option to export a backup GIF at the same time as you publish your file. We'll investigate this now.

1. Open the previous exercise.

2. Select File ➤ Publish Settings.

The Publish Settings dialog box will appear. By default it displays the Flash publishing settings.

3. Click on the Formats tab.

4. Check the GIF Image (.gif) check box, as shown in Figure 11-4.

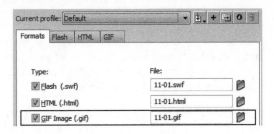

Figure 11-4. Selecting the GIF format

5. A GIF tab will appear. Click on it.

The GIF tab, shown in Figure 11-5, offers you GIF publishing settings. Let's check out a few of those settings.

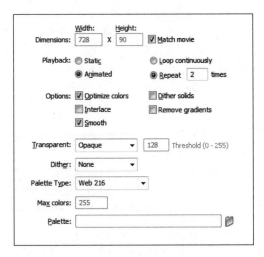

Figure 11-5. Setting your GIF to be animated and to loop twice

The Dimensions setting specifies the dimensions of your GIF. When the Match Movie check box is selected, your GIF will take on the exact dimensions of your Flash movie. When the check box is deselected, you can change the dimensions of your GIF to have dimensions that you can specify in the Width and Height fields.

The Playback section offers options for how your GIF will be played. Static means your GIF will be a single frame. Animated will animate your GIF—that is, an exact replica of your Flash animation will be reproduced in an animated GIF. Loop Continuously makes the animation play repeatedly (or you can specify in the Repeat section how many times the animated GIF will play).

11

The Options section allows you to remove unused colors from a GIF's color table by selecting the Optimize Colors check box, which effectively reduces the file size of your GIF. The Interlace option incrementally displays the GIF in a browser before it completely downloads, which may download the file quicker over a slow network connection. The user will see a basic representation of the image immediately, while the rest of the content is being downloaded. You must never interlace an animated GIF. Smooth applies anti-aliasing to produce a higher-quality image but may result in a halo of gray pixels around images. Dither Solids allows dithering to gradients along with solid colors, and Remove Gradients renders gradients in your Flash animation as solid colors in your GIF.

The Transparent drop-down list allows you specify the transparency of the Flash file's background when it's converted to a GIF. Opaque makes the background a solid color, Transparent makes the background transparent, and Alpha allows you to specify the degree of transparency.

Selecting a Dither option allows you to specify how pixels in the file are combined to simulate colors not available in the chosen palette.

You define the palette by choosing a Palette Type. Web 216 uses the standard web-safe color palette to create the GIF image, Adaptive analyzes the image to create a unique color palette for the GIF, Web Snap Adaptive creates a palette unique to the image but using only web-safe colors where possible, and Custom allows you to specify a palette.

6. Select the Animated radio button in the Playback section.

7. Enter 2 into the Repeat field.

8. Click Publish.

Your backup GIF will be saved in the same directory where you saved your Flash movie. Navigate to and double-click it to open it.

You will see your backup GIF launch and cycle through the animation. The GIF animation isn't as compelling as your Flash animation. Further, backup-GIF specifications usually dictate that they be 20KB or smaller, and this backup GIF is 173KB! In this circumstance, the GIF is unusable. So what do we do?

One option is to create a static GIF. If you were on the first frame and created a static backup GIF using the method you just learned, it would display as shown in Figure 11-6. This doesn't deliver the advertising message, and doesn't prompt the user to click.

Figure 11-6. A static backup GIF that doesn't tell the user our marketing message

Flash CS4 allows us to choose the frame that we want to convert to a GIF. We'll investigate this now.

1. With the Flash animation still open, scrub the playhead on the timeline to frame 216, as shown in Figure 11-7.

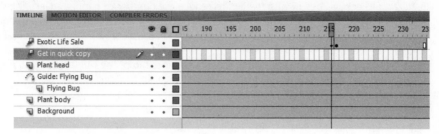

Figure 11-7. Selecting the frame we wish to be our static backup GIF

2. Open the Publish Settings dialog box by selecting File ➤ Publish Settings.

3. Click on the GIF tab.

4. Select the Static radio button.

5. Click Publish.

Navigate to where your FLA file is saved and launch the GIF that now resides there. Your static backup GIF will display the frame that you have chosen, as shown in Figure 11-8.

Figure 11-8. The completed backup GIF

As this backup GIF is only 6KB, it is fine to send to the publisher along with your Flash animation.

It's worthwhile to experiment with animated GIFs if your Flash animation is simple. Files that include photos and many-colored palettes, though, are often too large for publishers' specifications. Play around to find the right style for you.

Adhering to IAB standards for banner ads

Most banners that Flash designers are required to build will be displayed on sites that adhere to the Internet Advisory Board (IAB) standards. The IAB is composed of more than 350 industry professionals and is dedicated to fostering the standards, guidelines, and best practices that are adopted on commercial sites throughout the world. These standards are designed to ensure that your banners do not impact the experience of using sites, and to share information that will allow them to create successful online campaigns. For more information about the IAB, visit, www.iab.net.

Universal banner standards

In 2002 a project was begun with the aim to reduce the number of banner-advertising sizes in an effort to reduce inefficiencies and costs associated with creating and buying online media. The result was the Universal Ad Package, which consists of four banner sizes that are standard across most large publishers. You can find out more about the Universal Ad Package by clicking on the Guidelines, Products & Services tab of the IAB website. Table 11-1 details the pixel and file-size guidelines of the Universal Ad Package.

Table 11-1. The Universal Ad Package Dimensions

Ad Type	Dimension	Weight	Recommended Duration
Medium rectangle	300×250	40KB	15 seconds
Rectangle	180×150	40KB	15 seconds
Wide skyscraper	160×600	40KB	15 seconds
Leaderboard	728×90	40KB	15 seconds

In Chapters 3 and 6 we created a medium rectangle 300×250 and a leaderboard 728×90, respectively. They're shown in Figures 11-9 and 11-10.

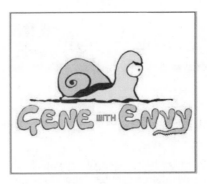

Figure 11-9. A medium-rectangle banner ad created in Chapter 3

Figure 11-10. A leaderboard banner ad created in Chapter 6

For more information about Internet advertising standards, visit www.iab.net.

Tracking your banner advertisement

In addition to standard sizes, several international advertising networks—for example, Yahoo!—recommend the use of standardized tracking. This consists of a *clickTAG* (a tracking code assigned by publishers, including Google, Yahoo!, and MSN) placed on the click event in your Flash movie to track the number of clicks on the advertisement. This enables marketers to know how successful their campaigns are at inspiring users to click on banner ads, and enables networks that serve the ad to know where the ad appears.

Let's assign a clickTAG to a banner.

1. Open 11-02.fla in Flash CS4.

We're going to create a new transparent layer to place the clickTag on.

2. Create a new layer above all of the other layers on the timeline.

3. Call this new layer Click here, as shown in Figure 11-11.

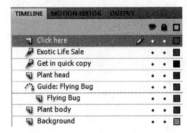

Figure 11-11. Creating a layer for the button

We are now going to create a button on frame 236 of the banner ad to give the user a clear call to action to click the banner ad to be taken to the advertised site. We have premade the button for you to apply the code to; you will find this button in the library for this document.

4. Scroll the playhead along to frame 236 on the new Click here layer and insert a keyframe.

5. Drag the button symbol from the Library onto frame 236 of the Click here layer onto the stage, as shown in Figure 11-12.

Figure 11-12. Positioning the button on the stage

11

> *You can choose to apply the same motion presets to the button as we have the to the rest of the text; simply revisit Chapter 6 for step by step instructions.*

We want to stop the movie clip where the button is displayed, so we'll add a bit of ActionScript (unrelated to the clickTAG) to the movie.

6. Select frame 236 of the Click here layer.

7. Select Window ➤ Actions and type the following code into the Actions panel, as shown in Figure 11-13:

```
stop();
```

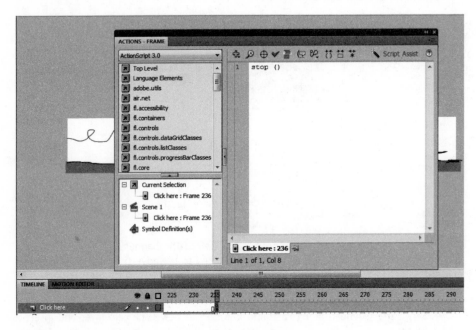

Figure 11-13. Inserting code to stop the movie from looping

Take a moment to test your movie. You will see that it no longer loops—we have stopped the looping because we want to leave the user with a clear call to action, and therefore impetus to click on the ad. We are now going to assign the clickTAG to the button.

Because, as mentioned earlier, currently publishers are dubious about accepting Flash movies containing ActionScript 3.0, we need to create the clickTAG in ActionScript 2.0.

8. Insert the following code above the stop(), as shown in Figure 11-14:

```
myButton_btn.onRelease = function(){
    getURL(clickTAG, "_blank");
};
stop()
```

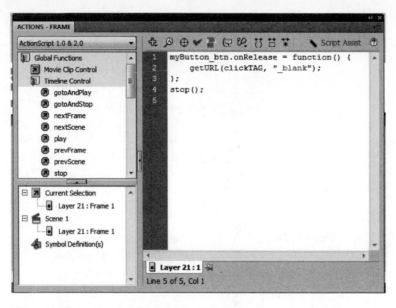

Figure 11-14. Inserting the clickTAG into the button

9. Test your move by selecting Control ➤ Test Movie.

The movie plays as before. But when the animation finishes and the button remains on the static end frame, when you mouse over, the mouse pointer turns into a hand to indicate that the button is now clickable. When the publisher uploads your Flash CS4 animation, they will insert into their system the destination URL that will be called when the user clicks the button.

Using the Accessibility panel

Flash CS4 allows designers and developers to include accessibility information in their Flash CS4 applications using the Accessibility panel

The Accessibility panel, shown in Figure 11-15, enables Flash CS4 designers and developers to apply descriptive text to make individual movie elements and element groups accessible. MSAA distributes these descriptions to the assistive technology the application user has installed.

Let's open the Accessibility panel now and investigate it.

1. Once again, open exercise601.fla in Flash CS4.

2. Select Window ➤ Other Panels ➤ Accessibility.

11

The Accessibility panel will appear as in Figure 11-15.

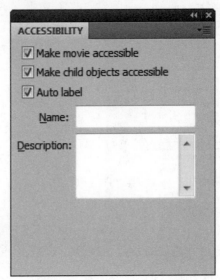

Figure 11-15.
The Accessibility panel provides an option to give elements and element groups descriptive text.

The Accessibility panel displays three fields—Make Movie Accessible, Make Child Objects Accessible, and Auto Label—with corresponding check boxes that are checked by default.

Because we haven't selected any objects on the Flash CS4 animation, the Accessibility panel assumes that we want to make the whole movie accessible via this panel.

Close the panel by clicking on the X in the top-right corner and then click on the Flying Bug symbol on the screen. Once again, select Window ➤ Other Panels ➤ Accessibility to produce the Accessibility panel. What do you see?

You will note that the Make Movie Accessible field has become Make Object Accessible. The field changes based on what you have selected, which allows you to drive accessibility deep down into complicated Flash animations.

- **Make Object/Movie Accessible:** When the Make Movie Accessible box is checked, Flash Player is directed to send the accessibility information for the object to a screen reader. If you disable the option, this information is not sent to the screen reader.

- **Make Child Objects Accessible:** Having this box checked when you publish your Flash CS4 movie tells Flash Player to send the information in the child object to the screen reader. Note that if the movie clip has button behavior assigned to it, this field is ignored.

- **Auto Label:** Checking this option instructs Flash CS4 to automatically label objects on the stage with the copy that you have associated with them.

- **Name:** Entering text into this field specifies the object name, which screen readers will read aloud. If you don't give your accessible object a name, the screen reader might read a generic word, which can be confusing.

> It's important that you don't confuse object names that are specified in the Accessibility panel with the instance name that you specify in the Properties Inspector. Assigning the Accessibility name does not automatically assign the object an instance name.

- **Description**: The copy that you enter into the Description field is read by the screen reader.
- **Shortcut**: If you have assigned a keyboard shortcut to your object, you can enter the shortcut in this field, and the screen reader will read it aloud. Entering a keyboard shortcut into this field in the Accessibility panel automatically creates the shortcut terminology that the reader reads. You must create actual functional keyboard shortcuts via ActionScript.
- **Tab Index**: Using this builds a tabbing order for objects that are accessed when the Tab key on the keyboard is pressed. This works for keyboard navigation through a Flash CS4 application but not for the order that the screen reader reads the content in your Flash movie.

Making Flash movies screen reader–friendly

The basic function of screen-reading software is to read websites and applications aloud. Making your Flash movies screen reader–friendly can be difficult, and unexpected errors can often be thrown in FLA files that have been developed for use in conjunction with screen readers.

When you are contemplating your Flash CS4 accessible application you must consider the way both the screen reader and the user interact with your application without the benefit of a mouse—in other words, enabling the user to tab through your Flash CS4 application using the Tab key on the keyboard. The order in which elements and objects appear on the page is not necessarily the default order in which information is tabbed through. When you build applications in Flash CS4, you can specify the order in which it is tabbed through and the Screen Reader reads it.

Optimizing the tab-control experience

The following exercise will show you how to create an intuitive tab-control order in your Flash CS4 navigation.

1. Open Ch11_ex1.fla in Flash CS4.

It will open as per Figure 11-16. You will notice that it has four static text elements: three dynamic input fields and a Submit button. We are going to assign Tab control so that it runs down the page—first the copy, then a static text field, then a dynamic text field, and so on until the Submit button is reached.

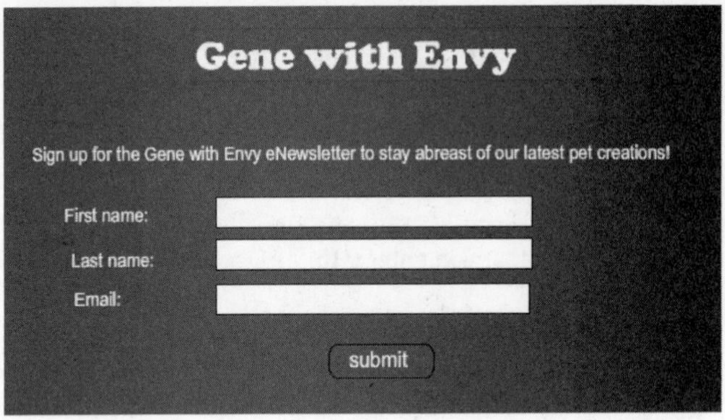

Figure 11-16. The Ch11_ex1.fla document in Flash CS4, awaiting you to assign accessibility

The Accessibility panel in Flash CS4 allows you to create a tab-order index on the following elements:

- Buttons
- Components
- Dynamic text
- Input text
- Movie clips
- Screens

To be able to assign tabbing order, each of the static text elements needs to be converted to a movie clip. We will do that now.

2. Convert the following static text elements on the stage into movie clips, as indicated in Figure 11-17.

- Sign up for the Gene with Envy eNewsletter to stay abreast of our latest pet creations.
- Gene with Envy header
- First Name
- Last Name
- Email

The remainder of the elements on the stage consist of dynamic text and a button, and therefore can already be assigned a tab order and a descriptor. Let's do this now!

3. Open the Accessibility panel by selecting Window ➤ Other Panels ➤ Accessibility.

4. Click on the Gene with Envy header.

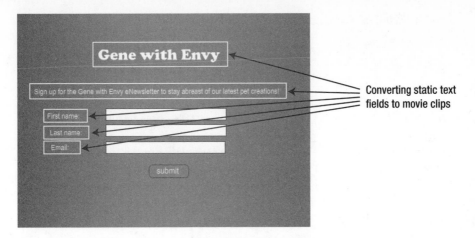

Figure 11-17. Converting static text fields to a movie clip in order to assign them a tabbing order

5. In the Accessibility panel type the following in each of the fields, as shown in Figure 11-18:

- Name: Gene with Envy
- Description: Gene with Envy Page Title
- Tab index: 1

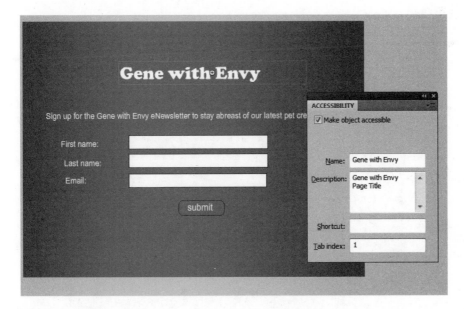

Figure 11-18. Assigning a tab order to the Gene with Envy heading

6. Repeat this for each section as per the following table.

Table 11-2. Creating Your Tabbing Order

Stage	Accessibility Panel		
Element	Name	Description	Tab Index
Gene with Envy header	Gene with Envy	Gene with Envy page header	1
Sign up for the Gene with Envy eNewsletter to stay abreast of our latest pet creations	Gene with Envy	Sign up for the Gene with Envy eNewsletter to stay abreast of our latest pet creations	2
First Name	First Name	Tell us your first name	3
First Name dynamic text	First Name text field	Type your first name here	4
Last Name	Last Name	Tell us your last name	5
Last Name dynamic text	Last Name text field	Type your last name here	6
Email	Email text field	Tell us your email address	7
Email dynamic text	Email text field	Type your email address here	8
Submit	Submit button	Click here to submit your details to our database	9

Let's check out our tabbing order on screen.

7. Select View ➤ Show Tab Order. Your Flash CS4 movie will display as shown in Figure 11-19.

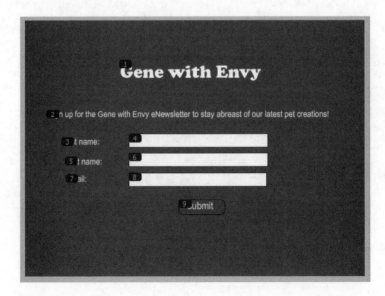

Figure 11-19. Viewing the tabbing order

For more information about creating accessible Flash CS4 animations, visit the Adobe Accessibility Resource Center at www.adobe.com/accessibility/.

Summary

Ensuring your Flash CS4 animation is accessible to a broad demographic is crucial to ensuring its success. In this chapter we have touched on creating accessible animation for screen readers and keyboard navigation, as well as investigating different publishing settings.

Also important is creating banner advertisements that are acceptable to a wide range of publishers. This will allow you to run your ad at many sites on the World Wide Web, and will streamline your development time, ensuring that you will not have to revise your ads for different networks.

In this book's final chapter, we will assemble the assets that we have developed throughout this book and publish them to www.gene-envy.com.

11

CHAPTER 12
THE END OF THE BEGINNING

This final chapter represents a culmination of all the ideas represented thus far. Here you will attempt to pull together the separate parts of a website that you have built to create a whole. Using the drawing, video, and 3D lessons from this book, you will create the basis of a complete Flash CS4 website.

The first thing you'll do is decide how your Flash site is going to look. In Chapter 2, you saw how creating sketches of your site can help you to think about how your site components are going to sit in situ. During the course of this book you have created a number of components that will be integrated into the final site. We will be using the following components:

- The logo that you built using the drawing tools in Chapter 4
- The countdown timer that you created in Chapter 8 using ActionScript 3.0
- The 3D carousel that you created in Chapter 9 using ActionScript 3.0
- The video and sound that you created in Chapter 10

If you have not completed these exercises, fear not—you can download the completed source files from the friends of ED website (www.friendsofed.com), along with the other assets required by this exercise. To complete this exercise correctly, all of the SWF files should be saved in the same directory.

We have created four sketches to demonstrate how each of these will sit in a custom background, as shown in Figures 12-1 through 12-4. Sketches are basic (usually hand-drawn) outlines that show the layout of your website. They enable you to get your ideas outlined before you invest time and effort in building them. Though they may look hasty, they are a good way to see if your ideas will work from a design point of view. The first sketch, in Figure 12-1, demonstrates the basic outline for our site. Our make-believe shop sells plant-animal hybrids, so we thought the perfect way to display them would be within a kind of "greenhouse." You will notice a familiar logo at the top—that's the logo that you created in Chapter 4!

Our site is going to contain movement—the countdown timer, the movie, and the 3D carousel, along with the interactive component of the contact form—and therefore we are not going to use the animated logo that we created in Chapter 9. If our site contained more static information, such as news articles or a photo gallery, we might consider using the animated logo. For this website, however, it would be too busy.

When you are considering the components of your website, you need to consider carefully the purpose of the site. If it is focused on moving content, as our site is, it's beneficial to make as much of the site static as possible—if everything is moving, it can be distracting for the user and draw them away from their purpose. Remember, when you are displaying your website, you have less than 10 seconds to engage your audience, or they may well move on to your competitors.

As you will have noticed in Figure 12-1, there are four buttons for each page of the site: the Home, Pets, Promo, and Contact buttons. We now need to consider how each of these pages sits within the initial sketch. In the case of this site, we decided that we would host the countdown timer on the home page, so our visitors can see instantly how long until they should return to get a bargain in our big sale. This is demonstrated in Figure 12-2.

Figure 12-1. The gene-with-envy site starts with a sketch that shows the stage upon which your animations will sit.

Figure 12-2. The home page sketch of our site

The Pets page, which is accessed by the Pets button, will display the available products for sale in the space above the countdown timer. This is displayed in Figure 12-3.

Figure 12-3. The product page of the site

The product page, as sketched in Figure 12-4, is going to display our promotional video. You will remember this from Chapter 10.

Figure 12-4. The video in your site

The final page, the Contact page, as shown in Figure 12-5, is very important, as it give users the ability to contact us to find out how to buy the product.

Figure 12-5. The Contact page of the gene-with-envy site

This section has established the way that the site will look—now it's time to bring it to life!

Preparation is key

In order to pull all the files together to build our site, we need to create a SWF file to hold our video file. In Chapter 10, you learned how to import the video file, which we will recap, but in the case of this site, we are also going to frame it with curtains. We will create a new Flash movie for this, and then we will pull this Flash movie into the larger movie that is our site. Let's do this now!

> *Please ensure that you have downloaded the source files for this chapter before proceeding.*

1. Create a new Flash (ActionScript 3.0) file and save it as promo.fla.

2. In the Properties Inspector, specify the stage size as 600×415 pixels.

> *We are now going to import the video file exactly the way that we did when we imported the video in Chapter 9—as an external video with a playback component. Refer to that chapter for more in-depth information about importing videos into Flash CS4.*

12

3. Select File ➤ Import ➤ Import Video from the File menu to import the video.

4. The video you are importing should be stored locally and in the same directory, so select On your computer and Load external video component, and click Next.

5. Choose SkinUnderPlayStopSeekMuteVol.swf, set the color of the controls to a dark gray, and click Next.

6. Import your video by clicking Finish.

After a short while, the video container will appear on the stage. You've seen this happen before, but this time we're going to add some pizzazz to our animation, in the form of curtains.

7. Create a new layer above the current video layer.

8. Load the curtains into the scene by selecting File ➤ Import ➤ Import to Stage.

9. Open the Curtains.swf file.

Curtains will appear over the sides of the video, looking something like Figure 12-6.

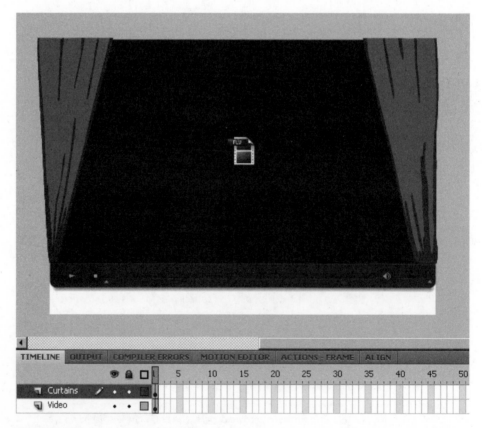

Figure 12-6. The curtains frame the video.

10. Publish the file by either selecting File ➤ Publish Movie or by using the keyboard shortcut Ctrl+Enter (on Windows) or Cmd+Enter (on the Mac).

> *Publishing files usually saves the SWF file in the same directory as your FLA file.*

11. Close your file.

Now that our video has been dressed to fit the shop look and feel, we can start to pull all the files together.

Importing the background

A solid construction is built from a sturdy, sound foundation. In this exercise, you will import a background image that will serve as a solid foundation and a content holder for the final Flash site.

1. Create a new Flash (ActionScript 3.0) document.

2. Set the size of the canvas to 1024×768 pixels in the Properties Inspector.

3. Give the movie a frame rate of 24fps, as shown in Figure 12-7.

Figure 12-7. Setting the frame rate of your animation

4. Save your file as Flash.fla.

5. Select File ➤ Import ➤ Import to Stage.

6. Browse to the Chapter 12 exercise files that you have downloaded from the friends of ED website and select the background.swf to import to the stage.

7. Name the layer Background in the timeline.

12

You should see what looks like a greenhouse shop, as shown in Figure 12-8. Parts of it are empty, waiting for you to import the rest.

Figure 12-8. Your site background, awaiting components to be imported

Importing the logo

Currently we have a background image on the stage waiting to be populated by components. The first site component that we are going to import is the logo. Let's do this now.

1. Leaving the previous exercise open, create another layer and name it logo.
2. Import the logo by going to File ➤ Import ➤ Import to Stage.
3. Browse the Chapter 12 exercise files to find the logo.swf file.
4. Once the logo has been imported to the stage, position it in the billboard at the top, as shown in Figure 12-9.

Figure 12-9. The logo imported to your stage

The static part of the site is now complete. Next, we are going to implement the buttons.

Creating buttons for your site

As you can see, four button labels exist in the top menu navigation, but these currently have no functionality. To begin with, we are going to make buttons of the graphics and give them individual instance names.

1. Select the Home button background. The square surrounding the button should highlight, as illustrated in Figure 12-10.

Figure 12-10. Selecting the Home graphic

2. Convert it to a button symbol and call it menu_Btn, as shown in Figure 12-11.

12

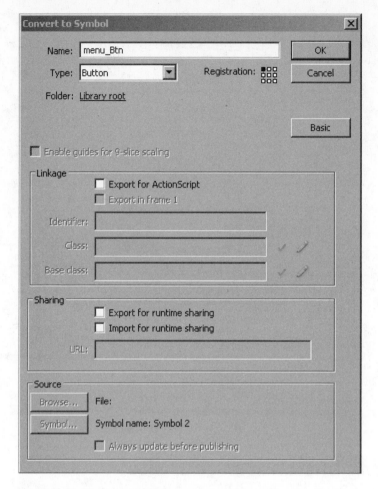

Figure 12-11. Naming your button

3. Click OK to exit the Convert to Symbol dialog box.

4. Double-click the button to take it to edit mode.

5. Insert a keyframe in each of the buttons states. Copy the Up state frame to each of the other frames (if it isn't done automatically), as shown in Figure 12-12.

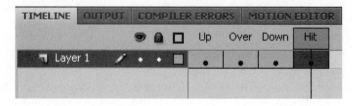

Figure 12-12. Copying states to your button

6. Select a dark blue for the Over state.

7. Quit the edit mode by clicking the Scene 1 link in the upper-left corner.

8. Make three copies of the button and place them behind the three other titles on the stage, like in Figure 12-13. Note that a fast way to do this is to drag the button while holding down the Alt key.

Figure 12-13. Placing buttons upon the stage

9. Now that you have four buttons, you need to give each one an instance name in the Properties Inspector of home_btn, pets_btn, promo_btn, and contact_btn, respectively.

Now that you have set up your buttons, you are going to create pages for users to click through using ActionScript.

Creating the site pages

In the following exercise, we are going to create the pages. First of all, we are going to create the page that loads the countdown timer Flash file. From there, we can use the same process to call the rest of the pages, which are the video, the carousel, and the contact form.

1. Create a new layer called actions.

2. Open the Actions panel by pressing F9.

3. Enter the following code into the Actions panel, as shown in Figure 12-14:

```
var page_loader : Loader = new Loader();
var urlRequest : URLRequest = new URLRequest("countdown.swf");
page_loader.load(urlRequest);
addChild(page_loader);
```

12

353

```
1  var page_loader : Loader = new Loader();
2  var urlRequest : URLRequest = new URLRequest("countdown2.swf");
3  page_loader.load(urlRequest);
4  addChild(page_loader);
5
```

Figure 12-14. Adding the ActionScript into the Actions panel

A new loader is created called page_loader. Loaders are used to import files into your Flash movies. Then a urlRequest variable is created, creatively called urlRequest. This variable just holds the location of the file. At the moment, the countdown.swf file is hosted locally, and the path is relative. You could also make the paths absolute and link to web-based URLs.

The next line, page_loader.load(urlRequest), tells Flash to grab the file and put it in a container called page_loader. Next, the page_loader container is added to the stage.

Now you need to carefully position the loader, which is housing the countdown timer, carefully in the mouth of the strategically placed TV-plant in the shop background.

4. Do this by typing

page_loader.x=400;
page_loader.y=450;

into the Actions panel, as shown in Figure 12-15.

```
6  page_loader.x=400;
7  page_loader.y=450;
8
```

Figure 12-15. Positioning the loader in ActionScript

5. Test the movie by selecting Control ➤ Test Movie. It should look like Figure 12-16.

This will be the first thing a user sees when they land on the home page. The buttons are still not functional.

6. Add some button functionality by adding the following code, as shown in Figure 12-17:

```
home_btn.addEventListener(MouseEvent.CLICK, loadHomeMovie);
function loadHomeMovie(event:MouseEvent):void
  {
          var urlRequest : URLRequest = new URLRequest("countdown.swf");
                       page_loader.load(urlRequest);
                       addChild(page_loader);
                       page_loader.x=400;
                       page_loader.y=450;

  }
```

Figure 12-16. Displaying the countdown timer on your site

```
9
10   home_btn.addEventListener(MouseEvent.CLICK, loadHomeMovie);
11
12   function loadHomeMovie(event:MouseEvent):void {
13
14       var urlRequest : URLRequest = new URLRequest("countdown.swf");
15       page_loader.load(urlRequest);
16       addChild(page_loader);
17
18       page_loader.x=400;
19       page_loader.y=450;
20
21   }
```

Figure 12-17. Adding functionality to your button

Buttons in ActionScript 3.0 listen for events. In the preceding code, you attach an event listener to the instance of the button labeled home_btn. This event listener calls the function loadHomeMovie whenever the button is clicked.

The loadHomeMovie function is a repeat of the first block of code that was executed at the start of the ActionScript. A new URLRequest is made for the countdown timer. It is then inserted into the page_loader container, added to the stage, and positioned into place.

12

You might be asking why the countdown timer code is added again. This is due to the fact that page_loader is a container. We swap our SWF movie files in and out of this container as the user clicks a button for each section. If the contact page were currently showing and a user clicked Home, then the code to display the countdown timer would need to be executed.

Let's now create the remaining pages of our website.

Calling the remaining pages

The next stage in building our Flash website is to alter the rest of the code to call to the stage the other SWF files that comprise our site. Code to run the other buttons can now be copied and pasted from the Home button ActionScript.

1. Copy the block of code you have just typed out, starting from the home_btn. addEventListener to the end brace, as shown in Figure 12-18.

```
10  home_btn.addEventListener(MouseEvent.CLICK, loadHomeMovie);
11
12  function loadHomeMovie(event:MouseEvent):void {
13
14      var urlRequest : URLRequest = new URLRequest("countdown.swf");
15      page_loader.load(urlRequest);
16      addChild(page_loader);
17
18      page_loader.x=400;
19      page_loader.y=450;
20
21  }
```

Figure 12-18. Copying code to implement it for the other pages of your site

2. Paste it three times into the Actions panel so that you have four blocks of code.

3. Alter the second block to read like the following, as shown in Figure 12-19. This code will call the 3D carousel to the stage.

```
pets_btn.addEventListener(MouseEvent.CLICK, loadPetMovie);

function loadPetMovie(event:MouseEvent):void {
        var urlRequest : URLRequest = new URLRequest("genosel.swf");
        page_loader.load(urlRequest);
        addChild(page_loader);
        page_loader.x=0;
        page_loader.y=-50;
    }
```

```
23   pets_btn.addEventListener(MouseEvent.CLICK, loadPetMovie);
24
25   function loadPetMovie(event:MouseEvent):void {
26
27       var urlRequest : URLRequest = new URLRequest("genose1.swf");
28       page_loader.load(urlRequest);
29       addChild(page_loader);
30
31       page_loader.x=0;
32       page_loader.y=-50;
33
34
35   }
```

Figure 12-19. Creating the movie page

We're now going to edit the third block of code to load the carousel into the site.

4. Edit the third block of code to read as shown in Figure 12-20.

```
promo_btn.addEventListener(MouseEvent.CLICK, loadPromoMovie);
function loadPromoMovie(event:MouseEvent):void {
              var urlRequest : URLRequest = new URLRequest("promo.swf");
              page_loader.load(urlRequest);
              addChild(page_loader);
              page_loader.x=208;
              page_loader.y=245;
}
```

```
37   promo_btn.addEventListener(MouseEvent.CLICK, loadPromoMovie);
38
39   function loadPromoMovie(event:MouseEvent):void {
40
41       var urlRequest : URLRequest = new URLRequest("promo.swf");
42       page_loader.load(urlRequest);
43       addChild(page_loader);
44
45       page_loader.x=208;
46       page_loader.y=245;
47
48   }
```

Figure 12-20. Editing the third block of code to call the carousel

Finally, we are going to edit the last block of code to call the contact form.

5. Alter the last block to read like the following, as shown in Figure 12-21:

```
contact_btn.addEventListener(MouseEvent.CLICK, loadContactMovie);

function loadContactMovie(event:MouseEvent):void {
```

12

```
        var urlRequest : URLRequest = new URLRequest("contact.swf");
        page_loader.load(urlRequest);
        addChild(page_loader);

        page_loader.x=130;
        page_loader.y=270;

    }
```

```
50  contact_btn.addEventListener(MouseEvent.CLICK, loadContactMovie);
51
52  function loadContactMovie(event:MouseEvent):void {
53
54      var urlRequest : URLRequest = new URLRequest("contact.swf");
55      page_loader.load(urlRequest);
56      addChild(page_loader);
57
58      page_loader.x=130;
59      page_loader.y=270;
60
61  }
```

Figure 12-21. Calling the contact form to the stage

Now save and then test your movie. If you have typed everything correctly, you will see that each button loads a new section of the website! Now we'll move on to getting the site onto the Web.

Embedding Flash documents into HTML

Embedding Flash documents into HTML is not dissimilar to embedding images into HTML documents, but like embedding images, it comes with its own particular set of rules. You can have Flash CS4 generate the HTML content for you, or you can design it yourself in an HTML editor such as Adobe Dreamweaver. As this book concentrates on the functionality of the Flash CS4 program, we will be creating the HTML document that houses your Flash files with Flash CS4.

As you already know, Flash CS4 comes with the ability to produce more than Flash documents. It has the functionality that allows you to create complete sites. Just as Flash allows you to create backup GIFs from banner animations, so too does it allow you to create the HTML document that your Flash animations are embedded in. Let's pause a moment to discover how to create an HTML document in Flash CS4.

1. If it is not already open in Flash CS4, open Flash.fla from the previous exercise.

2. Select File ➤ Publish Settings to display the Publish Settings dialog box, as shown in Figure 12-22.

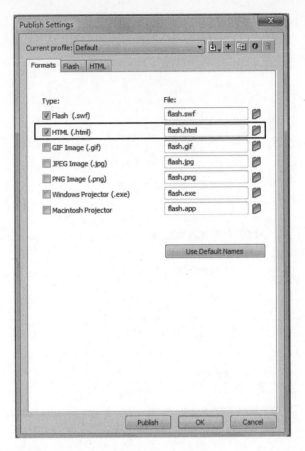

Figure 12-22. The Publish Settings dialog box

Notice that the HTML (.html) field is checked by default. We will leave this checked for this exercise because we want both an FLA file and an HTML document published. Also remember that in Chapter 11, we wanted a GIF image created, so we checked the GIF image (.gif) to create it.

Figure 12-23. Clicking the HTML tab will allow you to access the HTML document publishing settings.

3. Click the HTML tab, as shown in Figure 12-23, to display the publishing settings for HTML.

Publish settings for HTML

Before we publish the HTML document that houses the SWF file, let's take a moment to investigate the Publish Settings dialog box for HTML, as shown in Figure 12-24.

12

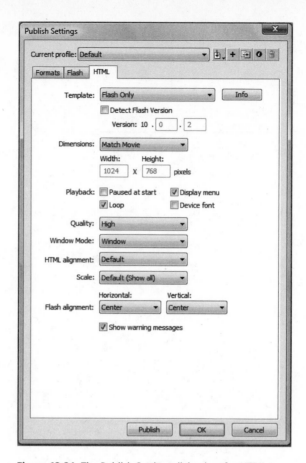

Figure 12-24. The Publish Settings dialog box for HTML

As its name would suggest, the HTML tab of the Publish Settings dialog allows you to describe the publishing specifications. We'll investigate these now.

The Template drop-down, shown in Figure 12-25, allows you to determine what preset HTML template you would like your HTML document published in. By default, it's set to Flash Only. Let's see what happens when we choose to publish it as the default.

Figure 12-25. The Template drop-down allows you to choose from HTML templates.

Ensure that the Flash Only template is selected and click Publish. Navigate to where your FLA file is saved, and you will see that a Flash.html document appears in the directory. It is named Flash.html, as this is the name you gave the Flash CS4 file. Double-click the HTML file to launch it in your default browser.

Table 12-1 gives a quick breakdown of what each of the HTML template settings export as.

Table 12-1. HTML Template Export Settings

Template name	Description
Flash For Pocket PC 2003	This template will display your Flash CS4 movie in an alignment suitable for viewing on Pocket PCs, as well as Internet Explorer and Netscape browsers on your computer.
Flash HTTPS	This HTML template automatically directs you to download Adobe Flash Player from a secure Adobe server if it cannot find it on your system.
Flash Only	This publishes your Flash movie in a standard HTML template.
Flash Only - Allow Full Screen	This publishes your Flash movie in this template when you require full-screen support.
Flash with AICC Tracking	This publishes your movie in this template when you require AICC-HACP support. This is used primarily when creating e-learning modules in Flash CS4. AICC-HACP stands for Aviation Industry CBT Committee and HTTP-Based AICC/CMI Protocol. The AICC is an industry-recognized committee that develops guidelines for aviation training modules, though their specifications are designed to be general purpose and not purely for the aviation industry.
Flash with FS Command	This displays the Flash movie in an HTML template that includes FS Command and JavaScript support. Basically, it is used to send messages to the program that is hosting the Flash document. In the case of the HTML template, it is the browser.
Flash with Named Anchors	This template enables you to insert HTML and script anchors, which enable you to bookmark, or save, the location of the Flash content published as Flash Player 6 and above. Using this means that the user can employ the browser's back button to navigate inside a Flash movie. Beware—not all browsers support this feature, so be sure to test across the most popular browsers (Internet Explorer, Mozilla, Chrome, and Safari) if you are considering using this functionality.
Flash with SCORM 1.2 Tracking	This template specifically supports Learning Interactions with SCORM (Sharable Content Object Reference Module) version 1.2. This is employed when you are creating Adobe Learning Interactions.
Flash with SCORM 2004 Tracking	This template specifically supports Learning Interactions with SCORM 2004 tracking.
Image Map	This template allows you to publish an image to your HTML file instead of your Flash file. We published an image in Chapter 11 when we created a backup GIF. To create an HTML page that displays an image file representation of your Flash movie, select this option, and then click the Formats tab and choose the image option you wish to publish.

12

Notice that when you select any of the templates aside from Image Map, you are offered the option to enable Flash Version Detection, as shown in Figure 12-26. If a user with a different version of Flash Player attempts to view your Flash movie, they will be sent to an alternative HTML page if they do not have the targeted player installed, which directs them to Adobe.com to download the current version of Flash Player.

Figure 12-26. Enabling Flash detection

The Dimensions drop-down in the Publish Settings dialog, shown in Figure 12-27, allows you to specify the width and height of the <object> and <embed> tags.

> When you are creating an HTML document to display your Flash CS4 movie, two tags are required within the HTML code to ensure that the Flash files display correctly: <object> and <embed>. Windows browsers such as Internet Explorer use the <object> tag to direct the browser to load Adobe Flash Player, while the <embed> tag performs the same task in Mac OS–specific browsers such as Safari.

As we are not manually creating the HTML code, we can give Flash CS4 some directions about the kind of information we want in the code. We'll investigate this now.

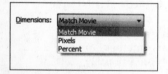

Figure 12-27. The Dimensions drop-down allows you to specify the <object> and <embed> tag dimensions.

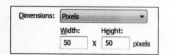

Figure 12-28. Defining a new display size for your movie to display in your HTML file

The Match Movie selection will display your Flash document in the HTML in the exact dimensions that you have specified the stage to be within Flash CS4. For example, if you have published a movie that was 100×100 pixels, choosing this option would ensure that it displayed at exactly 100×100 pixels within the HTML document.

The Pixels selection, shown in Figure 12-28, enables you to specify the number of pixels that you would like the height and width of your published Flash movie to be. If you took the example of the 100×100-pixel animation used in the Match Movie explanation, but decided that you wanted the animation to only display at 50×50 pixels in your HTML file, you could select this option and then specify the Flash movie dimensions in the Width and Height fields, as shown in Figure 12-28. However, there is a danger in doing this—even if you are resizing your Flash movie to display in the same proportions, it will not display with the clarity of the original size, and can appear pixelated and squashed (or stretched, if you choose to make the movie larger or use out-of-proportion dimensions). If you need your Flash movie to appear smaller or larger, you are best to manually resize it in Flash CS4 and export it at the new size. This setting does not change the dimensions of your original file, but the display dimensions in your HTML document.

The Percent selection enables you to choose the display size of your Flash movie as a percentage of the browser window. Again, be careful how you use this feature, as it can distort the manner in which your Flash files display in the HTML document.

The Playback options section, shown in Figure 12-29, controls the playback features of your Flash movie. We'll investigate these now.

Figure 12-29. The playback options in the Publish Settings dialog box

Selecting Paused at start requires the user to click a button to start the movie, or play the file via the shortcut menu. This option is deselected by default.

Checking the Loop option loops your animation so that it repeats itself upon reaching the end of the animation. You must deselect this option if you do not wish your Flash CS4 animation to loop.

The Display menu option displays a shortcut menu upon right-clicking the mouse (Windows), or Ctrl-clicking (Mac OS) in the Flash movie.

Device font is a Windows-only option that directs the file to substitute anti-aliased fonts for fonts that are in your movie but are not installed on the user's machine.

The Quality drop-down list of the Publish Settings dialog (shown in Figure 12-30) allows you to choose a balance between the time your movie takes to process and its appearance. The shorter the time your movie takes to process, the poorer its appearance quality tends to be and vice versa.

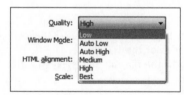

Figure 12-30. The Quality options allow you to create a balance between process time and movie quality.

The Low quality option offers optimum playback but sacrifices the movies quality to the greatest degree out of all the settings.

Auto Low allows for great movie speed, but where it can, strikes a balance between appearance quality and speed. The really cool thing about Auto Low is that the movie automatically begins with anti-aliasing off, but if the Flash player detects that the CPU can handle it, it turns it on for vastly improved appearance.

Auto High is the opposite to Auto Low. As Auto Low automatically sacrifices appearance for performance, Auto High automatically sacrifices performance for an animation that looks the best it possibly can. Again, this option has the functionality to change the quality settings depending on the performance of the user's computer. It begins with the highest possible quality, but will switch to a lower quality if the user's computer cannot process it.

12

The Medium quality option will not smooth bitmaps in your Flash CS4 animation, but it will allow some anti-aliasing.

The High quality option is the default for Flash CS4 movies. It always uses anti-aliasing and favors the file's appearance over animation.

The Best quality option provides the best appearance and will greatly sacrifice playback speed.

Figure 12-31. The Window Mode drop-down box

The Window Mode drop-down box, shown in Figure 12-31, controls the wmode attribute in the <object> and <embed> tags. As discussed previously, the <object> and <embed> tags direct the user's operating system to access Flash Player. The wmode attribute controls the window in HTML in which your Flash movie displays.

Window, selected by default, ensures that your Flash movie plays in an opaque square within the HTML document and does not allow other content to appear within that square.

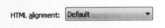

Figure 12-32. The HTML alignment options allow you to position where the Flash movie will appear in the browser window.

Opaque Windowless allows the HTML document to display content over the embedded Flash movie, but also creates an opaque background behind the movie so that elements do not display from behind it.

Transparent Windowless renders the background color of your Flash file transparent so that objects such as background images specified within the HTML code will display from behind the Flash file.

The HTML alignment options, shown in Figure 12-32, allow you position the Flash CS4 file in the browser window. It defaults to the center, but you can choose between left, center, and right horizontal alignments; or top, middle, and bottom vertical alignments.

Figure 12-33. The Scale drop-down

Selecting an option from the Scale drop-down (shown in Figure 12-33) allows you to place the movie content within specified boundaries of the HTML file. The Scale options work with the Dimensions options to determine how the file will be displayed within the boundaries in each of the options that you have set.

Default (Show all) allows you to display the entire Flash movie in the different dimensions, but within the ratio of the original file.

No border maintains the original ratio of your Flash file. If the allocated size within the HTML is smaller than your Flash file, choosing this option will display your file at the original size, but will resize it to fit the specified area.

Exact fit displays your Flash document in the specified area but will not preserve the original ratio of the movie, which will cause distortion.

No scale will not allow the Flash CS4 document to scale up or down when the size of the Flash Player window in the HTML document is changed.

The Flash alignment option allows you to set the way the content is placed in the window and how it will be cropped if it is larger than the browser.

Upload me

Now that the party is pumping and all your website files are sitting in a directory of their own, it is time to upload the final website directory to your web server.

Web servers come in all shapes and forms, all priced accordingly. You may find that your Internet service provider offers you free space to host your website. Be aware that you will often have to also get a domain name. A domain name is the name of the URL that identifies your website. Have a look through you favorite search engine to find a host and domain package that works for you. While you are there, have a look for an FTP client. **FTP** stands for **File Transfer Protocol**, and standardizes the way computers share information over the Web. An FTP client is a piece of software that will aid you in uploading your website from your personal computer to the server computer living on the Internet. You may come across a fantastic freeware solution called FileZilla. It's cheap and reliable. What more can we say? Get it from http://filezilla-project.org/.

If you use Mozilla/Firefox, then you should also note that the free FTP plug-in, FireFTP, can be found here: http://fireftp.mozdev.org/. This allows you to upload and download files from within the browser window.

Once you install your FTP client, it should look similar to Figure 12-34.

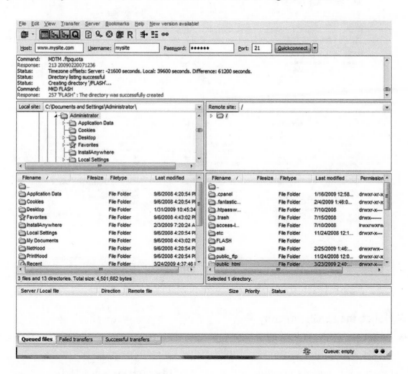

Figure 12-34. The FileZilla interface

FTP clients will have two halves: your computer on one side of the screen, and the server computer on the other. Follow these steps to log in and upload your files:

1. Find the host or address dialog box and enter your details.

2. Enter the username you have been supplied with.

3. Enter the password.

4. Most websites will use port 21, so you can typically leave this as the default (see Figure 12-35). Ports are like doors; you can knock, and if you smile politely, someone might let you in.

Figure 12-35. An example of FTP login details

5. Click Quickconnect or Connect. After a short while, the server window will fill with the available directory on the host server.

6. In your personal computer window (usually on the left side), browse to find your Chapter 12 directory.

7. Now, on the server side (usually the right), create a new directory and call it FLASH, as shown in Figure 12-36.

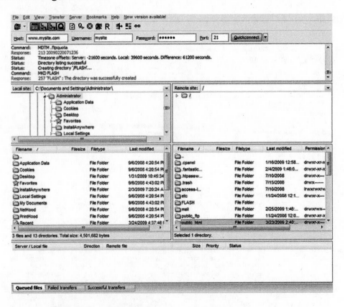

Figure 12-36. The FLASH directory on the FTP

8. Notice the FLASH directory.

9. Copy the contents of your website directory to the new FLASH directory on the server. After the transfer is complete, that's all you need to do!

10. Open your favorite browser and point it to the domain name URL.

The final gene-with-envy site displayed in your browser is shown in Figure 12-37.

Figure 12-37. The final gene-with-envy site

Summary

Using the projects created in the exercises, you have constructed the beginnings of an engaging multimedia website. You can add to it by creating more buttons in the navigation bar, and linking to more SWF files or to HTML. You could even go all Web 2.0 and make the Flash home page be the landing page for a WordPress or similar CMS (content management system).

You have now completed the final exercises of this book. Congratulations! Over the last 12 chapters, you have learned how to use Flash CS4 to create functional and compelling Flash animations. You have learned how to take a niggling idea and, through the design flow process, give that idea legs that translate to business ideas. You have learned how to give your ideas substance and translate them into real-world applications. It's now time for you to take your fledgling ideas and implement them in Flash CS4.

But the next step is up to you. When you are considering your next project, be sure to consider beyond its application to how it will function in real life. Is your concept viable? What aspects of Flash CS4 can you utilize to make it truly unique? There are no wrong or right answers here; it's a process of refining, optimizing, and taking advantage of the tools you have at hand—Flash CS4.

12

INSTALLING AWAY3D AND OTHER
CLASS LIBRARIES USING SUBVERSION

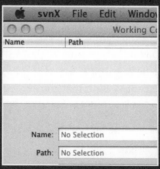

Away3D is a package of classes used to create three-dimensional environments in Flash Player. The simplest way to install it is to download the library folder and copy it to every Away3D project you work on. This is an easy process if you limit yourself to working on a handful of projects, but things can start to spiral out of control when you have more than that. The reason is that engines and APIs like Away3D are constantly changing, evolving, and going through a design process. Updates can happen on a daily basis. So, if you had an army of Away3D projects, you would have to update the folder in every directory, every day. Imagine a system that arranged the latest libraries for you. A version control system such as Subversion, which is often abbreviated "svn," is an organized solution for your needs.

Installing Subversion and Away3D for MAC OS X

Follow the steps in this exercise to install Subversion. This will let you download and keep tabs on Away3D, Papervision3D, and many other code repositories. A **code repository** is a central location for the latest class and library files. Having only one spot to store files avoids all version control issues.

1. Begin by creating a directory called Away3D in your root folder, or in another place you are likely to remember, as shown in Figure A-1.

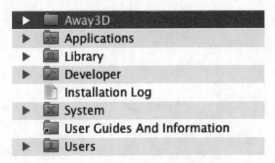

Figure A-1. Create a directory called Away3D.

2. Download a client version of Subversion.

Subversion has two options: one is a program that runs on a distant server computer; the other is a client version that runs on your local machine. Download it from http://homepage.mac.com/martinott/Subversion-1.5.5.pkg.zip.

3. Double-click the Subversion-1.5.5.pkg.zip file to install it.

You need svnX, another program, to control Subversion. svnX is a free, open source client for Apple that runs on your computer to integrate with Subversion, and ensures that you are always using the most up-to-date Away3D classes.

At the time of writing, a good place to find svnX is on the Apple website, at www.apple.com/downloads/macosx/development_tools/svnx.html.

4. Download svnX and install it by copying the svnX file to your Applications directory.

5. Open svnX.

After opening the program, you will be presented with two windows, as shown in Figure A-2.

> It's good practice to check regularly for svnX updates. You can easily do this by clicking the *SvnX* menu item and choosing *Preferences*. You can then ensure that the *Check for updates at startup* check box is checked.

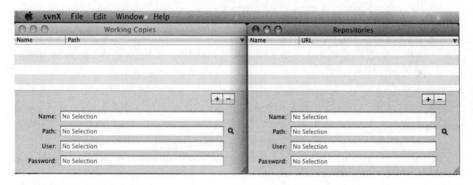

Figure A-2. The svnX repository

The Repositories window will contain a list of libraries being looked after by Subversion. The Working Copies window shows where the repositories are stored locally on your machine.

6. Inside the Repositories window, click the + icon to add a new library to your system.

7. Type Away3D in the name field, and http://away3d.googlecode.com/svn in the Path field.

Your Repositories window should look like Figure A-3.

A

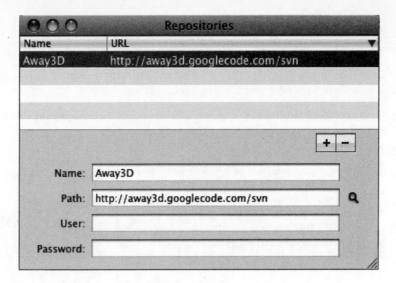

Figure A-3. Adding a library to your repository

8. Double-click the highlighted Away3D entry. A window will appear showing all the latest Away3D files with a description of updates and history. This window should look like Figure A-4.

9. Now click the Checkout button [image].

10. Browse the finder window to the root Away3D directory that you created in the first step, and select it. The latest Away3D libraries will now be copied to this location on your machine.

As this happens, the other svnX window will show you that the Away3D repository is now ready to be used, as shown in Figure A-5.

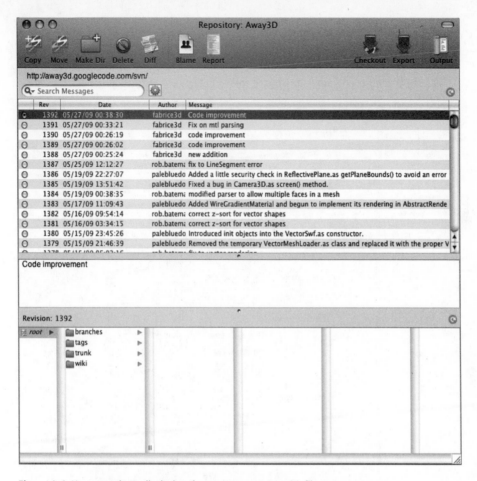

Figure A-4. Your repository displaying the most current Away3D files

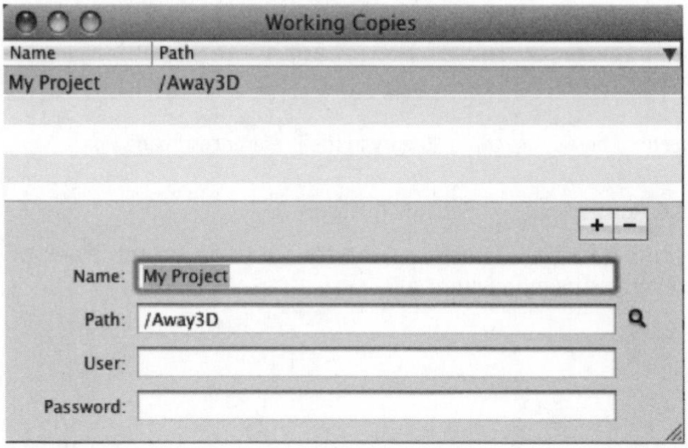

Figure A-5. svnX indicating that the Away3D repository is ready for use

The only thing that we need to do is let Flash CS4 know where the Away3D repository can be found.

11. Open Flash CS4 and go to Edit ➤ Preferences.

12. Select the ActionScript category, as shown in Figure A-6.

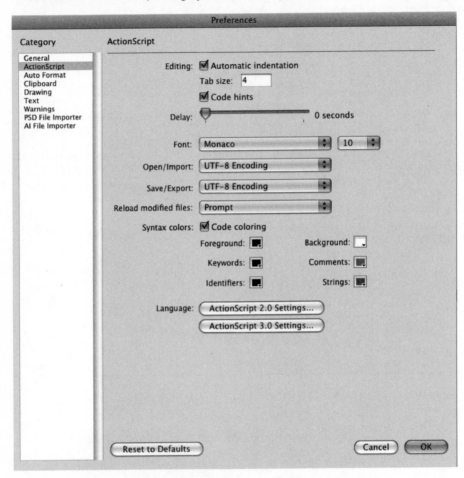

Figure A-6. Selecting the ActionScript category in the Preferences dialog box

13. Click the ActionScript 3.0 Settings button.

14. Add a new class path and select the source folder in the trunk of your Away3D repository, as shown in Figure A-7.

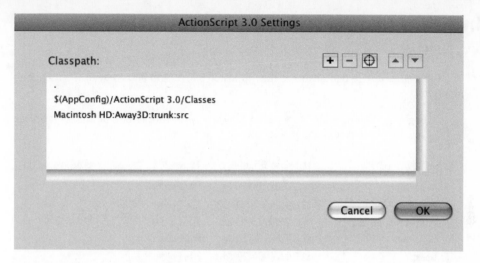

Figure A-7. Away3D is now ready to be used in Flash CS4.

Away3D is now ready to be used in all your projects. To install Papervision3D, use the same process outlined from step 7, but this time add details for Papervision3D (the name and path http://papervision3d.googlecode.com/svn/trunk/, as shown in Figure A-8).

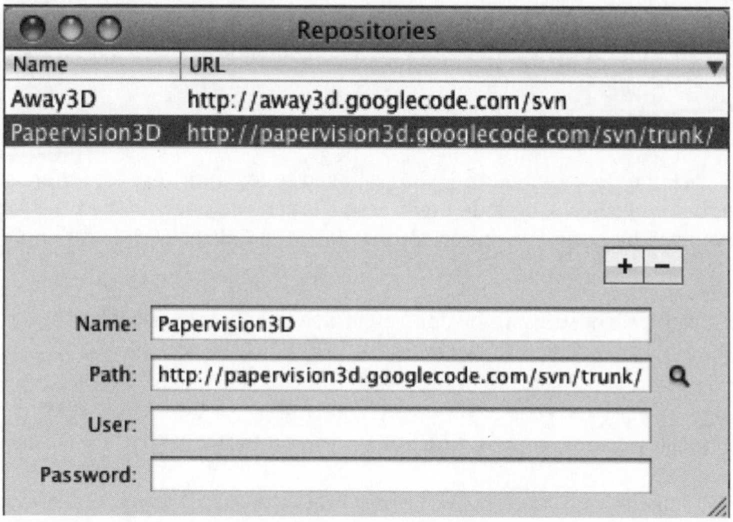

Figure A-8. The Papervision library in the svnX repository

A

Installing Subversion and Away3D for Windows

The following exercise demonstrates how to install Subversion and Away 3D for Windows computers.

1. Begin by creating a directory called Away3D in your root folder, or in another place you are likely to remember, as shown in Figure A-9.

Name	Date modified	Type	Size
Away3D	6/1/2009 10:11 PM	File Folder	
Program Files	11/29/2008 8:00 AM	File Folder	
Program Files (x86)	6/1/2009 10:09 PM	File Folder	
Windows	4/11/2009 3:12 AM	File Folder	
Users	11/16/2008 1:12 AM	File Folder	

Figure A-9. Creating the Away3D directory

2. Download the CollabNet Subversion Command-Line Client v1.6.2 (for Windows) from www.collab.net/downloads/subversion/.

> At the time of writing, Client v1.6.2 is the current version of Subversion. This may well be updated by the time that you purchase this book. If so, simply install the updated version.

After you click the Download button, you will need to log in or register for an account at CollabNet before you can continue the exercise. When you have finished the registration process, you will be given the option to download the CollabNet Subversion Command-Line Client.

3. Install the client software by double-clicking the CollabNetSubversion-client-1.6.2-1.win32 file, as shown in Figure A-10.

Name	Date modified	Type
CollabNetSubversion-client-1.6.2-1.win32	6/1/2009 10:32 PM	Application

Figure A-10. Double-click CollabNetSubversion-client-1.6.2-1.win32 to commence the installation.

4. Follow the instructions given by the install screens to complete this portion of the installation.

You require one last program to control Subversion: TortoiseSVN. TortoiseSVN is a program that runs on your computer and talks to Subversion. It asks to share the most recent copy of the Away3D classes with you. At the time of writing, a good place to find TortoiseSVN is the TortoiseSVN website, at http://tortoisesvn.net/downloads.

5. Download TortoiseSVN and install it. Follow the installation screens to complete the installation.

6. Windows will need to be restarted because TortoiseSVN is a shell extension and is integrated into Windows. Restart Windows, and once your machine has rebooted, right-click the Away3D folder you created in the first step. The TortoiseSVN command will appear in the context menu, as shown in Figure A-11.

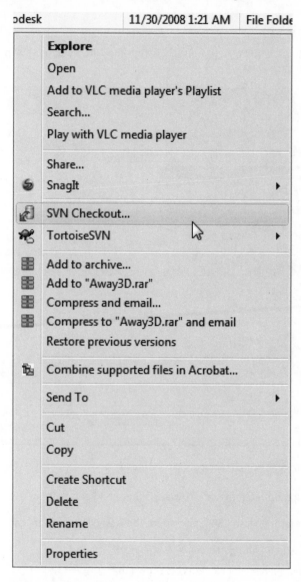

Figure A-11. TortoiseSVN is installed on Windows.

> *TortoiseSVN will not show up in 64-bit versions of Windows Explorer in Vista. The solution to this problem is to run a 32-bit Explorer window. You can do this by creating a shortcut and pointing its target to launch a 32-bit version of Explorer. In 64-bit Vista, create a shortcut with the target %Systemroot%\SysWOW64\explorer.exe.*

7. Click SVN Checkout.

8. Enter http://away3d.googlecode.com/svn in the URL field, as shown in Figure A-12, and then click OK.

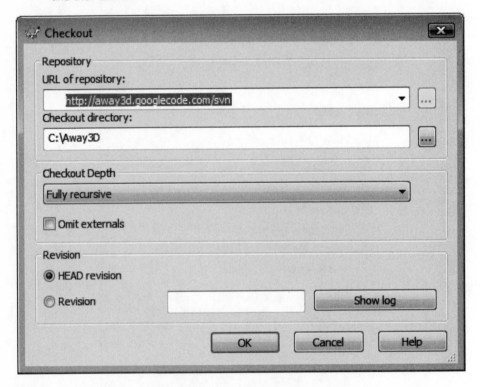

Figure A-12. Adding the Away3D library to the SVN repository

TortoiseSVN will then fetch the latest Away3D files and keep them in the one location.

The final step is letting Flash CS4 know where the Away3D repository can be found.

9. Open Flash CS4 and go to Edit ➤ Preferences.

10. Select the ActionScript category, as shown in Figure A-13.

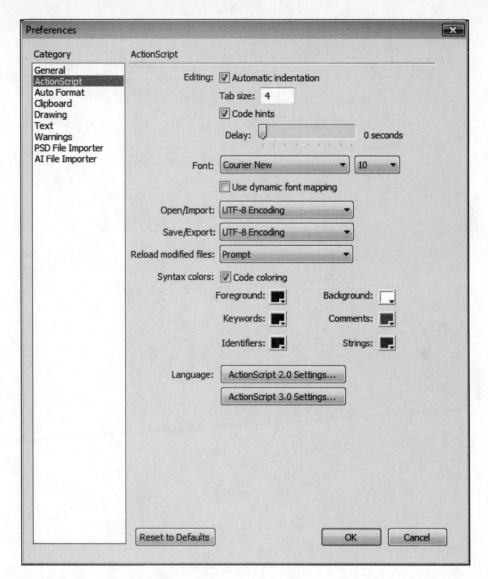

Figure A-13. Select the ActionScript category in the Preferences dialog box.

11. Click the ActionScript 3.0 button.

12. Add a new class path and select the source folder (src) in the Away3D repository folder.

Away3D is now ready to be used in all your projects. You can also follow the same process to add more repositories, such as the Papervision3D class libraries, to your system.

A

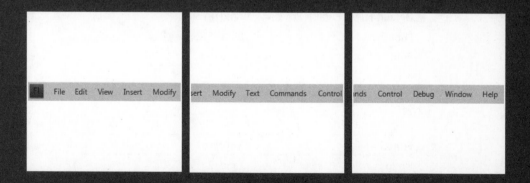

Once memorized, shortcuts can save you development time. Flash CS4 contains numerous shortcuts for both Windows and Mac OS X operating systems, as detailed in the following.

Shortcuts for Mac OS X

The shortcuts have been arranged as per the File menu order, as shown in Figure B-1.

Figure B-1. Shortcuts arranged by the File menu order

File

Function	Shortcut
New	Cmd+N
Open	Cmd+O
Browse in Bridge	Cmd+Opt+O
Close	Cmd+W
Close All	Cmd+Opt+W
Save	Cmd+S
Save As	Cmd+Shift+S
Import to Stage	Cmd+R
Open External Library	Cmd+Shift+O
Export Movie	Cmd+Opt+Shift+S
Publish Settings	Opt+Shift+F12
Default HTML Publish Preview	Cmd+F12
Publish	Shift+F12
Print	Cmd+P

Edit

Function	Shortcut
Undo	Cmd+Z
Redo	Cmd+Y
Cut	Cmd+X
Copy	Cmd+C

Function	Shortcut
Edit Symbol	Cmd+E
Paste in Center	Cmd+V
Paste in Place	Up Arrow+Shift+V
Clear	Delete, Backspace, or press the Delete key
Duplicate	Cmd+D
Select All	Cmd+A
Deselect All	Cmd+Shift+A
Find and Replace	Cmd+F
Find Next	F3

Edit ➤ Timeline

Function	Shortcut
Remove Frames	Shift+F5
Cut Frames	Cmd+Opt+X
Copy Frames	Cmd+Opt+C
Paste Frames	Cmd+Opt+V
Clear Frames	Opt+Delete
Select All Frames	Cmd+Opt+A

View

View ➤ Go to

Function	Shortcut
First	Home
Previous	Page Up
Next	Page Down
Last	End
Zoom In	Cmd+=
Zoom Out	Cmd+-
Hide Edges	Up Arrow+Shift+E
Show Shape Hints	Cmd+Opt+H

B

View ➤ Magnification

Function	Shortcut
100% Magnification	Cmd+1
400% Magnification	Cmd+4
800% Magnification	Cmd+8
Show Frame	Cmd+2
Show All	Cmd+3

View ➤ Preview Mode

Function	Shortcut
Outlines	Cmd+Opt+Shift+O
Fast	Cmd+Opt+Shift+F
Anti-Alias	Cmd+Opt+Shift+A
Anti-Alias Text	Cmd+Opt+Shift+T

View ➤ Grid

Function	Shortcut
Show Grid	Cmd+'
Edit Grid	Cmd+Opt+G

View ➤ Guides

Function	Shortcut
Show Guides	Cmd+;
Lock Guides	Cmd+Opt+;
Edit Guides	Cmd+Opt+Shift+G

View ➤ Snapping

Function	Shortcut
Snap to Grid	Cmd+Shift+'
Snap to Guides	Cmd+Shift+;
Snap to Objects	Cmd+Shift+U
Edit Snapping	Cmd+/

Insert

Function	Shortcut
New Symbol	Cmd+F8

Insert ➤ Timeline

Function	Shortcut
Frame	F5
Keyframe	F6

Modify

Function	Shortcut
Document	Cmd+J
Convert to Symbol	F8
Break Apart	Cmd+B
Group	Cmd+G
Ungroup	Cmd+Shift+G

Modify ➤ Shape

Function	Shortcut
Advance Smooth	Cmd+Opt+Shift+M
Advance Straighten	Cmd+Opt+Shift+N
Optimize	Cmd+Opt+Shift+C
Add Shape Hint	Cmd+Shift+H

Modify ➤ Transform

Function	Shortcut
Scale and Rotate	Cmd+Opt+S
Rotate 90 CW	Cmd+Shift+9
Rotate 90 CCW	Cmd+Shift+7
Remove Transform	Cmd+Shift+Z

B

Modify ➤ Arrange

Function	Shortcut
Bring to Front	Opt+Shift+Up Arrow
Bring Forward	Cmd+Up Arrow
Send Backward	Cmd+Down Arrow
Send to Back	Opt+Shift+Down Arrow
Lock	Cmd+Opt+L
Unlock All	Cmd+Opt+Shift+L

Modify ➤ Align

Function	Shortcut
Left	Cmd+Opt+1
Horizontal Center	Cmd+Opt+2
Right	Cmd+Opt+3
Top	Cmd+Opt+4
Vertical Center	Cmd+Opt+5
Bottom	Cmd+Opt+6
Distribute Widths	Cmd+Opt+7
Distribute Heights	Cmd+Opt+9
Make Same Width	Cmd+Opt+Shift+7
Make Same Height	Cmd+Opt+Shift+9
To Stage	Cmd+Opt+8
Print	Cmd+P

Text

Text ➤ Style

Function	Shortcut
Bold	Cmd+Shift+B
Italic	Cmd+Shift+I

Text ➤ Align

Function	Shortcut
Align Left	Cmd+Shift+L
Align Center	Cmd+Shift+C
Align Right	Cmd+Shift+R
Justify	Cmd+Shift+J

Text ➤ Letter Spacing

Function	Shortcut
Increase	Cmd+Opt+Right Arrow
Decrease	Cmd+Opt+Left Arrow
Reset	Cmd+Opt+Up Arrow

Control

Function	Shortcut
Play	Enter
Rewind	Shift+,
Go to End	Shift+.
Step Forward One Frame	.
Step Backward One Frame	,
Test Movie	Cmd+Enter
Test Scene	Cmd+Opt+Enter
Enable Simple Buttons	Cmd+Opt+B
Mute Sounds	Cmd+Opt+M
Make Same Height	Cmd+Opt+Shift+9
To Stage	Cmd+Opt+8
Print	Cmd+P

B

Debug

Function	Shortcut
Debug Movie	Cmd+Shift+Enter
Continue	Opt+F5
End Debug Session	Opt+F12
Step In	Opt+F6
Step Over	Opt+F7
Step Out	Opt+F8
Pasteboard	Cmd+Shift+W
Rulers	Cmd+Opt+Shift+R

Window

Function	Shortcut
Duplicate Window	Cmd+Opt+K
Timeline	Cmd+Opt+T
Tools	Cmd+F2
Properties	Cmd+F3
Library	Cmd+L, Opt+F11
Actions	Opt+F9
Behaviors	Shift+F3
Compiler Errors	Opt+F2
Movie Explorer	Opt+F3
Output	F2
Align	Cmd+K
Color	Shift+F9
Info	Cmd+I
Swatches	Cmd+F8
Transform	Cmd+T
Components	Cmd+F7
Component Inspector	Shift+F7

Window ➤ Debug Panels

Function	Shortcut
AS 2.0 Debugger	Shift+F4

Window ➤ Other Panels

Function	Shortcut
Accessibility	Shift+F11
History	Cmd+F10
Scene	Shift+F2
Strings	Cmd+F11
Web Services	Cmd+Shift+F10

Window ➤ Workspace

Function	Shortcut
Hide Panels	F4

Help

Function	Shortcut
Flash Help	F1

B

Shortcuts for Windows

The shortcuts have been arranged as per the File menu order, as shown in Figure B-2.

Figure B-2. Shortcuts arranged by the File menu order

File

Function	Shortcut
New	Ctrl+N
Open	Ctrl+O
Browse in Bridge	Ctrl+Alt+O
Close	Ctrl+W
Close All	Ctrl+Alt+W
Save	Ctrl+S
Save As	Ctrl+Shift+S
Publish Settings	Ctrl+Shift+F12
Publish	Shift+F12
Print	Ctrl+P
Exit	Ctrl+Q

File ➤ Import

Function	Shortcut
Import to Stage	Ctrl+R
Open External Library	Ctrl+Shift+O

File ➤ Export

Function	Shortcut
Export Movie	Ctrl+Alt+Shift+S

File ➤ Publish Preview

Function	Shortcut
Default	F12, Ctrl+F12

Edit

Function	Shortcut
Undo	Ctrl+Z
Redo	Ctrl+Y
Cut	Ctrl+X
Copy	Ctrl+C
Paste in Center	Ctrl+V
Paste in Place	Ctrl+Shift+V
Clear	Backspace, Delete
Duplicate	Ctrl+D
Select All	Ctrl+A
Deselect All	Ctrl+Shift+A
Find and Replace	Ctrl+F
Find Next	F3
Edit Symbols	Ctrl+E
Preferences	Ctrl+U

Edit ➤ Timeline

Function	Shortcut
Remove Frames	Shift+F5
Cut Frames	Ctrl+Alt+X
Copy Frames	Ctrl+Alt+C
Paste Frames	Ctrl+Alt+V
Clear Frames	Alt+Backspace
Select All Frames	Ctrl+Alt+A

View

Function	Shortcut
Zoom In	Ctrl+=
Zoom Out	Ctrl+-
Pasteboard	Ctrl+Shift+W
Rulers	Ctrl+Alt+Shift+R
Hide Edges	Ctrl+H
Show Shape Hints	Ctrl+Alt+H

B

View ➤ Go to

Function	Shortcut
First	Home
Previous	Page Up
Next	Page Down
Last	End

View ➤ Magnification

Function	Shortcut
100%	Ctrl+1
400%	Ctrl+4
800%	Ctrl+8
Show Frame	Ctrl+2
Show All	Ctrl+3

View ➤ Preview Mode

Function	Shortcut
Outlines	Ctrl+Alt+Shift+O
Fast	Ctrl+Alt+Shift+F
Anti-Alias	Ctrl+Alt+Shift+A
Anti-Alias Text	Ctrl+Alt+Shift+T

View ➤ Grid

Function	Shortcut
Show Grid	Ctrl+'
Edit Grid	Ctrl+Alt+G

View ➤ Guides

Function	Shortcut
Show Guides	Ctrl+;
Lock Guides	Ctrl+Alt+;
Edit Guides	Ctrl+Alt+Shift+G

View ➤ Snapping

Function	Shortcut
Snap to Grid	Ctrl+Shift+'
Snap to Guides	Ctrl+Shift+;
Snap to Objects	Ctrl+Shift+/
Edit Snapping	Ctrl+/

Insert

Function	Shortcut
New Symbol	Ctrl+F8

Insert ➤ Timeline

Function	Shortcut
Frame	F5
Keyframe	F6

Modify

Function	Shortcut
Document	Ctrl+J
Convert to Symbol	F8
Break Apart	Ctrl+B
Group	Ctrl+G
Ungroup	Ctrl+Shift+G

Modify ➤ Shape

Function	Shortcut
Advanced Smooth	Ctrl+Alt+Shift+M
Advanced Straighten	Ctrl+Alt+Shift+N
Optimize	Ctrl+Alt+Shift+C
Add Shape Hint	Ctrl+Shift+H

B

Modify ➤ Timeline

Function	Shortcut
Distribute to Layers	Ctrl+Shift+D
Convert to Keyframes	F6
Clear Keyframe	Shift+F6
Convert to Blank Keyframes	F7

Modify ➤ Transform

Function	Shortcut
Scale and Rotate	Ctrl+Alt+S
Rotate 90 CW	Ctrl+Shift+9
Rotate 90 CCW	Ctrl+Shift+7
Remove Transform	Ctrl+Shift+Z

Modify ➤ Arrange

Function	Shortcut
Bring to Front	Ctrl+Shift+Up Arrow
Bring Forward	Ctrl+Up Arrow
Send Backward	Ctrl+Down Arrow
Send to Back	Ctrl+Shift+Down Arrow
Lock	Ctrl+Alt+L
Unlock All	Ctrl+Alt+Shift+L

Modify ➤ Align

Function	Shortcut
Left	Ctrl+Alt+1
Horizontal Center	Ctrl+Alt+2
Right	Ctrl+Alt+3
Top	Ctrl+Alt+4
Vertical Center	Ctrl+Alt+5
Bottom	Ctrl+Alt+6
Distribute Widths	Ctrl+Alt+7
Distribute Heights	Ctrl+Alt+9
Make Same Width	Ctrl+Alt+Shift+7

Function	Shortcut
Make Same Height	Ctrl+Alt+Shift+9
To Stage	Ctrl+Alt+8
Unlock All	Ctrl+Alt+Shift+L

Text

Text ➤ Style

Function	Shortcut
Bold	Ctrl+Shift+B
Italic	Ctrl+Shift+I

Text ➤ Align

Function	Shortcut
Align Left	Ctrl+Shift+L
Align Center	Ctrl+Shift+C
Align Right	Ctrl+Shift+R
Justify	Ctrl+Shift+J

Text ➤ Letter Spacing

Function	Shortcut
Increase	Ctrl+Alt+Right
Decrease	Ctrl+Alt+Left
Reset	Ctrl+Alt+Up Arrow

B

Control

Function	Shortcut
Play	Enter
Rewind	Shift+, Ctrl+Alt+R
Go To End	Shift+.
Step Forward One Frame	.
Step Backward One Frame	,
Test Movie	Ctrl+Enter
Test Scene	Ctrl+Alt+Enter
Enable Simple Frame Actions	Ctrl+Alt+F
Enable Simple Buttons	Ctrl+Alt+B
Mute Sounds	Ctrl+Alt+M

Debug

Function	Shortcut
Debug Movie	Ctrl+Shift+Enter
Continue	Alt+F5
End Debug Session	Alt+F12
Step In	Alt+F6
Step Over	Alt+F7
Step Out	Alt+F8

Window

Function	Shortcut
Duplicate Window	Ctrl+Alt+K
Timeline	Ctrl+Alt+T
Tools	Ctrl+F2
Properties	Ctrl+F3
Library	Ctrl+L or F11
Actions	F9
Behaviors	Shift+F3
Compiler Errors	Alt+F2
Movie Explorer	Alt+F3

Function	Shortcut
Output	F2
Align	Ctrl+K
Color	Shift+F9
Info	Ctrl+I
Swatches	Ctrl+F9
Transform	Ctrl+T
Components	Ctrl+F7
Component Inspector	Shift+F7
Hide Panels	F4

Window ➤ Debug Panels

Function	Shortcut
AS 2.0 Debugger	Shift+F4

Window ➤ Other Panels

Function	Shortcut
Accessibility	Shift+F11
History	Ctrl+F10
Scene	Shift+F2
Strings	Ctrl+F11
Web Services	Ctrl+Shift+F10

Help

Function	Shortcut
Flash Help	F1

B

INDEX